Aerospace Law and Policy Series

VOLUME 14

Editors

Pablo Mendes de Leon, Professor of Air and Space Law, and Tanja Masson-Zwaan, Assistant Professor of Space Law, Leiden University, The Netherlands.

Introduction

The *Aerospace Law and Policy Series* critically examines the fundamental changes that international aviation and space activities have undergone since the last century, growing up as mature industries while freeing themselves from traditional regulatory constraints and displaying a variety of innovative applications that call for creative legal solutions.

Objective

The objective of the Series is to make a contribution to legal thinking on public international air and space law and policy, and their implementation at the regional and national levels, responsibility and liability of public bodies and service providers, competition law, insurance law, company law, and the complex relationship between EU law and public international law.

Readership

Aviation and space lawyers, academics, representatives of governments, international organizations, and companies involved in aviation and space activities.

The titles published in this series are listed at the end of this volume.

European Union Competition Law in the Airline Industry

European Union Competition Law in the Airline Industry

John Milligan

Wolters Kluwer

Published by:
Kluwer Law International B.V.
PO Box 316
2400 AH Alphen aan den Rijn
The Netherlands
Website: www.wolterskluwerlr.com

Sold and distributed in North, Central and South America by:
Wolters Kluwer Legal & Regulatory U.S.
7201 McKinney Circle
Frederick, MD 21704
United States of America
Email: customer.service@wolterskluwer.com

Sold and distributed in all other countries by:
Quadrant
Rockwood House
Haywards Heath
West Sussex
RH16 3DH
United Kingdom
Email: international-customerservice@wolterskluwer.com

ISBN 978-90-411-6618-0

e-Book: ISBN 978-90-411-6628-9
web-PDF: ISBN 978-90-411-8823-6

To Gerry, Una, Russell, Dawn, with thanks for their encouragement in the writing of this book, and the other Milligans.

About the Author

John Milligan is a solicitor qualified in England and Wales, also admitted in Ireland and formerly a barrister, and has since 2001 been an EU & competition partner at Clyde & Co LLP, one of the leading aviation practices in the world. He has over 20 years' experience advising in the aviation, marine transport, energy and insurance sectors. He specialises in all aspects of competition law, including mergers and alliances, distribution and other commercial agreements, cartel investigations, damages actions, abuse of dominance, market investigations and the EU State aid rules.

Prior to joining Clyde & Co, John was an associate at the Law Offices of SG Archibald in Brussels. He studied law at Queen's University Belfast, Northern Ireland and completed a Master's degree ('Licence spéciale en droit européen') at the Université Libre de Bruxelles, Belgium. John is a guest lecturer in EU competition law at the Institute of Air and Space Law at the University of Leiden, the Netherlands.

Table of Contents

Introduction

The European Union (EU) competition rules apply to all practices in the air transport sector – cartels, information exchange between competitors, commercial agreements between airlines such as code-sharing, alliances, joint ventures, vertical agreements with manufacturers, other suppliers or agents and other means of distribution such as computer reservation systems, abusive conduct by dominant companies whether airports, airlines or other companies, and mergers. They also apply to State action such as the grant of exclusive rights to entities to operate airports or to airlines to operate routes and State aid.

Since the EU liberalisation of air transport which took place in the late 1980s, competition has intensified and the industry has evolved, with the emergence of low cost carriers, global airline alliances oneworld, SkyTeam and Star Alliance, and greater consolidation between airlines through mergers and alliances.

The enforcement of competition law in the air transport sector, which was far behind other industry sectors until 2004, has similarly increased, both within the EU – at EU and EU Member State level – and internationally, with inter-jurisdictional cooperation in the framework of the International Competition Network and bilateral Treaties between the EU and third countries, such as the United States and Canada. The investigations of air cargo surcharges and transatlantic mergers and alliances are examples of such cooperation. Private enforcement is also increasing with entities bringing legal proceedings in national courts based on alleged infringements of competition law, in the form of either 'stand-alone actions' or 'follow on' claims based on decisions of the Commission or national competition authorities. Competition law may also be raised as a defence to other claims.

Competition law is relevant when it comes to drafting commercial agreements, planning and structuring joint ventures and mergers, informal collaboration with competitors and unilateral conduct of dominant companies. This book sets out the law and principles of competition assessment of such practices. While it aims so far as possible to be a stand-alone text minimising the need for cross-referencing, it does not pretend to be a detailed text on all issues relating to competition law and readers are recommended to refer to the European Commission website (DGCOMP) and current editions of leading competition texts such as Bellamy & Child, Van Bael & Bellis and Whish & Bailey (also discusses United Kingdom (UK) law). Other books, articles or sources are cited in the text.

Chapter 1 deals with the fundamentals of the EU, its laws and institutions, and so as not to ignore the UK position vis-à-vis the rest of Europe following its referendum of 23 June 2016 on EU membership, includes a Note on 'Brexit'. Chapter 2 traces the development of competition regulation of the air transport industry, including the factual and political context and the eventual advent of competition law in the sector, with discussion of cases such as *Nouvelles Frontières, Ahmed Saeed* and *'Open Skies'*, air transport block exemptions, the last of which (tariff consultations) expired in 2007, through to the current legal framework and the influence of the above on the industry structure. Chapter 3 sets out the principles of market definition, the basis for all competition assessment. Chapter 4 discusses the key concepts and principles of Article 101 of the Treaty on the Functioning of the European Union (TFEU) which regulates anticompetitive agreements and practices, Chapter 5 discussing 'horizontal' agreements with focus on cartels and code-sharing, Chapter 6 discussing 'vertical agreements'. Chapter 7 discusses abuse of a dominant position and the principles of Article 102 TFEU. Chapter 8 discusses mergers and alliances, including a section on market definition in the case of agreements between airlines. Chapter 9 discusses the enforcement of competition law, public and private, including the recent harmonisation of private actions for damages by the EU Damages Directive 2014. Finally, Chapter 10 discusses State aid (Articles 107–109 TFEU) and mentions the regulatory position as regards State subsidies by non-EU countries to airlines. The law is as stated at 1 March 2017 and the author has endeavoured to include developments to 31 March 2017 to the extent there have been any.

The author is grateful to John Balfour, Consultant at Clyde & Co, and the editor, Pablo Mendes de Leon, for their comments on the text.

The author welcomes comments on the text and can be contacted at: john.milligan@clydeco.com

CHAPTER 1

Introduction to the European Union and Competition Law

1.1 OVERVIEW

The EU is a customs union and free trade area of 28 Member States, with its own legal system and institutions responsible for law-making, enforcing laws and judicial protection. Primary legislation is contained in the Treaty on the Functioning of the European Union (TFEU), with secondary legislation in the form of Regulations, Directives, and Decisions addressed to Member States. A fundamental part of the EU is the creation of a system of undistorted competition. This comprises the prohibition of agreements which restrict or distort competition, abuse of a dominant position, control of mergers which significantly impede competition in particular by strengthening a dominant position and the prohibition of State aids by governments which favour undertakings and distort competition.

1.2 THE EUROPEAN UNION AND ITS ORIGINS

1.2.1 Creation of the EEC Through to the EU

The EU has developed out of the European Economic Community (EEC) which was established by the Treaty of Rome 1957.[1] This was precipitated by the political instability following the Second World War. Speeches and initiatives from European

1. There were previously competition provisions of sectoral application in the Treaty establishing the European Coal and Steel Community 1951 and the Treaty establishing the European Atomic Energy Community (Euratom) 1957).

leaders[2] to create a closer union, or a 'family of nations', led to the adoption of the Statute of the Council of Europe,[3] the European Coal and Steel Community, the European Atomic Energy Community and the EEC.

The Preamble of the Treaty of Rome called for 'common action to eliminate the barriers which divide Europe' and Article 2 required the creation of a 'common market'. This comprised a free trade area based on fundamental freedoms – free movement of goods, people, companies and capital across borders – and a customs union without taxes or duties on intra-EU trade and a customs tariff on imports from third countries. It also provided for a system of undistorted competition and for common policies such as a common agricultural policy, common commercial policy towards third countries and transport (discussed below).

The EEC originally comprised six Member States and has expanded to include as at 1 January 2016 a total of 28 Member States with a population of approximately 500 million inhabitants. The members and their dates of accession are below:

- 1957 Belgium, France, Germany, Italy, Luxembourg, Netherlands
- 1973 Denmark, Ireland, United Kingdom (UK)
- 1981 Greece
- 1986 Spain, Portugal
- 1995 Austria, Finland, Sweden
- 2004 Czech Republic, Cyprus, Estonia, Hungary, Latvia, Lithuania, Malta, Poland, Slovakia, Slovenia
- 2007 Bulgaria, Romania
- 2013 Croatia.

2. Winston Churchill, Zurich September 1946; Schuman Plan which led to the Coal and Steel Community 1951; Spaak Report and intergovernmental conference which led to the creation of the Treaty of Rome.
3. The Council of Europe created the European Convention for the Protection of Human Rights and Fundamental Freedoms in 1950.

See Figure 1.1.

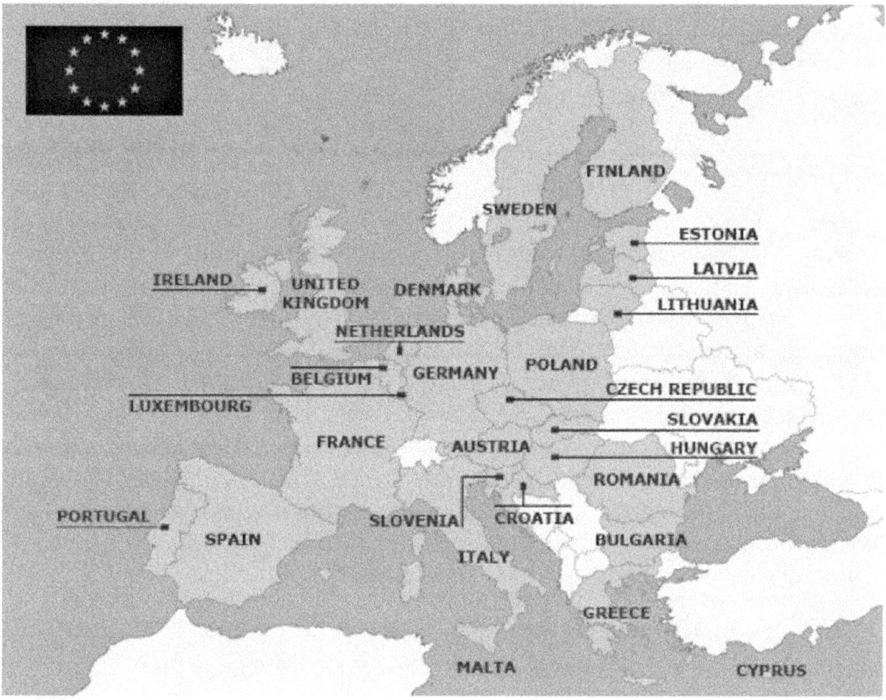

The Preamble to the Treaty of Rome set as one of its goals the achievement of 'an ever closer Union among the peoples of Europe'. With the Maastricht Treaty (signed in February 1992 and effective from November 1993), the Community was placed within the framework of a broader Union. The EU not only comprised the 'first pillar' of the existing European Communities, but also included, at intergovernmental level and separate from the EU legal structures, a 'second pillar' comprising the EU's system of a common foreign and security policy and a 'third pillar' comprising cooperation on justice and home affairs.

1.2.2 The European Economic Area

In 1994, the Agreement on the European Economic Area (EEA) brought together the EU Member States and Iceland, Liechtenstein and Norway into the EEA, which is subject to the European competition rules and the fundamental freedoms, but not common policies on taxation, customs duties or agriculture and fisheries. The three EEA non-EU Member States do not enjoy voting rights in the legislation making process.

1.2.3 A Note on 'Brexit': Exit from the EU

A referendum in the UK on membership of the EU on 23 June 2016 resulted in a majority (52 per cent of votes cast) in favour of leaving the EU. It is too early to do more than speculate on what will happen, but some brief comments can usefully be made on the subject of competition law.

(1) Procedure and timeline

In order to leave the EU, a Member State has to notify the European Council of its intention to do so, under Article 50 of the Treaty on European Union (TEU set out in Appendix III – Treaty on European Union Provisions). The UK made this notification on 29 March 2017. Formal negotiations on leaving the EU then commence, and the exiting Member State (UK) has a maximum of two years from the date of notification in which to conclude an agreement on its withdrawal from the EU. Any exit deal has to be approved unanimously by the Council, and the European Parliament has veto powers over any deal struck. In the absence of an agreement on withdrawal being reached, unless the Council unanimously agreed that the two-year period could be extended, or the Article 50 notification could be revoked, the EU Treaties and legislation would cease to apply to the UK two years from the date Article 50 was triggered (29 March 2019). In that scenario, the UK's relationship with the EU would then, as other non-EU countries, be governed by World Trade Organisation (WTO) rules.

(2) Impact on competition law

If the UK exits the EU, the application of EU law generally will depend on any trade agreement reached with the EU and the extent to which this incorporates existing EU law. As regards competition law, however, there will be less change as EU competition law applies in any event to any agreement (formal or informal), including cartels, alliances, or abuse of a dominant position, which affects trade between Member States, irrespective of whether the party or parties are located within the EU. Agreements or abuses which produce effects confined to the UK would, as currently, be outside the scope of EU competition law, but UK competition law on agreements and abuses closely mirrors EU law (Articles 101 and 102 TFEU), so such practices would continue to be subject to those very similar national laws. 'Block exemption' Regulations exempting categories of agreements such as vertical or technology transfer agreements would no longer apply in the UK, but agreements which comply with them would remain exempt under EU law.

Articles 101 and 102 TFEU would, however, no longer apply in the UK and the jurisdiction of the European courts would cease. The UK would, therefore, have the ability to investigate and reach its own conclusions in cases which currently fall within the exclusive jurisdiction of the EU, which could be a benefit, but would require additional resources. It may be that the UK authorities and courts would be required to have regard to the jurisprudence of the European General Court and Court of Justice, but in any event, there could potentially be a divergence of jurisprudence.

Mergers or joint ventures within the meaning of the EU Merger Regulation 139/2004 (EUMR) would continue to be subject to the compulsory notification regime to the Commission, if the relevant global, EEA and/or EEA Member State turnover thresholds are met. The 'one-stop principle', whereby EU national authorities have no jurisdiction over mergers caught by the EUMR, may no longer exclude the UK authorities from claiming jurisdiction over such mergers, thus requiring notification to both the UK authorities and the Commission, a question which will depend on any EU/UK agreement that may be reached. As regards mergers falling outside the EUMR, they would continue to be governed by national merger control regimes, including the UK, according to those countries' laws.

The effect of a UK airline no longer being majority owned or effectively controlled by EU nationals or Member States, or the effect of changes in ownership of an EU airline if it is acquired by a UK airline, will be an issue to be addressed in the event of the UK leaving the EU and will depend on the terms on which it does so. This is not a matter of competition law.[4]

As regards State aid (Articles 107–109 TFEU), the UK would no longer be prohibited by EU law from granting subsidies or other advantages to undertakings such as airlines or airports. It may be that such matters would be the subject of a trade agreement reached with the EU in the event of the UK leaving the EU. In any event, action could, in theory, be brought against the UK under Regulation 868/2004 (or such successor instrument as may be adopted in future) which prohibits unfair subsidies granted by third countries to airlines (*see* Chapter 10 *EU State Aid Rules*). A UK company would, however, continue to be able to enforce the EU State aid rules, in so far as aid threatened to distort competition within the EU.

1.3 TERMINOLOGY IN THIS BOOK

Terminology and Treaty numbering have changed periodically since 1993. Following the Treaty on European Union (TEU, Maastricht 1992) the 'EEC' was renamed the European Community (EC) and the EEC Treaty became the EC Treaty, reflecting its widening aims including economic and monetary union, leading to the introduction of the Euro on 1 January 1999 in the majority of Member States. With effect from 1 December 2009, the TFEU replaced the EC by the EU (EU law replacing EC law) and the 'common market' by 'internal market'. Treaty numbers have also changed. TFEU terminology and Treaty article numbers will be used throughout this book. The

4. For a discussion of this and other areas of EU law which may be impacted by Brexit, including access to the single EU air transport market and agreements concluded with third countries such as the US, market access and Open Skies *see*: 'The EU air law consequences of Brexit for the UK' 27 June 2016, available on http://www.clydeco.com/blog/brexit/article/the-eu-air-law-consequences-of-brexit-for-the-uk.

institutions are described by the commonly used terminology namely the Council, the Commission, the European Parliament, the General Court and the Court of Justice.

1.4 INSTITUTIONS

1.4.1 Council of the European Union

The Council (also known as the Council of Ministers) is the main decision-making body and, with the European Parliament, the principal legislator of the EU.[5] The Presidency of the Council rotates between Member States every six months. It is comprised of ministers from, and who therefore represent and follow the instructions of, the governments of their respective Member States. It acts on proposals submitted by the Commission. In the field of competition law, the Council is empowered under Article 103 TFEU to adopt appropriate Regulations or Directives to implement the competition rules set out in Articles 101 and 102. The Council and its functions are to be distinguished from the European Council, which does not negotiate or adopt EU laws, but sets the EU's policy agenda and priorities, in the course of meetings attended by heads of Member State governments.[6]

1.4.2 European Commission

The Commission is the EU's politically independent executive arm. Its role is to propose legislation, for adoption by the Parliament and the Council, to adopt measures implementing Council Regulations – in the field of competition law, block exemption Regulations – and to ensure that EU law is properly applied in all the member countries, which will include taking specific enforcement action against undertakings or governments.

The Commission also represents the EU internationally, in particular in areas of trade policy and negotiating international agreements on behalf of the EU, in so far as it has competence to do so. Air services agreements (ASAs) with third countries are an example of the Commission negotiating on Member States' behalf in the air transport sector (discussed in Chapter 2 *Liberalisation of Air Transport*).

The Commission is composed of the College of Commissioners of 28 members, including the President and Vice-Presidents. The Commissioners, one nominated by the government of each Member State, sit for a five-year term and are assigned responsibility for specific policy areas by the President. The Commission is organised into Directorate-Generals which cover the main areas of the EU's activity. The

5. The Commission also legislates, for example 'block exemptions', but only on the basis of a mandate from the Council and EP.
6. *See* generally TFEU Articles 235–243 on European Council and Council of Ministers.

Directorate-General for Competition (DG COMP) is charged with enforcing the competition rules (discussed in greater detail at Chapter 9 *Enforcement of EU Competition Law*).[7]

1.4.3 European Parliament

Members of the Parliament are elected every five years by voters across the EU and they sit according to their political allegiance, rather than their Member State of origin. The Parliament shares power with the Council in the adoption of legislation in certain defined areas through the 'co-decision procedure'. The Parliament has much less influence than the Commission and the Council in the field of competition law, being involved in competition legislation only through a more limited 'consultation' procedure, although it has called for competition law to be brought within the co-decision procedure. The Damages Directive was, however, a rare case of competition law adopted under this procedure.[8] The Parliament's other main duty is scrutiny of the other EU institutions. This includes the election of a European Ombudsman, whose remit is to investigate and report on complaints concerning instances of maladministration in the activities of the other EU institution or agencies, with the exception of the Court of Justice acting in its judicial role.[9]

1.4.4 General Court

There was until 1989 only one European Court responsible for the interpretation and enforcement of EU law. In 1988, the General Court (initially named the Court of First Instance) was established to assist the Court of Justice. The Court has one judge from each Member State. It rules on actions for annulment brought by individuals, companies and, in some cases, EU governments. Notably in the field of competition law and State aid, it hears appeals against Commission decisions. Appeals must be brought within two months of the decision being challenged.[10] The Court can annul or uphold fully or in part, decisions of the Commission and can cancel, increase or reduce any fine imposed by the Commission. Appeals are on points of law but, unlike the higher Court of Justice, the General Court also has exclusive jurisdiction to find and appraise the relevant facts and to assess the evidence. In competition cases, this will include whether the conditions for the application of Article 101 or 102 TFEU, prohibiting anticompetitive agreements and abuse of a dominant position, respectively, are met. A notable example of a Commission decision being annulled by the General Court in the

7. *See* generally TFEU Articles 244–250.
8. Directive 2014/104/EU of the European Parliament and of the Council on certain rules governing actions for damages under national law for infringements of the competition law provisions of the Member States and of the European Union, OJ L 349, 5.12.2014, pp. 1–19.
9. TFEU Article 228; *see* generally TFEU Articles 223–234.
10. Article 263 TFEU.

field of air transport is its series of judgments of 16 December 2015 annulling the landmark Commission *Airfreight* decision in 2010, in which carriers worldwide had been fined EUR 799 million.[11]

1.4.5 Court of Justice

The Court of Justice consists of one judge from each Member State and eight Advocates General. The role of the Advocate General is to provide an opinion on how he/she believes the case should be resolved, and his/her Opinion is more often than not followed.

The Court of Justice rules on alleged breaches of the EU Treaties and any laws made under them by a Member State government, or on failure to implement EU law or incorrect implementation. The *Open Skies* judgments of 2002 against Member States against whom infraction proceedings were brought by the Commission were a notable example in the field of air transport (discussed in Chapter 2 *Liberalisation of Air Transport*). The Court of Justice also hears both preliminary references from Member States' national courts when they refer questions on the interpretation of EU law, and allegations of a failure to act by an EU institution, body, office or agency.

The Court of Justice also hears appeals, on points of law only, against judgments and orders of the General Court.[12] In principle, the appeal does not have suspensive effect. If the appeal is admissible and well founded, the Court of Justice sets aside the judgment of the General Court. In such a case, it generally refers the case back to the General Court, which is bound by the decision given by the Court of Justice on the appeal, and there is no guarantee that the result on the facts will necessarily, therefore, be different. If the state of the proceedings so permits, the Court of Justice may itself give final judgment in the case.

The Court of Justice also gives preliminary rulings on the interpretation of EU law and the validity of acts of institutions of the EU, at the request of a Member State court or tribunal, remitting the matter to the national court to apply the ruling to the facts before it.[13] A national court action in the course of which there is a request for a preliminary ruling can be a direct means of having the point(s) of law being heard by the Court of Justice. Rulings on requests for a preliminary reference have been significant in the development of the application of competition law to the air transport sector, including judgments such as *Nouvelles Frontières* and *Ahmed Saeed* (discussed in Chapter 2 *Liberalisation of Air Transport*).

11. Cases T-9/11 Air Canada, T-28/11 Koninklijke Luchtvaart Maatschappij, T-36/11 Japan Airlines, T-38/11 Cathay Pacific Airways, T-39/11 Cargolux Airlines International, T-40/11 Latam Airlines Group and Others, T-43/11 Singapore Airlines and Others, T-46/11 Deutsche Lufthansa and Others, T-48/11 British Airways, T-56/11 SAS Cargo Group and Others, T-62/11 Air France-KLM, T-63/11 Société Air France and T-67/11. Martinair Holland v Commission, as yet unpublished. There were fines in other jurisdictions globally which are outside the remit of the Commission decision.
12. Article 256(1) TFEU; *see* also Protocol (No 3) on the Statute of the Court of Justice of the European Union, Article 58.
13. Article 267 TFEU.

1.5 SOURCES OF EU LAW

1.5.1 Treaty Articles, Regulations, Directives

EU law takes precedence over the national laws of the Member States.[14] Member States are also under a duty to refrain from any measure which could jeopardise the attainment of the EU's objectives.[15]

The primary source of EU competition law are the Treaty articles, notably Articles 101–109 TFEU. There is also a large amount of secondary legislation in particular, Regulations establishing the current competition regime. Regulations are directly applicable and establish uniform rules across the EU. Regulations, which shall be discussed include 1/2003[16] which sets out the provisions implementing Articles 101 and 102, sectoral block exemptions in the field of air transport (which have now lapsed although Regulation 487/2009[17] enables further Regulations to be adopted) and block exemptions for other types of agreements, notably vertical agreements covered by Regulation 330/2010[18] and the EU Merger Regulation 139/2004.[19]

Directives are harmonising measures establishing minimum standards which must be met by Member States, and must be implemented by Member States in their national laws. Directives are rarely adopted in the field of competition law.

1.5.2 Commission Notices, Decisions and Case Law of the ECJ

The European Commission, which, together with the national competition authorities (NCAs) and national courts, is responsible for the enforcement of the competition law provisions of the Treaty, has also published Notices giving guidance on the interpretation of primary and secondary legislation on a wide range of matters such as market definition, horizontal and vertical agreements, State aid and mergers. It also publishes documents and memoranda on developments such as judgments of the Court of Justice.[20]

There are also Decisions of the European Commission, for example, concerning particular agreements, conduct, merger activity or State aid. These are binding on the party(ies) to whom they are addressed. More rarely, the Council has adopted decisions mandating the Commission to take action, albeit not directly in the field of competition

---

14. Case C-35/76 Simmenthal [1978] ECR 629.
15. Article 4 Treaty on European Union.
16. Council Regulation (EC) No. 1/2003 of 16 December 2002 on the implementation of the rules on competition laid down in Articles 81 and 82 of the Treaty (OJ L1, 4.1.03, p1).
17. Council Regulation (EC) No. 487/2009 of 25 May 2009 on the application of Article 81(3) of the Treaty to certain categories of agreements and concerted practices in the air transport sector.
18. Commission Regulation 330/2010 of 20 April 2010 on the application of Article 101(3) TFEU to categories of vertical agreements and concerted practices 2010 OJ L 102 page 1.
19. Council Regulation (EC) No. 139/2004 of 20 January 2004 on the control of concentrations between undertakings 20 January 2004 (OJ L 24, 29.1.2004, p. 1).
20. Commission decisions, notices and other communications are available on the Commission's website at: http://ec.europa.eu/competition/.

law, such as the mandate it granted the Commission to negotiate with third countries in relation to ASAs following the *Open Skies* judgments (discussed in Chapter 2).

Finally, there is the jurisprudence of the General Court, formerly the Court of First Instance of the European Communities, and the Court of Justice. This is binding on the parties and on the courts of the Member States.[21]

1.6 OUTLINE OF THE EU COMPETITION RULES

One of the EU's exclusive competences is to establish the competition rules necessary for the functioning of the EU internal market.[22] The legislative framework of European competition policy is provided by the Articles 101–109 TFEU, with further rules provided by Council and Commission Regulations. EU competition comprises the following main areas of action: the prohibition of agreements which restrict competition (Article 101); the prohibition of abuse of a dominant position (Article 102); the prohibition of mergers which would significantly impede effective competition by creating or strengthening a domination position (EU Merger Regulation); the liberalisation of monopolised sectors (Article 106); and the prohibition of State aid (Articles 107–109).

This section gives a brief outline of objectives of the EU competition rules as well as an overview of the principal prohibitions and Regulations. These are discussed in more detail in subsequent chapters dealing with agreements, abuse of a dominant position, mergers and joint ventures, enforcement and State aid respectively.

1.6.1 Objectives of EU Competition Policy

One of the fundamental principles set out in Article 3(f) of the EEC Treaty in 1957 was 'the institution of a system ensuring that competition is not distorted in the Community'. Article 119 TFEU also provides 'The activities of the Member States and the Union shall include, as provided in the Treaties, the adoption of an economic policy which is based on the close coordination of Member States' economic policies, on the internal market and on the definition of common objectives, and conducted in accordance with the principle of an open market economy with free competition.' The Treaty provisions on competition since the EEC Treaty have remained virtually unchanged.

The underlying premise of competition law is that in the open market economy, rules are needed to prevent practices such as price fixing, market sharing, abuse of a dominant position, anticompetitive mergers, the granting of unjustified monopoly rights and State aid measures which distort competition by artificially keeping companies in business.[23]

21. For further discussion, *see* textbooks such as The European Union and its Court of Justice 2nd edition by Anthony Arnull 2006; European Union Law of Competition 7th edition by Bellamy & Child 2013.
22. Article 3(1)(b) TFEU.
23. 30th Report on Competition Policy, European Commission 2000 para. 1.

All or most of these principles are generally common to antitrust systems globally. A second objective of EU competition law, distinct from other systems such as the US, is the integration of national markets into a single European market without barriers between Member States – a factor which led to liberalisation and competition rules in the air transport sector in Europe (*see* Chapter 2).

1.6.2 Article 101 TFEU: Prohibition of Anticompetitive Agreements

Article 101(1) prohibits agreements and concerted practices, which are looser forms of collaboration, between two or more 'undertakings' or decisions of associations of undertakings, which may affect trade between Member States and which have as their object or effect the prevention, restriction or distortion of competition within the EU. This prohibits cartels such as price fixing, market sharing, limiting output or capacity and bid rigging and substantial fines are imposed for such infringements. It may also prohibit commercial agreements such as cooperation agreements or other alliances and joint ventures as well as 'vertical' agreements such as supply or distribution agreements which contain territorial or exclusivity restrictions. Article 101(2) provides that any agreement or decision prohibited under Article 101(1) shall be void.

An agreement which restricts competition may nevertheless escape the prohibition and nullity under Article 101(1)–(2) if the benefits of the agreement outweigh the anticompetitve effects, assessed by reference to four cumulative criteria, set out in Article 101(3). These criteria are as follows: (a) the agreements must contribute to improving the production or distribution of goods or promote technical or economic progress; (b) consumers must receive a fair share of the resulting benefits; (c) the restrictions imposed by the agreements must be indispensable to the attainment of these objectives; and (d) the agreements must not afford the parties the possibility of eliminating competition in respect of a substantial part of the products or services in question.

Prior to 1 May 2004, it was possible for parties to notify agreements to the Commission for approval. Since that date, there is no system of prior approval, so to check their compliance with competition law, the parties must themselves conduct an assessment of their cooperation under Article 101(1) and (3). Joint ventures involving coordination of the parents (as opposed to 'full-function' joint ventures falling within the scope of the EU Merger Regulation 139/2004 (discussed in Chapter 8 *Mergers and Alliances*)) would fall within this category. The Commission (or a national competition authority (NCA)) may, however, open an investigation (either of its own initiative or following a complaint) into proposed or already implemented cooperation if it appears that the cooperation may breach the EU competition rules. If the cooperation falls within Article 101(1), the burden will be on the parties to demonstrate that the exemption criteria under Article 101(3) TFEU are fulfilled.

Agreements may also be exempt if they meet the conditions set out in 'block exemptions' covering certain common types of agreement. There are block exemptions applicable to 'vertical' (supply and distribution/agency) agreements, technology transfer, research and development and specialisation agreements.[24] Block exemptions formed the majority of EU competition law applicable to agreements between airlines, but were gradually phased out and with effect from 2007 all block exemptions have now all been abolished, so that all agreements are now a matter for self-assessment under Article 101(3) by the parties.[25] These block exemptions are discussed in Chapter 2.

1.6.3 Article 102: Prohibition of Abuse of a Dominant Position

Article 102 TFEU prohibits the abuse of a dominant position by an undertaking (or undertakings in rare cases where 'collective dominance' is established) within the EU or a substantial part (a single Member State or region thereof may suffice), in so far as it may affect trade between Member States. Article 102 applies to unilateral conduct in the market, but may also include terms in agreements between dominant firms and other trading partners, potentially rendering such terms unenforceable by the dominant firm.

Abuses fall into two broad categories – 'exclusionary' abuses, which exclude competitors from the market, such as tying obligations or loyalty rebates, and 'exploitative' abuses, where the dominant company exploits its market power by, for example, charging excessive prices, discriminating without objective justification, or imposing other unfair conditions on trading partners. Article 102 TFEU does not contain an equivalent exemption for anticompetitive agreements as set out in Article 101(3) TFEU, whereby a company's conduct may be exempted because of procompetitive benefits. However, a dominant company may avoid an infringement under Article 102 if it can show that its conduct, which on the face it may appear abusive, is in all the circumstances, objectively justified and proportionate.

1.6.4 Enforcement and Penalties for Breach of Articles 101 and 102

As well as rendering the relevant agreement or terms thereof void, infringement of Articles 101 and 102 may expose the parties to very substantial fines (up to 10 per cent of group worldwide turnover) and actions for damages in the courts of the Member States. These may be 'stand-alone' actions, not relying on a finding of an infringement

---

24. *See* Commission Regulation 330/2010 on the application of Article 101(3) of the Treaty on the Functioning of the European Union to categories of vertical agreements and concerted practices OJ L 102, 23.4.2010, pp. 1–7; Commission Regulation 316/2014 on the application of Article 101(3) of the Treaty on the Functioning of the European Union to categories of technology transfer agreements; OJ L 93, 28.03.2014, pp. 17–23 Commission Regulation 1217/2010 on the application of Article 101(3) of the Treaty on the functioning of the European Union to categories of research and development agreements OJ L 335, 18.12.2010, p. 36; Commission Regulation 1218/2010 on the application of Article 101(3) of the Treaty to categories of specialisation agreements OJ L 335, 18.12.2010, p. 43.
25. Regulation 479/2009 nevertheless enables the Commission to adopt block exemptions in respect of agreements between airlines.

by the Commission or a national competition authority (NCA), or 'follow-on' damages claims, which rely on a decision of the Commission or NCA condemning a given infringement.

The Commission and/or NCAs in certain cases, also have extensive powers to carry out investigations in relation to suspected breaches of Articles 101 and 102, order termination of infringements and impose fines. These powers are set out in Regulation 1/2003.[26] This Regulation also confers full powers of investigation on the Commission in respect of agreements and practices and conduct affecting air transport services between EU and non-EU countries.

Both Articles 101 and 102 have 'direct effect' in the laws of the Member States of the EU, which means that they create rights which must be enforced in the national courts. Agreements or conduct contrary to those prohibitions are, therefore, prohibited, without any prior decision to that effect being required. By virtue of the supremacy of EU law, both national courts and administrative authorities are under a duty to disapply national legislation which requires undertakings to act in such a way as to breach Articles 101 or 102.

1.6.5 Public Undertakings: Article 106 TFEU

Public undertakings are subject to competition law. Article 106(1) provides that with regard to public undertakings or undertakings to which a Member State has granted special or exclusive rights – for example a right to operate a port, or historically rights granted by Member States to airlines to operate on given routes – may not enact any measure benefiting such undertakings, which are contrary to the EU competition rules. Article 106(2) offers an exemption where it is necessary for the provision of services of general economic interest (SGEI), such as the operation of unprofitable, often remote, routes. By virtue of Article 106(3), the Commission has the power to adopt Directives or Decisions addressed to Member States, where necessary, to ensure the application of Article 106(1)–(2). The notion of 'undertakings' is discussed below in Chapter 4 section 4.2.

1.6.6 Mergers: EU Merger Control Regulation 139/2004

'Concentrations' – acquisitions, mergers and 'full-function' joint ventures[27]– having an EU dimension (defined by reference to global, EEA and potentially, national, turnover thresholds) must be pre-notified to the Commission for assessment of their compatibility with the internal market. Mergers will be cleared if they are unlikely to significantly impede effective competition in the EEA or in a substantial part of it, in particular as a result of the creation or strengthening of a dominant position. This is

26. Council Regulation 1/2003 of 16 December 2002 on the implementation of the rules on competition laid down in Articles 81 and 82 of the Treaty OJ L 1, 4.1.2003, p. 1.
27. Joint ventures which are not full-function, such as alliances between airlines involving extensive integration of networks, will fall outside the scope of the EUMR and may be subject to Article 101 and/or Article 102 TFEU.

likely to be the case if the merging parties have high market shares and if existing competitors would be unable to challenge the merging parties' exercise of market power. If mergers give rise to serious concerns as to their compatibility with the internal market, they will be subject to a second phase in-depth investigation by the Commission. At either phase one or phase two, however, conditions may be offered by the parties to remedy competition concerns. Mergers will be prohibited where competition concerns cannot be addressed. The majority of mergers are cleared, and the majority of those, by phase one decisions, though in the case of mergers between airlines, commitments from the parties will often be required to address competition concerns as a condition of clearance and these may be significant. There have also been prohibitions, however.[28]

Concentrations lacking an EU dimension are subject to national merger control regimes to the extent they may be applicable, a question which will depend on turnover and/or market share thresholds. There is no harmonisation of national merger control regimes, so each Member State must be considered. Most non-EU countries also have merger control regimes, many of which will also require notification of mergers.

1.6.7 Articles 107–109: Prohibition of State Aid

Article 107(1) TFEU prohibits State-funded aid, such as capital injections, loans, tax exemptions or other measures, granted to undertakings, that distort or threaten to distort competition by favouring certain undertakings. Article 107(2)–(3) provides that certain categories of aid such as aid of a social character, to remedy a crisis in the economy of a Member State or to facilitate the development of certain economic activities (such as rescue and restructuring aid) or of certain economic areas may be deemed to be compatible with the internal market. Such aid must nevertheless be notified in advance by the Member State granting the aid, for clearance by the Commission pursuant to Article 108 TFEU, unless it falls within a limited exceptions such as '*de minimis*' (small amounts of aid). There are also specific EU guidelines on aid to airlines and airports. If a government has been found to grant aid in breach of Article 107 it will be ordered to recover aid from the recipient. National courts also have the power to declare unnotified aid illegal.

28. Decision of 2 October 1991 Case No. IV/M053 – Aerospatiale-Alenia/de Havilland; see also Ryanair/Aer Lingus I and III; Aegean Olympic I – Chapter 8 *Mergers and Alliances*.

CHAPTER 2
Liberalisation of Air Transport

2.1 OVERVIEW

Despite EU competition law being in force from 1958, air transport largely operated beyond the reach of competition law until the late 1980s. Under the international system of air transport, regulated by mostly bilateral and reciprocal agreements between States, the generally incumbent 'flag carrier' airlines benefited from State protection and in many cases ownership, and market access was denied to potential competitors - although some countries agreed to more liberal arrangements. From 1987 to 1992 a process of liberalisation of air transport took place whereby regulatory restrictions on air transport were removed, and legislation enabled the Commission to apply EU competition law to air transport, initially only to intra-EU transport and latterly between the EU and third countries as well, and to grant 'block exemptions' for certain categories of agreements, under which the Commission introduced several exemptions, which have now expired.

2.2 REGULATORY BACKGROUND

2.2.1 Chicago Convention and State Sovereignty over Airspace

The operation of international air services has been and continues to be regulated by air service agreements concluded between States. The principal legal instrument governing international aviation is the Convention on International Civil Aviation of 1944 (Chicago Convention).[29] At the date of writing, the Convention had 191 members, including the 28 Member States of the EU.[30] The Convention also established the International Civil Aviation Organization (ICAO) whose remit is to coordinate and

29. *See* www.icao.int/publications/Documents/7300_orig.pdf.
30. *See* www.icao.int/secretariat/legal/list%20of%20parties/chicago_en.pdf.

regulate international aviation. The International Air Transport Association (IATA) was established in 1947 to provide technical support to ICAO and to adopt industry standards.[31]

The underlying principle, enshrined in Article 1 of the Convention, is that each contracting State has complete and exclusive sovereignty over the airspace above its territory. This codified the traditional view, airlines, most of which were State owned, being regarded as 'flag carriers' and valuable national assets.[32] No scheduled international air service could, therefore, be operated to, from or over a State without its permission.[33] Non-scheduled, including among others charter carriers, were able to operate more freely.

2.2.2 'Freedoms of the Air' and Air Services Agreements

As States drawing up the Chicago Convention could not agree on the freedom to operate international air services, a list of 'freedoms of the air' in relation to the rights of airlines to enter and land in another country's airspace were formulated.[34] They include most significantly the third and fourth freedoms of the air - the rights respectively of an airline to carry passengers and cargo from its own State to another, and vice versa. These 'freedoms' were in fact restrictions on commercial aviation rights, air space being closed unless and until international agreement on such operations was reached between States, by bilateral or multilateral ASAs, and strictly in accordance with and the terms and conditions set out those agreements.[35]

The freedoms are summarised below:[36]

- First Freedom: to overfly one country en route to another.
- Second Freedom: to make a technical stop in another country.
- The first two Freedoms have been granted automatically as between States which are party to, and have ratified, the International Air Services Transit Agreement,[37] also known as the Two Freedoms Agreement, which accompanied the Chicago Convention.
- Third Freedom: the carriage of traffic, that is, passengers and cargo, from the home country of the airline to another country.
- Fourth Freedom: the carriage of traffic to the home country of the airline from another country.

31. *See* generally: http://www.iata.org/about/Pages/index.aspx.
32. OECD Paper 'Airline liberalisation and Competition: the EU experience' John Balfour DAF/COMP(2014)22 4 June 2014, http://www.oecd.org/competition/airlinecompetition.htm.
33. Chicago Convention Article 6 provides: 'No scheduled international air service may be operated over or into the territory of a contracting State, except with the special permission or other authorization of that State, and in accordance with the terms of such permission or authorization'.
34. *See* http://www.icao.int/Pages/freedomsAir.aspx.
35. OECD Paper 'Competition in the Air Transport Sector', Pablo Mendes de Leon 7 September 2011.
36. *Ibid.*
37. *See* http://www.icao.int/secretariat/legal/List%20of%20Parties/Transit_EN.pdf.

- Fifth Freedom: the carriage of traffic between two foreign countries by an airline of a third country, which carriage is linked with third and fourth Freedom traffic rights of the airline.
- Sixth Freedom: the carriage of fifth Freedom traffic between two foreign countries via the home country of the airline.
- Seventh Freedom: the carriage of traffic between two foreign countries by an airline of a third country, which carriage is not linked with third and fourth Freedom traffic rights of the airline.
- Eighth Freedom: the carriage of passengers and cargo between two points in a foreign country on a route with origin and/or destination in the home country of the airline.
- Ninth Freedom: the carriage of passengers and cargo between two points in a foreign country on a route, which is unrelated to the home country of the airline.

These rights – the first four of which would generally be granted – were generally granted on a limited reciprocal basis and with the aim of protecting the national airline and, therefore, severely restricting competition. They also limited capacity and frequency and often limited operations to a single designated airline (resulting in a duopoly on the routes in question), required the use of designated airports only and the approval by both States of fares.[38]

In the *Airfreight cartel* decision (discussed in Chapter 5.2.4), fines were reduced by the European Commission by up to 15 per cent to take into account the regulatory environment of bilateral ASAs.[39] It is understood that certain airlines which had appealed against the finding of an infringement of EU competition law argued that the agreements on pricing resulted from provisions of ASAs relating to the setting of air fares. If adherence to such agreements was mandated by State laws, with no possibility for individual choice, private operators would not be guilty of a breach of competition law.[40]

Most ASAs also include provisions whereby one State may withhold or withdraw operating rights if the airlines from the other State is not 'substantially owned and effectively controlled' by one of the contracting parties, thus excluding third parties. While such restrictions could be justified to some extent by safety and security requirements, they limit airlines' ability to operate in other countries and restrict their freedom as regards mergers given that traffic rights under ASAs could be lost if more than the permitted degree of ownership or control was transferred to foreign nationals.[41]

---

38. *See* note 30 *supra.*
39. Case COMP/39258 – Airfreight *see* official summary at: http://ec.europa.eu/competition/antitrust/cases/dec_docs/.../39258_6547_3.pdf; official decision as yet unpublished. The Airfreight Cartel case is discussed in Chapter 5 below.
40. Joined Cases C-359/95 P and C-379/95 P Commission and French Republic *v.* Ladbroke Racing Ltd ECR I-6301 1998, para. 33.
41. *See* Airline Competition – Background Paper by the Secretariat OECD – 18–19 June 2014 DAF/COMP(2014)14.

2.2.3 Absence of Competition Regulation in International Air Transport

By creating a system under which market access by airlines, capacity and frequencies, were agreed by individual governments, the Chicago Convention led to results that were incompatible with competition law, with State carriers protected, other airlines excluded and fares very high. Air transport continues to be excluded from the World Trade Organisation (WTO) General Agreement on Trade in Services (GATS), the Annex on Air Transport Services excluding traffic rights and traffic related services.[42]

2.3 EXCLUSION OF AIR TRANSPORT FROM THE APPLICATION OF EU COMPETITION LAW

2.3.1 Enforcement of EU Competition Law from 1962

Competition law was established in Europe in 1958, with the Treaty of Rome establishing the European Communities (the 'Treaty') and containing the primary provisions on competition (now Articles 101 and 102 TFEU, as well as provisions regulating public undertakings and State aid) and provided for the creation of a competition enforcement regime.[43] Regulation 17/62, the procedural Regulation for the implementation and enforcement of competition law[44] gave the Commission power to investigate, order termination of, and impose fines for suspected infringements. Regulation 17/62 was not restricted sector-wise in its application.[45] However, it was retrospectively limited by Council Regulation 141/62 so as to exclude transport from the procedural rules for enforcing Articles 101 and 102 which it laid down.[46] This was stated to be on the grounds that the characteristics of the common transport policy, which was yet to be established, might require different rules from other sectors.[47]

While the Treaty had provided for the establishment of a common transport policy,[48] there was no agreement between Member States on what this should comprise. Further, the Council had discretion as to whether provisions may be laid

42. WTO General Agreement on Trade in Services (GATs) Annex of Air Transport Services 1994; for the time being, ancillary services such as distribution and selling of air services, maintenance and repair of aircraft and the operation of Computerised Reservation Systems (CRSs), now Global Distribution Systems (GDSs) may be made subject to the liberalisation set forth by the WTO/GATS regime. *See also* Chapter 10.6.2 Subsidies to Third Country Airlines.
43. Article 87 EEC Treaty, now as amended Article 103 TFEU obliged the Council to adopt regulations or directives for the application of competition rules within three years.
44. Council Regulation No. 17: First Regulation implementing Articles 85 and 86 of the Treaty Official Journal 21/02/1962 page 204–211.
45. The regime for notification of agreements to the Commission for exemption or negative clearance was abolished in 2004 by Regulation 1/2003 (discussed Chapter 4).
46. Council Regulation No. 141/62 exempting transport from the application of Council Regulation No. 17. OJ 124, 28.11.1962, p. 2751.
47. *Ibid* recital 1.
48. Article 3(e) of the EEC Treaty provided 'the activities of the Community shall include ... the inauguration of a common transport policy'.

down for transport, and unanimity was required for the adoption of legislation.[49] EU Member States, therefore, continued to regulate both their own domestic and international aviation by means of ASAs, leaving the air transport sector largely competition free.

Prior to the adoption of Regulation 141/62 and aware of the controversy surrounding the application of competition law to transport, the Commission had stated that the existence of the special and rather weak, provisions on transport, did not rule out the applicability of the Treaty's general rules, including competition law, in the transport field, on the basis that those rules were universally applicable unless otherwise stipulated in the Treaty.[50]

2.3.2 Services Ancillary to Air Transport

The Commission did take action against airlines in respect of services ancillary to air transport, such as ground handling services[51] and computer reservation systems (CRSs),[52] – now also referred to as Global Distribution Systems (GDSs) – thus making it clear that the exclusions of 141/62 did not include such services.

2.3.3 'Transitional' Rules on Competition in the Transport Sectors

There were 'transitional' rules for the application of competition law in the transport sector but these were limited in scope. Then Articles 88 and 89 EEC (now amended Articles 104 and 105 TFEU – old numbering used in the following sections of this chapter) set out the powers conferred on national authorities and the Commission, respectively. National authorities were obliged to 'rule upon the admissibility' of potential infringements having regard to EU competition law, and the Commission had the power to investigate infringements in conjunction with Member State authorities and could 'propose appropriate measures to bring them to an end', authorising Member States to take enforcement measures (if they wished to do so). The Commission itself had no power to order the termination of an infringement.

2.3.4 Commission Action in Relation to Air Transport Services under 'Transitional' Rules

The Commission made attempts to apply the competition rules to air transport, but in the absence of powers to investigate, order the termination of infringements or impose

49. [then] Article 84(2) of the Treaty provided that the Council, acting by means of a unanimous vote, 'may decide whether, to what extent and by what procedure appropriate provisions might be adopted for sea and air transport'.
50. Memorandum on the general lines of the common transport policy COM (61) 50 final, 10 April 1961, paras 33–35.
51. Olympic Airways Decision 85/121 OJ 1985 l46 p51.
52. London European Sabena Decision 88/589 Infringement Article102 with fine OJ L 317, 24/11/1988 Page 47 – *see* Chapter 7 *Abuse of a Dominant Position*.

fines, which Regulation 17 would have provided, without success. It put questions to Member States and airlines in relation to tariff fixing and capacity-sharing agreements which could infringe competition law[53] and brought infraction proceedings against seven Member States for refusing to respond, to which the majority stated that the competition rules did not apply to air transport, so they were under no obligation to cooperate.[54] The Commission also pursued discussions with the Council to bring air transport within the procedural Regulation 17/62[55] and action was brought by the Parliament against the Council for failure to implement a common transport policy, although the Court held that the action failed on the grounds that the obligation was too vague to be enforceable.[56]

2.4 EARLY APPLICATION OF COMPETITION LAW TO AIR TRANSPORT

2.4.1 *Nouvelles Frontières* Decision of the Court of Justice[57]

A French Court had been asked to enforce a criminal law to convict travel agents for not adhering to tariffs approved by the Minister for Civil Aviation,[58] and considering the French law breached Article 101, made a reference to the Court of Justice for a preliminary ruling. The case attracted attention from not only the airlines involved (Air France and KLM) and the French Government who had brought the prosecution, but also the governments of Italy, the Netherlands and the UK, as well as the European Commission, who all made submissions to the Court.

The Court held, for the first time, that air transport was indeed subject to competition law and that if Member States approved tariffs which breached competition law, this would also breach Article 106 TFEU which prohibits Member States from adopting, with regard to public undertakings or undertakings enjoying special or exclusive rights, any measure that would lead to an infringement of EU law.[59] The Court stated that Treaty provisions could only be excluded from other Treaty provisions by an express provision of the Treaty and noted that there had been no such

53. European Commission Annual Report on Competition Policy 1981, para. 5.
54. European Commission Annual Report on Competition Policy 1985, para. 32.
55. Discussed *Ibid* paras 27–33. The Commission's proposals were set out, amongst others, in the Civil aviation memorandum No. 2 (1984) which proposed an approach of reducing governments' control over tariffs and conditions for exemption for airlines from Article 85.
56. Case 13/83 European Parliament v Council [1985] ECR 1513.
57. Joined cases 209 to 213/84 Ministère Publique v Asjes and others ('Nouvelles Frontières') [1986] ECR 1245.
58. The French Civil Aviation Code provided that air transport could only be provided by undertakings approved by the Minister for Civil Aviation, that airlines must submit their tariffs for approval, and that approval rendered that tariff binding on all traders selling tickets of that airline for the journey specified.
59. In so doing, it cited the French Merchant Seamen case 1974 where the ECJ had already held that even though sea and air transport were not covered by the Treaty's common transport policy until such time as the Council decided they should be included, they were nevertheless subject to other treaty provisions Case C-167/73 Commission v France ('French Merchant Seamen') [1974] ECR 359.

exclusion of transport from the competition rules and that the Treaty rules on competition therefore applied to air transport.[60]

In the absence of legislation implementing the competition rules, however, the Court held that the Commission could not order termination of infringements, unless there was a prior decision of a national authority under (then) Article 88, or of the Commission under Article 89. Nor was it open to a national court to declare an agreement incompatible with Article 101(1)[61] because it had no power to make a full assessment under Article 101 given it had no power to grant an exemption under Article 101(3) in respect of agreements.[62]

2.4.2 Commission Action Post *Nouvelles Frontières*

Following the Court's judgment in *Nouvelles Frontières*, the Commission commenced proceedings against 10 airlines under Article 89(1) in respect of capacity and revenue-sharing joint ventures and tariff concertations, and proposals were made for legislation liberalising air transport and extending competition enforcement powers to air transport, with sector specific exemptions under Article 101(3). Legislation was adopted in December 1987, and actions against the airlines were allowed to lapse.[63]

2.5 LIBERALISATION OF AIR TRANSPORT IN THE EU

2.5.1 Background

As mentioned above, the *Nouvelles Frontières* decision of the Court of Justice was a catalyst for liberalisation. Two further developments were also significant.

The Single European Act 1986: The most significant obstacle to opening up air transport to competition was the unanimity of Member States voting in the Council, which was required to approve such legislation. This was, however, removed by the Single European Act 1986[64] so that an individual government could no longer veto changes to the status quo, and was replaced by 'qualified majority' voting.[65]

US Deregulation: An economic driver for liberalisation was the threat posed by the more efficient US airlines, coupled with their clear ambitions to expand their services into Europe. The Airline Deregulation Act 1978 liberalised US domestic

60. *Nouvelles Frontières supra,* paras 40–42.
61. *Ibid* para. 68.
62. *Ibid* paras 76–77.
63. *See* generally Sixteenth Report of Competition Policy point 36; Seventeenth report on competition policy point 46).
64. The SEA was adopted due to the failures to achieve a Single Market, with plan set up to achieve this by 1 January 1993 by means of harmonising laws across all sectors.
65. A 'qualified majority' is currently defined as at least 55 per cent of the members of the Council representing the participating Member States, comprising at least 65 per cent of the population of these States. A blocking minority must include at least the minimum number of Council members representing more than 35 per cent of the population of the participating Member States, plus one member, failing which the qualified majority shall be deemed attained – Article 238(3)(a) TFEU.

aviation, bringing an end to strict price and entry controls, followed by the International Air Transportation Competition Act 1979 which sought to open up international markets to US airlines, who were seeking to operate increased and more cost effective services, by promoting liberalised bilateral ASAs.[66] The apparent success of the US deregulation encouraged the Commission in its attempts to liberalise air transport in the EU.

2.5.2 EU Approach to Liberalisation

Liberalisation in the EU followed a more gradual approach than the US due to differences in the industry in the EU, which comprised independent States with sovereign rights over their airspace, and was dominated by State owned flag carrier airlines. Liberalisation of air transport in the EU, therefore, took the form of legislation phased in three packages from 1987 to 1992, accompanied by legislation enabling the Commission to enforce EU competition law and to issue block exemptions for categories of agreements.[67]

2.5.3 First Liberalisation Package 1987

The measures adopted by the Council in the first liberalisation package were: Regulation 3975/87 laying down the procedure for the application of the rules on competition to undertakings in the air transport sector;[68] Regulation 3976/87 on the application of Article 101(3) to certain categories of agreements and concerted practices in the air transport sector;[69] Directive 87/601 on fares for scheduled air services between Member States, reducing fare restrictions, laying down criteria which must be applied by Member States when approving fares, and requiring them to approve them if they were reasonably related to the long term fully allocated costs of the carrier;[70] and Decision 87/602 on the sharing of passenger capacity between air carriers on scheduled air services between Member States and on access for air carriers to scheduled air service routes between Member States. This allowed capacity to vary between 55 per cent and 45 per cent (and subsequently 60 per cent and 40 per cent) as opposed to a rigid 50/50 split, and obliged Member States to designate more than one national airline on a given route, known as 'multiple designation'.[71]

The competition Regulations are discussed in section 2.6 below.

66. In the early 1990s, the US concluded a number of 'Open Skies' Agreements with several EU Member States, discussed below.
67. *See* generally John Balfour, European Community Air Law 1995.
68. OJ 1987, L 374, p. 1.
69. OJ 1987, L 374, p. 9.
70. OJ 1987, L 374, p. 12.
71. OJ 1987, L 374, p. 19.

2.5.4 Second Liberalisation Package 1990

The Regulation on fares 2342/90 gave greater flexibility to airlines to set their own fares and introduced the principle of 'double disapproval', whereby a fare introduced would be authorised unless the authorities of both Member States connected by the route disapproved of it.[72] Regulation 2343/90 on access for air carriers to scheduled intra-EU air service routes and on the sharing of passenger capacity air carriers on scheduled services between Member States provided, amongst other things, for the removal of bilateral restrictions on capacity quotas, eliminating them totally by 1 January 1993.[73]

2.5.5 Third Liberalisation Package 1992: Single European Aviation Market

Most significantly, Regulation 2407/92 introduced a common system for the licensing of air carriers within the EU, laying down common specifications and criteria for the licensing of air carriers with effect from 1 January 1993.[74] These included requirements, notably, that airlines be owned and effectively controlled by a majority of EU nationals,[75] as well as minimum insurance, safety and fitness requirements. Any airlines which met these standards would be entitled to an operating licence to serve any international route within the EU. Any discrimination on grounds of nationality or preferential treatment of national flag carriers was prohibited. Restrictions on charter airlines and limits on the number of 'seat only' sales were also abolished.

Second, Regulation 2408/92 on route access, allowed free access to international intra-EU routes for EU carriers, as well as the more far-reaching right to offer services between airports in two other Member States without taking off or landing in their own country, for example, the right of a UK carrier to fly between other EU Member States without starting or ending at a UK airport – so-called 'seventh freedom' rights.[76] It also abolished the sharing of capacity between airlines on intra-EU routes and allowed without restrictions, the multiple designation of airlines on intra-EU routes. From 1997, it also granted EU carriers the right of 'cabotage' – the ability to offer services on domestic routes within any Member State of the EU (known as the 'eighth' freedom of the air), without the need for a preceding or following flight from the UK.

Finally, Regulation 2409/92 on fares introduced the freedom for airlines to set their own fares on services within and between Member States.[77]

72. Council Regulation 2342/90 on fares for scheduled air services OJ L 217, 11.8.1990, p. 1–7.
73. Council Regulation 2343/90 on access for air carriers to scheduled intra-Community air service routes and on the sharing of passenger capacity between air carriers on scheduled air services between Member States OJ L 217, 11.08.1990 pp. 8–14.
74. Council Regulation 2407/92 on licensing of air carriers OJ L 240, 24.8.1992, pp. 1–7.
75. *Ibid*, as amended by Regulation 1008/2008 Article 4(f).
76. Council Regulation 2408/92 on access for Community air carriers to intra-Community air routes OJ L 240, 24.08.1992 pp. 8–14.
77. Council Regulation 2409/92 on fares and rates for air services. OJ L 240, 24.08.1992 P. 15–17. This was subject to safeguards against unfair pricing, including notification to the European Commission.

These Regulations were repealed and consolidated into a single air services Regulation 1008/2008 which also introduced new requirements concerned with pricing transparency.[78]

The 'third package' removed all remaining regulatory restrictions on operations within the EU by EU airlines, and established what has come to be known as the 'EU single aviation market'. This has subsequently been extended, in some cases wholly and in others mostly, and by various different international agreements, to many neighbouring and nearby countries, including Norway, Iceland, Switzerland, Morocco, Serbia and Israel. 'Open skies' agreements have also been concluded between the EU and the US and Canada. Air transport between the EU and other third countries continues to be governed by the relevant bilateral ASAs. Air transport between the EU and third countries continued to be governed by the ASAs, however. These and the *Open Skies* judgments of the ECJ are discussed in section 2.7 below.

2.6 EU COMPETITION RULES IN AIR TRANSPORT (1988–2004)

2.6.1 Regulation 3975/87 on the Application of Articles 101 and 102 to Air Transport

This Regulation gave the Commission powers to enforce competition law, similar to those in other sectors, but differing in three respects. The Regulation applied to intra-EU air transport until 30 April 2004 and indicates the approach which the Commission adopted in relation to specific types of agreements, so is discussed briefly below.

First, Article 2 exempted 'technical agreements' the sole object and effect of which was 'to achieve technical improvements or cooperation'. These included the application of technical standards for aircraft, aircraft parts and equipment, for fixed installations for aircraft, the exchange, pooling or training of personnel for technical or operational purposes, conditions governing the application of transport tariffs provided that such rules do not directly or indirectly fix transport fares and conditions, arrangements for the sale and acceptance of tickets between air carriers, known as 'interlining', as well as the refund, prorating and accounting schemes established for such purposes and the clearing and settling of accounts between air carriers by means of a clearing house.[79]

Second, the exemption of agreements under Article 101(3) was dealt with by means of an 'opposition procedure' whereby undertakings would submit an application to the Commission, which would publish a summary on the Official Journal of the

78. Council Regulation 1008/2008 of 24 September 2008 on common rules for the operation of air services in the Community (Recast) OJ L 293, 31.10.2008, pp. 3–20; *see* Articles 22 and 23. For detailed discussion of liberalisation *see* John Balfour European Community Air Law 1995.
79. Article 2 of Regulation 3975/87 and Annex. This was repealed by Regulation 411/2004 on the basis it was of a purely declaratory nature.

EU and an exemption would be deemed to be granted - for a period of six years and with retrospective effect - on the expiry of 90 days unless the Commission notified the parties to the contrary. Examples of such notifications, to which objection was not raised, included a joint operating agreement between British Midland and Sabena on a service between Birmingham and Brussels,[80] a joint venture between British Airways, KLM and Sabena creating Sabena World Airlines, which never came into effect[81] and IATA cargo tariff coordination.[82]

Most significantly, however, and in contrast with all other industry sectors, the Commission's powers were restricted to intra-EU transport, services to third countries being excluded.[83]

2.6.2 Block Exemption 'Enabling' Regulation 3976/87

The Commission was also granted power to exempt the following categories of agreements:[84] joint planning and coordination of airline schedules; consultations on tariffs for the carriage of passengers, baggage and freight on scheduled services; joint operations on new or less busy scheduled air services; slot allocation at airports and airport scheduling in accordance with a Code of Conduct adopted by the Council; and common purchase, development and operation of CRSs relating to timetabling, reservations and ticketing by air transport undertakings.[85]

2.6.3 Commission Block Exemptions

The Commission made liberal use of its power to adopt block exemptions, adopting Regulations 2671/88 on agreements relating to joint planning and coordination of capacity, sharing of revenue and consultations on tariffs on scheduled air services and slot allocation at airports, 2672/88 on CRSs for air transport services and 2673/88 on ground handling services.[86] Commission Regulation 2671/88 was subsequently

80. OJ C 29, 8.2.1990, pp. 3–4.
81. OJ C 82, 31.3.1990, pp. 7–8.
82. OJ C 228, 5.9.1989, pp. 2–7.
83. Domestic services within a single Member State were also excluded, but were included within the scope of the competition law by Regulation 2410/92 amending Regulation 3975/87.
84. According to the preamble, the Regulation was based on the idea that the air transport sector had to date been governed by a network of international agreements, bilateral agreements between States and bilateral and multilateral agreements between air carriers and that the changes required to that system to ensure competition should be effected gradually so as to provide time for the air transport sector to adapt.
85. Article 2, Regulation 3976/87 as amended. Regulation 3976/87 had originally authorised the block exemption of revenue sharing subject to narrow conditions, as well as ground handling and in-flight catering services. It had not, however, authorised the block exemption of freight tariff consultations or joint operations, both of which were added.
86. These 1988 block exemptions were amended and replaced by Regulations 82/91, 83/91 and 84/91 two of which were themselves extended, the ground handling Regulation 82/91 expiring on 31 December 1992.

amended by Regulation 1617/93[87] and 2672/88 by 3652/93.[88] These block exemptions have now expired, but are discussed briefly given their relevance to agreements pre-1 May 2004 and as an indication of the Commission's approach to the agreements listed.

2.6.3.1 IATA Tariff Consultations

The Commission considered that consultations on passenger and cargo tariffs within the IATA tariff conference structure, while caught by Article 101(1), may contribute to the acceptance of interlinable fares and rates, to the benefit of air carriers and passengers. 'Interlining' is the facility whereby a passenger can arrange transport using more than one airline on an itinerary involving stops at one or more than one airport. The Commission exemption required that consultations must not exceed the aim of facilitating interlining, users must be able to purchase a single ticket combining services of more than one carrier and change the reservation to another service on the same route operated by another carrier, provided this was permitted by the terms and conditions of the initial reservation. Consultations could not result in binding agreements and fares had to be available to all EU passengers irrespective of their nationality or country of residence.

In 1989, IATA had applied for an exemption under Article 101(3) in respect of IATA Tariff Coordination which was found to benefit from the block exemption.[89]

In 1993, IATA resolutions adopted at tariff conferences providing for the imposition of a worldwide fixed surcharge on all freight movements, were, however, considered to be outside the scope of the block exemption, on the basis that while the surcharge formed part of an interlinable tariff, its main purpose was to raise revenue (as opposed to facilitate interlining) and it failed to take account of the different cost impact on different carriers. An amended resolution giving individual carriers greater discretion in applying the surcharge did not remove the Commission's concerns, most carriers treating the surcharge as binding and was abandoned.[90]

The block exemption, originally granted by Regulation 2671/88 was modified on subsequent occasions and in its final form, Regulation 1459/2006 exempted only IATA consultations on passenger (and not cargo) tariffs and allocation of slots at congested airports. This Regulation was not renewed beyond 2007 on the basis that the need for tariff consultations was unclear. Thereafter, compatibility with competition law has been a matter of assessment by parties to such agreements under Article 101(3).

87. Commission Regulation 1617/93 on the application of Article 85(3) of the Treaty to certain categories of agreements and concerted practices concerning joint planning and coordination of schedules, joint operations, consultations on passenger and cargo tariffs on scheduled air services and slot allocation at airports [OJ L 155 of 26.06.1993].
88. Commission Regulation (EC) No. 3652/93 of 22 December 1993 on the application of Article 85 (3) of the Treaty to certain categories of agreements between undertakings relating to computerised reservation systems for air transport services OJ L 333, 31.12.1993.
89. Notice pursuant to Article 5 (2) of Council Regulation (EEC) No. 3975/87 concerning case No. IV/32.680 IATA cargo tariff coordination 1989 OJ C 228/2 (notice inviting third party comments).
90. *See* Comp Rep EC 1993 p155.

2.6.3.2 Joint Planning and Coordination of Schedules

This was permitted in cases where airlines could not reasonably be expected to operate the route independently, to ensure the maintenance of services to new or less busy routes, periods or times of the day, and help develop onward connections.[91] Such planning could include connecting flights between different airlines. Planning and coordination of minimum capacity to be provided on services the connection of which was coordinated between airlines could be permitted, provided that it did not limit the capacity to be provided by participating carriers or lead to them sharing capacity. The Regulation also permitted carriers to agree schedules and the minimum capacity to be utilised on such schedules, so as to facilitate interlining.

2.6.3.3 Joint Operations

There was an exemption of agreements on the joint operation of a scheduled air service on a new or low density route between EU airports, such joint operation taking the form of one carrier sharing the revenues and costs of a scheduled service operated by another carrier.[92] This was subject to a maximum duration of three years, airlines being able to exit at the end of a traffic season, and the parties being free to offer additional services on the routes in question and set fares, capacity and schedules independently.

2.6.3.4 Slot Allocation and Airport Scheduling

Regulation 1617/93 also exempted arrangements on slot allocation at airports and airport scheduling, so as to improve the utilisation of airport capacity and airspace, facilitate air-traffic control and help to spread the supply of air transport services from the airport.[93] It required that entry to congested airports must remain open to all interested airlines, and in order to ensure transparency, such arrangements could only be accepted if all air carriers concerned could participate in the negotiations, and if the allocation was made on a non-discriminatory and transparent basis. A condition of exemption was that new entrants must have priority regarding 50 per cent of newly created or available slots in accordance with Regulation 95/93 on common rules for the allocation of slots at Community airports (*see also* Chapter 7.4.5.4).

2.6.3.5 Computer Reservation Systems (CRSs, Now GDSs)

Regulation 2672/88 permitted joint ventures to create and operate CRSs (now more commonly known as 'GDSs', on the basis that few individual European undertakings could achieve the economies of scale required to compete with the more advanced

91. Regulation 1617/93 Article 4(1)f.
92. Regulation 1617/93 Article 1, 3.
93. Regulation 1613/96 Recital 6.

existing systems.[94] The Commission required that CRSs allow free access on non-discriminatory terms and display of information to be unbiased in favour of particular airlines.[95] A Regulation imposing a Code of Conduct for CRSs operating in the EU, including Amadeus and Galileo, was adopted by the Council in 1989.[96] This has been amended and the current Regulation applicable is 80/2009, which is subject to review. CRS issues are further discussed in Chapter 6 *Article 101 TFEU: Vertical Agreements* and Chapter 7 *Abuse of a Dominant Position.*

2.6.3.6 *Ground Handling*

Regulation 2673/88 exempted agreements between airlines and suppliers of ground handling services, similarly requiring equal treatment of airlines.[97] There was also a Directive on groundhandling (referred to in Chapter 7 *Abuse of a Dominant Position*).

2.6.4 Enforcement Powers as Regards EU-Third Country Routes

Given that Regulations 3975/88 and 3976/88 did not apply to agreements with third country carriers the Commission had no means directly taking action in respect of such agreements.

In the *Airfreight cartel* decision, the Commission accepted it did not have the powers to sanction alleged cartel behaviour concerning air transport between EU airports and airports in third countries that took place before 1 May 2004. Under these circumstances, the Commission did not find an infringement or impose fines for anticompetitive agreements and practices concerning air transport between EU airports and airports in third countries before 1 May 2004.[98]

Clarification of the pre-1 May 2004 enforcement framework on EU-third country routes and the application of Article 102 was provided by the ECJ in the *Ahmed Saeed* case (discussed in the section below).

---

94. Regulation 3652/93 Recital 5.
95. Commission Regulation 2672/88 of 26 July 1988 on the application of Article 85(3) of the Treaty to certain categories of agreements between undertakings relating to computer reservation systems for air transport services [OJ L 239/9] as amended by Regulation 83/91 and Regulation 3652/93 Commission Regulation (EC) No. 3652/93 of 22 December 1993 on the application of Article 85 (3) of the Treaty to certain categories of agreements between undertakings relating to computerised reservation systems for air transport services OJ L 333, 31.12.1993, pp. 37–44 [OJ 1993 L333/37].
96. Council Regulation (EEC) No. 2299/89 of 24 July 1989 on a code of conduct for computerised reservation systems OJ L 220 of 29.07.1989; amended by Regulation 3089/93 and Regulation 323/1999.
97. Commission Regulation (EEC) 2673/88 of 26 July 1988 on the application of Article 85 (3) of the Treaty to certain categories of agreements between undertakings, decisions of associations of undertakings and concerted practices concerning ground handling services [OJ L 239/17].
98. Case COMP/39258 – Airfreight *see* http://ec.europa.eu/competition/antitrust/cases/dec_docs/.../39258_6547_3.pdf paras 816–817;official decision as yet unpublished.

2.6.5 *Ahmed Saeed* Decision of the Court of Justice[99]

This case had arisen from a reference for a preliminary ruling from the Court of Justice shortly before the Court's judgment in *Nouvelles Frontières*, from a German court where a case had been brought against travel agents in Germany, including Ahmed Saeed Flugreisen, for selling tickets from Frankfurt to Tokyo (indirect flights commencing at Lisbon, Portugal, agents benefitting from and passing on savings from differences in currency rates) at prices which were lower than the tariff approved by the German government. The German court questioned whether the provisions of the German law were contrary to the EU competition rules.

The Court confirmed that the Commission's powers, as regards EU-third country services, were the same as those under the 'transitional regime' as discussed in the *Nouvelles Frontières* case, given that agreements on tariffs on air transport between EU and non-EU countries were outside the scope of the Commission's newly acquired enforcement powers under Regulation 3785/87. While Article 101 in conjunction with Article 106 prohibited national authorities from encouraging the conclusion of agreements on tariffs contrary to Article 101 (or 102 as the case may be), the Commission had no power to investigate or order the termination of such infringements, its powers being limited to those set out in then Article 89 (now as amended 105 TFEU).

As regards Article 102, however, the Court held that an agreement could also be considered an abuse of a dominant position, if one of the airlines was in a dominant position.[100] In such a case, the Court held that the Commission or national court could indeed take action in respect of such abuse, despite the absence of legislation implementing Articles 101 and 102 as regards third countries. This was on the basis that there was no scope for exemption under Article 102, abuse simply being prohibited (*see also* discussion of *Nouvelles Frontières* above). Both national authorities and the Commission, therefore, had the power to prohibit such abuse.[101]

Following this case, the Commission sought powers to apply Articles 101 and 102 to EU/non-EU routes. It stated that given it was not empowered to grant exemption under Article 101(3), there was uncertainty for airlines and Member States when approving tariffs filed by carriers for such routes which may otherwise benefit for exemption.[102] The Commission was not granted these powers.

---

99. Case 66/86 Ahmed Saeed Flugreisen and Silver Line Reisebüro GmbH v Zentrale zur Bekämpfung unlauteren Wettbewerbs e.V. 1989 ECR 803.
100. *Ibid* para. 37. The Court suggested that this may be the case where one airline succeeded in imposing on another the application of a particular tariff. This may not suffice today.
101. Ahmed Saeed, paras 30–32.
102. Proposal for a Council Regulation amending Regulation (EEC) No. 3975/87 of 14 December 1987 laying down the procedure for the application of the rules on competition to undertakings in the air transport sector; Proposal for a Council Regulation amending Regulation (EEC) No. 3976/87 on the application of Article 85(3) of the Treaty to certain categories of agreements and concerted practices in the air transport sector OJ 1989 C248 p7.

2.6.6 Commission Investigations of EU/Non-EU Carrier/Agreements Pre-1 May 2004

There are examples of the Commission investigating agreements with non-EU carriers albeit lacking full enforcement powers. In the case of the proposed alliance between British Airways and American Airlines in 1998, proceedings were commenced in 1996 under then Article 89 (as amended, now Article 105 TFEU), extensive commitments were required by the Commission, and the alliance did not proceed.[103] In Lufthansa /SAS /United Airlines and KLM /NorthWest alliances (procedures commenced at the same time as BA/AA), the Commission for the first time took a formal position pursuant to then Article 89 in 2002.[104] In these cases, the Commission was reliant on the parties to cooperate as regards provision of information and having no power to adopt a decision requiring measures to be taken, was reliant the Member State authorities to do so. Alliances are discussed in Chapter 8 *Mergers and Alliances*.

2.6.7 Extension of EU Competition Enforcement Powers to EU-Third Country Services

On 1 May 2004, the Commission obtained full powers to enforce the EU competition rules in respect of air transport services between EU and third countries, in accordance with the procedural framework that had applied to other industry sectors since 1962. When Regulation 1/2003 was adopted, air transport had been excluded from its application and it was included by means of an amendment of Regulation 1/2003 by Regulation 411/2004.[105]

2.7 EU-THIRD COUNTRY AIR TRANSPORT AND *OPEN SKIES* JUDGMENTS

2.7.1 Obstacles to EU Third Country Competition Enforcement

One important reason why powers had not been given to the Commission to enforce Articles 101 and 102 to EU / non-EU air transport, was due to the conflict that this would create between competition law and Member States' ASAs with third countries, which were a matter of Member State competence, and Member States resisted the

103. Commission notice concerning the alliance between British Airways and American Airlines OJ C 239, 30.7.1998, pp. 10–16. A factor in the competition assessment was restriction on the ability of new entrants to access the market due to the rather limited bilateral agreement in place at the time between US and UK. In 2010, an alliance involving BA / Iberian Airlines and AA was approved. *See* Chapter 8 *Mergers and Alliances*.
104. Commission Notice concerning the alliance between Lufthansa, SAS and United Airlines –procedure under Article 85 (ex 89) EC); Commission Notice concerning the Alliance between KLM Royal Dutch Airlines and Northwest Airlines, Inc. – procedure under Article 85 (ex 89) of the EC Treaty OJ C 181 of 30.07.2002, pp. 2–8; Commission Press Release IP/02/1569.
105. Council Regulation (EC) No. 411/2004 of 26 February 2004 repealing Regulation (EEC) No. 3975/87 and amending Regulations (EEC) No. 3976/87 and (EC) No. 1/2003, in connection with air transport between the Community and third countries (OJ L 68, 6.3.2004, pp. 1–2).

expansion of Commission powers in this area. The restrictive arrangements under bilateral ASAs, which had been dismantled in respect of intra-EU transport, continued to apply unchanged, therefore, in respect of EU-third country traffic.

The Commission issued a proposal that it be granted competence to negotiate and conclude ASAs with third countries and observed that international air transport was fragmented by bilateral agreements, with market opportunities very unevenly distributed for EU carriers. It stated; 'certain third countries are using this to gradually further their own Interests. In this context the member states have similar interests and must stand together. The Community must be considered as one market both internally and externally'.[106] No such powers were granted by the Council.

2.7.2 Nationality Clauses in Third Country Air Services Agreements

The Commission was particularly concerned by the nationality clause in ASAs restricting the rights granted by the third country to nationals of the Member State concerned, as opposed to throughout the EU. This also prevented consolidation between EU airlines given that if an airline was no longer majority owned or controlled by nationals of its home country, it could lose traffic rights which that home country had concluded with third countries. In 2000, a possible acquisition by BA of KLM was reportedly abandoned due to, amongst other things, the fear of a loss of KLM's traffic rights under an Open Skies agreement concluded by the Netherlands with the US if it became majority British owned, the UK not then enjoying similar rights with the US.[107]

The Commission had requested Member States to amend ASAs by replacing existing nationality clauses by a 'Community clause' whereby the air carriers designated to operate the services must be based in the EU and be majority owned and effectively controlled by EU nationals or States.[108] Member States generally did not comply with this request.

Obstacles in the Commission's way were ultimately removed, however, by the judgments of the Court of Justice in the case of *Open Skies*.[109]

2.7.3 '*Open Skies*' Judgments

The Netherlands, Austria, Belgium, Denmark, Sweden, Finland, Luxembourg, and Germany had entered into 'Open Skies' agreements with the US, liberalising air

106. Communication accompanying Commission Proposal for a Council Decision on a consultation and authorisation procedure for agreements concerning commercial aviation relations between Member States and third countries COM (90) 17 final, para. 1.
107. Substantial ownership and effective control of international airlines: The Netherlands. George Middeldorp, the Netherlands Comparative Law Association www.ejcl.org/64/art64-16.html.
108. COM (90) 17 final, *supra*, para. 14.
109. 'Open Skies' Judgements of the Court of Justice in Case C-466/98 Commission v United Kingdom [2002] ECR I-9427; Case C-467/98 Commission v Denmark [2002] ECR 9519; Case C-468/98 Commission v Sweden [2002] ECR 9575; Case C-469/98 Commission v Finland [2002] ECR 9627; Case C-471/98 Commission v Belgium [2002] ECR 9681; Case C-472/98 Commission v Luxemburg [2002] ECR 9741; Case C-475/98 Commission v Austria [2002] ECR 9797; Case C-476/98 Commission v Germany [2002] ECR 9855.]

transport services so as to grant unlimited route and traffic rights, the fixing of prices in accordance with a system of 'mutual disapproval' and the possibility of sharing codes. The Commission brought infraction proceedings against the Member States in question, but not against the Netherlands as it had concluded its Open Skies agreement with the US in September 1992 prior to the the entry into force of the Third Liberalisation Package on 1 January 1993. The UK had entered into a more limited 'Bermuda II' type agreement and was also named as a Defendant.[110]

The Commission charged the Member States with (i) having infringed the external competence of the Community to conclude such agreements (a charge not made against the UK) and (ii) having infringed the provisions of the EU Treaty on the right of establishment by a clause on ownership and control of airlines ('nationality clause') permitting the US to refuse traffic rights to air carriers designated by the Member State signatory, if such carrier was substantially owned and controlled by another Member State. Article 49 TFEU provides: '...restrictions on the freedom of establishment of nationals of a Member State in the territory of another Member State shall be prohibited... Freedom of establishment shall include the right to take up and pursue activities ... under the conditions laid down for its own nationals by the law of the country where such establishment is effected'.

As regards the infringement of the external competence of the Community, the Court confirmed that there was no express legal base to enter into such agreements. In the absence of such a base, competence could nevertheless result by implication if it was necessary to conclude an international agreement in order to ensure the effective exercise of the EU's internal competence. In so doing, the Court applied the principle which it had established in the AETR judgment whereby competence for external relations would shift to the Community to the extent that relations with a third country would affect EU legislation.[111] This was found not to be the case as regards the grant of traffic rights and operating licences to non-EU carriers as these were beyond the scope of the liberalisation packages[112] but was found to be the case for the establishment of air fares on intra-EU routes, CRSs and slot allocation[113] which applied to carriers throughout the EU irrespective of whether they were EU owned or not, and did therefore apply to non-EU carriers, thus being within the exclusive competence of the EU.

As regards the Commission's second ground of challenge, the Court held that the nationality clause was indeed contrary to the rules governing the freedom of establishment. This was on the basis that the clause limiting the benefits to carriers owned and controlled by nationals of the signatory Member State discriminated against carriers

110. This type of agreement restricted rights to named carriers and airports.
111. Case 22/70 Commission v Council [1971] ECR 263.
112. Regulations 2408/92 and 2407/92 dealing with access to intra-EU routes and grant of licences to EU carriers respectively.
113. Regulations 2409/92, 2289/79 (later consolidated into Regulation 1008/2008). Allocation of slots, governed by Regulation 95/93 was also found to apply to US carriers but was not a matter covered by the bilateral agreements. *See also* Chapter 7.4.5.4.

from other Member States, denying them the same treatment as nationals of the home Member State, namely, the same right to offer air transport services from that country to US destinations.

The Court's interpretation of the application of the principle of freedom of establishment had the far-ranging consequence of conferring the potential for third country traffic rights from each Member State on all licensed EU carriers.[114] As a result of these judgments, Member States could not now solely negotiate international air service agreements in respect of the areas highlighted by the Court, and more significantly, could no longer reserve benefits in such agreements to their national carriers alone. The Commission now had to be involved in the negotiation of agreements dealing with issues such as slots, CRSs and fares on intra-EU routes.

2.7.4 Negotiation and Conclusion of Air Services Agreements with Third Countries

The *Open Skies* judgments had clarified the question of the respective competence shared between the Member States and the EU, and resulted in the Member States in question being obliged to bring their bilateral agreements into line with EU law. On 5 June 2003, the Council granted the Commission a mandate to negotiate with the US and with all other third countries on the revision of nationality clauses.[115] Regulation 847/2004 provided a new framework for relations between the EU and third countries, recognising the competence of Member States to negotiates ASAs, but providing for coordination between Member States and the Commission in relation to negotiations with third countries[116] so that existing bilateral agreements between Member States and third countries that contained nationality clauses should be amended or replaced by new agreements with EU designation clauses.[117] This state of affairs led to the conclusion of the agreements discussed below.

2.7.4.1 EU-US Agreement 2007

As regards the US, an EU agreement was concluded in 2007, replacing agreements concluded by individual Member States. This provided for extensive liberalisation, under which US and EU airlines could operate services between any EU and US airport without restriction (third and fourth freedom rights), as well as certain fifth freedom

114. *See* generally Beyond Open Skies: A New Regime for International Aviation, Brian F Havel 2009.
115. Council Decisions of 5 June 2003 authorising the Commission to open negotiations with third countries on the replacement of certain provisions in existing bilateral agreements with a Community agreement, and authorising the Commission to open negotiations with the United States in the field of air transport. *See* IP/03/806.
116. Council Regulation 847/2004 on the negotiation and implementation of air service agreements between Member States and third countries OJ 2004 L 195/3.
117. *Ibid* recital 6. The means of achieving this was by providing for the exchange of information between Member States and the Commission to avoid infringements, and for Member States to have the power to revise agreements, which were numerous, or to enter into new agreements, provided such negotiations were notified to the Commission so as to comply with EU law.

rights whereby airlines could continue from destinations within the US or the EU to other third country destinations. It did not achieve full liberalisation, domestic cabotage rights and restrictions on foreign ownership or control of airlines remaining unresolved (US restricting foreign ownership of airlines to 25 per cent of the shares with voting rights, and the EU requiring Member States or their nationals to own more than 50 per cent and effectively control airlines).[118]

The agreement has also established a framework for regulatory cooperation on competition matters between the Commission and the US Department of Transportation (DOT), providing for general exchange of views and experience between the two authorities, with a view to reducing the potential conflicts in the application of the competition regimes in the EU and the US and promoting compatible regulatory approaches through a better understanding of the methodologies, analytical techniques and remedies used in the respective competition reviews of the Commission and the DOT.[119]

This liberalisation paved the way for Transatlantic alliances beginning with the Star Alliance transatlantic joint venture agreement and greater consolidation between EU carriers.[120] A second stage agreement was signed in June 2010 covering a range of matters, including improvement of labour and security arrangements, and a provision for liberalisation of airline ownership and control, which is yet to be realised.[121]

2.7.4.2 Other EU-Third Country Agreements

Agreements have been concluded with a number of countries including Switzerland (which also contains provisions identical to Articles 101 and 102 TFEU)[122] and Canada.[123] The EU has also concluded agreements with Balkan States establishing a 'European Common Aviation Area' (ECAA), which include provisions on competition

118. Air Transport Agreement between the European Community and the United States of America, 2007 OJ L 134/1. Norway and Iceland became signatories in 2009; *see* Commission press release IP/09/1962. *See also* Commission MEMO/10/103 25 March 2010 – FAQs on the second stage EU-US "Open Skies" Agreement and existing first stage air services agreement.
119. *Ibid* Annex 2. *See* generally Transatlantic Airline Alliances: Competitive Issues and Regulatory Approaches: A report by the European Commission and the United States Department of Transportation 16 November 2010, ec.europa.eu/competition/sectors/transport/.../joint_alliance_report.pdf.
120. *See* Chapter 8 *Mergers and Alliances*.
121. *See* Commission MEMO/10/103 25 March 2010 – FAQs on the second stage EU-US 'Open Skies' Agreement and existing first stage air services agreement. Article 21(2) provides: '...The European Union and its Member States shall allow majority ownership and effective control of their airlines by the United States or its nationals, on the basis of reciprocity, upon confirmation by the Joint Committee that the laws and regulations of the United States permit majority ownership and effective control of its airlines by the Member States or their nationals.'
    See http://ec.europa.eu/transport/sites/transport/files/modes/air/international_aviation/country_index/doc/2010_03_25_us_protocol_attach_b.pdf.
122. The EU-Switzerland agreement had in fact pre-dated the Open Skies judgments entering into force on 1 June 2002 OJ L114/1.
123. December 2009; http://ec.europa.eu/transport/modes/air/international_aviation/country_index/canada_en.htm.

law and State aids,[124] and Morocco, Georgia, Israel, Jordan and Moldova.[125] These agreements seek to achieve gradual market opening between the EU and its neighbours linked with regulatory convergence through the gradual implementation of EU aviation rules. The status of EU aviation relations by country can be viewed on the Commission's website.[126]

2.8 IMPACT OF LIBERALISATION ON BUSINESS MODELS

With the introduction of competition rules and full market access since the early 1990s, air travel and the number of new entrants have increased and prices have decreased.[127]

On one hand, low-cost carriers (LCCs) have emerged as a result of full access to the EU aviation market, including unrestricted cabotage rights as of 1 April 1997, being able to establish bases for crew and aircraft throughout the EU and with online booking facilitating direct sales. The low-cost model is one of low fares, point-to-point flights, often between 'secondary' airports, on short-haul routes to price-sensitive passengers, with the ability to purchase one-way – as opposed to the more restrictive full service carrier return tickets where a one-way ticket may be as expensive as a return. This has been achieved in part by creating new demand by adding not only new routes, but also at the expense of the full service carriers operating on parallel routes. The LCCs operate on lower profit margins than legacy carriers (due to them not generally operating premium class), thus requiring a high load factor. 'LCCs' have grown rapidly and according to ICAO, Ryanair, easyJet, and other European LCCs had expanded to account for 37 per cent of the seat capacity on scheduled services in the EU as at 2012.[128]

On the other hand, and in response to LCC entry, the traditional 'full service' / legacy carriers have used the liberalised market to establish 'hub-and-spoke' systems where the airline selects a 'hub' to or from which traffic would be concentrated for transport from or to another major hub. Passengers would be transported to or from these hubs from or to secondary airports (or 'spokes'). This replaced point-to-point

124. Multilateral Agreement between the European Community and its Member States, Albania, Bosnia and Herzegovina, Bulgaria, Croatia, Macedonia, Iceland, Montenegro, Norway, Romania, Serbia and Kosovo on the Establishment of a European Common Aviation Area; OJ L 285, 16.10.2006, pp. 1–46, Article 14, Annex III. *See also* Máté Gergely 'The 2006 ECAA Agreement: Centrepiece of the European Community's Aviation Policy Towards its Neighbours', Air & Space Law VOL.XXXIII/3 (June 2008).
125. *See* generally http://ec.europa.eu/transport/modes/air/international_aviation/external_aviation_policy/neighbourhood_en.htm and weblinks therein.
126. *See* http://ec.europa.eu/transport/modes/air/international_aviation/country_index/.
127. *See* http://ec.europa.eu/transport/modes/air/internal_market_en.
128. *See* generally 'Airline Cost Performance IATA economics briefing no 5: An analysis of the cost base of leading network airlines versus no-frills, low-cost airlines (LCCs); *see also* OECD Executive summary of the discussion on Airlines Competition DAF/COMP/M(2014)/ANN4/FINAL 28 November 2014.
https://www.iata.org/whatwedo/Documents/economics/airline_cost_performance.pdf; 'Analyses of the European air transport market Airline Business Models' German Aerospace Centre December 2008 http://ec.europa.eu/transport/modes/air/doc/abm_report_2008.pdf.

travel enabling more efficient use of aircraft capacity. There has also been increasing consolidation of the industry through airline alliances.[129]

There has also been a blurring of the boundaries between the low-cost and full service carriers, with each adapting to compete with the other's model, and to a lesser degree, between scheduled and non-scheduled carriers. Certain LCCs have introduced premium categories, as observed by the Commission in relation to Ryanair in its IAG/Aer Lingus decision where it noted that a substantial number of business customers increasingly chose LCCs for their business trip, thus reducing the differences between network carriers' traditional focus on business / premium customers and LCCs' focus on leisure customers, and that LCCs had developed business type classes to attract business customers.[130] Full service carriers have also entered the low-cost market, for example Aer Lingus, now merged with IAG, and Lufthansa, which set up a subsidiary carrier Germanwings to offer travel on the LCC model.

129. *See* generally 'EU Air Transport Liberalisation Process, Impacts and Future Considerations' OECD International Transport Forum Discussion Paper 2015 No. 4 Guillaume Burghouwt, Pablo Mendes de Leon, Jaap De Wit; OECD Airline Competition 18–19 June 2014 DAF/COMP(2014)14.

130. *See* Chapter 8 *Mergers and Alliances*; M.7541 IAG /Aer Lingus, paras 23–25.

Chapter 3
Market Definition

3.1 OVERVIEW

The principles of market definition are relevant to the assessment of an agreement, practice, conduct or merger under competition law. The definition of the 'relevant market' enables the Commission, Court or parties to assess the competitive constraints on the party(ies), hence the effect of the agreement, practice or transaction in question, and the market share of the parties and their competitors.

The 'relevant market' comprises the 'product' and 'geographic' market and is assessed primarily by reference to consumer or customer preferences, known as 'demand-side substitutability'. If products or services are reasonably substitutable from the point of view of customers, they will form part of the relevant market. Market definition is a complex process and will be determined on a case-by-case basis, though case law will clearly be relevant. The ability of undertakings which do not currently compete with the party or parties being assessed, to enter the market within a short period so as to compete with the party(ies), known as 'supply-side substitutability', may exceptionally be found to enable the market definition to be widened to include such competitors. This is often not proved due to the requirement for market entry to exert an effect that is immediate.

The principles set out below are applicable across all industry sectors so will be relevant to agreements or practices involving air transport undertakings. Specific principles have also been developed in relation to airline – airline agreements or mergers, on the basis of the principles set out below (*see* 'Definition of the relevant market' in Chapter 8 *Mergers and Alliances*).

3.2 ROLE OF MARKET DEFINITION IN COMPETITION LAW

Defining the 'relevant market' is the starting point for assessing the effect on competition of any agreement, conduct or merger and will often dictate whether there is a competition infringement or not. According to the Commission, the exercise of market definition consists in identifying the effective alternative sources of supply for the customers of the undertakings involved, both in terms of products or services and the geographic location of suppliers.[131] If there are such alternative sources of supply, they should be included within the relevant market. The process of defining the market focuses on the 'product' market and 'geographic' market, to identify those actual competitors of the undertaking(s) whose agreement, conduct or merger is being assessed, that are capable of constraining those undertakings' behaviour. This also makes it possible to calculate the market share which is a first indication of the market power of companies in a market.

A narrow market definition will result in a higher market share, whereas wider groups of products or services or geographic areas will result in lower shares. Given the potentially adverse implications of high market shares on the competition assessment of agreements, conduct and mergers, a very significant aspect of competition cases is the determination the relevant market. It does not necessarily follow that a significant market share equates to market power, if for example, potential competition - the ability of potential competitors to enter the market quickly and effectively - may significantly constrain the behaviour of the company(ies) being assessed.

3.2.1 Article 101 TFEU Cases: Agreements

Market share is key to the application of Article 101(1), which applies only to agreements which have as their object or effect an 'appreciable' prevention, restriction or distortion of competition. Agreements, which are prima facie anticompetitive where the market shares of the parties are low, will be presumed to be outside Article 101 in the absence of 'hardcore restrictions' or restrictions by object.[132] The test of whether a restriction is 'appreciable' - that the agreement would indeed have an appreciable effect on competition within that market - requires definition of the relevant market. Other Commission Notices such as the Horizontal Guidelines also lay down market share thresholds by way of guidance below which agreements should not be expected to raise concerns.[133] There are also market share thresholds which must not be exceeded for certain categories of agreements to qualify for exemption under block exemption regulations, such as 'vertical' agreements[134] (*see* Chapter 6 *Article 101 TFEU: Vertical Agreements*).

---

131. Commission's Notice on the Definition of the Relevant Market for the purposes of Community law 1997 OJ C 372/3, para. 13.
132. Notice on agreements of minor importance which do not appreciably restrict competition under Article 101(1) of the Treaty on the Functioning of the European Union ('*De Minimis* Notice') (2014/C 291/01).
133. Communication from the Commission — Guidelines on the applicability of Article 101 of the Treaty on the Functioning of the European Union to horizontal cooperation agreements OJ C 11, 14.1.2011, pp. 1-72.
134. Commission Regulation 330/2010 of 20 April 2010 on the application of Article 101(3) of the Treaty on the Functioning of the European Union to categories of vertical agreements and concerted practices. Other block exemptions include Commission Regulation 1217/2010 of 14

Given that the purpose of defining the market is to determine whether an agreement is likely to appreciably restrict competition and trade, in cases where agreements have as their object the prevention, restriction or distortion of competition, market definition is not necessarily a prerequisite for finding an infringement.[135] Certain case law of the Commission and Court of Justice had expanded the scope of agreements which are deemed restrictive 'by object', removing in such cases, the need for proof of an anticompetitive effect, hence to a large degree the importance of market definition.[136] In 2014, however, the Court of Justice made clear that the concept of restriction of competition 'by object' could be applied only to certain types of coordination between undertakings which revealed a sufficient degree of harm to competition that it may be found that there was no need to examine their effects. Otherwise, the Commission would be exempted from the obligation to prove the actual effects on the market of agreements which were in no way established to be, by their very nature, harmful to the proper functioning of normal competition.[137]

3.2.2 Article 102 TFEU Cases: Abuse of a Dominant Position

In the case of Article 102 which applies only to 'dominant' undertakings, an undertaking cannot be dominant unless it has substantial market power. The definition of the relevant market(s) is, therefore, a necessary first step in assessing whether an undertaking is dominant. Undertakings with low market shares (below 40 per cent) will only exceptionally be found to be 'dominant' hence within the scope of Article 102, and the one notable case where this occurred was British Airways in the *Virgin/ British Airways* case (*see* Chapter 7 *Abuse of a Dominant Position* section 7.4.2).

3.2.3 Mergers

Determination of market shares is also key to the assessment of mergers, which must be prohibited by the Commission if they would 'significantly impede effective competition in the EU in a substantial part of it, in particular as a result of the creation or strengthening of a dominant position' (Merger Regulation 139/2004 Article 2(2)),[138]

December 2010 on the application of Article 101(3) of the Treaty on the Functioning of the European Union to certain categories of research and development agreements.

135. *see* Case T-62/98 Volkswagen AG v Commission [2000] ECR II-2707 at paras 230–232.
136. Case C-226/11 Expedia Inc. v Autorité de la concurrence and others, 13 December 2012.
137. Case C-67/13 P, Groupement des Cartes Bancaires 11 September 2014, para. 58. Revised version of 03/06/2015 Guidance on restrictions of competition "by object" for the purpose of defining which agreements may benefit from the *De Minimis* Notice, accompanying the Commission Notice on agreements of minor importance which do not appreciably restrict competition under Article 101(1) of the Treaty on the Functioning of the European Union (*De Minimis* Notice). *See also* Chapter 4 *Elements of Article 101 TFEU*, section 4.5.
138. Council Regulation (EC) No. 139/2004 of 20 January 2004 on the control of concentrations between undertakings 20 January 2004 (OJ L 24, 29.1.2004, p. 1.

Merger Guidelines also providing that mergers where the market share of the merging parties concerned does not exceed 25 per cent should not be expected to raise concerns.[139]

3.3 COMMISSION NOTICE ON MARKET DEFINITION

To provide guidance on how markets should be defined and increase transparency of its approach, the Commission issued in 1997 the Notice on definition of the relevant market (the 'Notice'), codifying its own administrative practice and case law of the Court of Justice on market definition.[140] The approach is similar whether applying Articles 101 or 102 or the EU Merger Regulation and it may be relevant when assessing whether there is a distortion of competition in State aid cases.[141] The majority of case law in recent years, generally, and certainly in the air transport sector, has been under the EU Merger Regulation. This is discussed in Chapter 8 *Mergers and Alliances*.

3.4 'PRODUCT' AND 'GEOGRAPHIC' MARKETS

The relevant market is established by a combination of the 'product' and 'geographic' market. Each of these is considered from the point of view of purchasers or consumers, known as 'demand-side substitutability' and from suppliers, 'supply-side substitutability', with focus on characteristics of the product or service in question, including price.

The Commission has defined the product market, in accordance with case law of the Court of Justice, as follows:

'A relevant market comprises all those products and/or services which are regarded as interchangeable or substitutable by the consumer, by reason of the product's characteristics, their prices and their intended use.'[142] This is known as 'demand-side substitutability'.

It has defined the relevant geographic market as follows: 'The relevant geographic market comprises the area in which the undertakings concerned are involved in the supply and demand of products or services, in which the conditions of competition are sufficiently homogeneous and which can be distinguished from neighbouring areas because the conditions of competition are appreciably different in those areas.'[143] Increasingly, with the reduction in national barriers and globalisation of trade, the Commission focuses on wider geographic definitions comprising the EEA

139. Recital 32 of the Merger Regulation; Guidelines on the assessment of horizontal mergers under the Council Regulation on the control of concentrations between undertakings OJ C 31, 5 February 2004 p5.
140. Commission's Notice on the Definition of the Relevant Market for the purposes of Community law 1997 OJ C 372/3.
141. According to the Commission, the focus of assessment in State aid cases is the aid recipient and the industry/sector concerned rather than identification of competitive constraints faced by the aid recipient, but the principles of market definition may serve as a basis of assessment of State aid cases where issues of market power and therefore of the relevant market are raised (Notice on definition of the relevant market, page 1 footnote 1).
142. Notice on the definition of the relevant market, para. 7.
143. *Ibid* para. 8.

or wider.[144] It has, for example, found markets for the conversion of Airbus passenger aircraft to freighters and for aircraft components to be global.[145]

3.5 'DEMAND-SIDE' SUBSTITUTABILITY

The primary test for determining what the relevant market should be is 'demand-side' substitutability - namely to determine close substitutes readily available in the geographic area, or another area to which consumers can turn should prices increase. According to this test, if a customer would view the two products or services as substitutable and would readily switch between them following a 5–10 per cent permanent increase (discussed below at section 3.5 - 'SSNIP' test), they would be likely to form part of the same relevant product market.[146] Products having the same characteristics or responding to the same customer needs are likely to be regarded as belonging to the same product market. Products which satisfy different needs will, therefore, belong to distinct markets, except for the fairly exceptional circumstances where supply-side substitutability may be relevant (discussed at section 3.6. below).

In the *Virgin /British Airways* case, BA was found to hold a dominant position on the UK market for air travel agency services.[147] Arguments that dominance should be assessed by reference to the position that BA held on particular routes in respect of which sales were made, were rejected, the General Court holding that agency or distribution services provided in relation a product or service, were a distinct market from that product or service itself. Agents were found to constitute independent intermediaries carrying on an independent business of providing services, collecting the price of the transport and remitting it to the airlines, and providing those airlines with advertising and commercial promotion services. The Court also found that this was an economic activity for which, at the time of the contested decision, airlines could not substitute another form of distribution of their tickets, and that they therefore constituted a market for services which was distinct from the air transport market.[148] The relevant geographic market was found to be the UK, on the basis that travel agents tended to operate within national boundaries, and customers normally booked tickets in their country of residence. The boundaries of travel agency markets may have become more blurred given the increase in sales through online travel agents.

In the case of scheduled passenger air transport services, demand-side substitutability has been the principal means of defining the market, with focus on the origination and destination (O&D) approach whereby passengers consider all

144. According to the Commission, in the two years 2013–2015 its merger decisions found the geographic market to be the EEA or wider in 61 per cent of cases, compared to 48 per cent 10 years previously. *See* Competition Policy Brief 2015-12 March 2015.
145. COMP/M.6554 - EADS/STA/Elbe Flugzeugwerke JV, decision of 3/09/2012; COMP/M.6844 - GE/Avio, decision of 1/7/2013 and COMP/M.6410 - UTC/Goodrich, decision of 26/7/2012.
146. Notice on the definition of the market para. 15.
147. Commission Decision 2000/74/EC of 14 July 1999 relating to a proceeding under Article 102 of the EC Treaty (IV/D-2/34.780 — *Virgin/British Airways*) (OJ 2000 L 30, p. 1, para. 72).
148. Case T-219/99, British Airways plc v Commission [2003] ECR II 5917 para. 100; upheld by ECJ Case C-95/04 P, British Airways v Commission [2007] ECR I-2331.

alternatives of travelling from a city of origin to a city of destination. The specific aspects of this approach are discussed in Chapter 8 *Mergers and Alliances*, section 8.4.1.

3.6 SSNIP/HYPOTHETICAL MONOPOLIST TEST

In order to measure demand substitution, the Commission and other competition regulators (including in the US) use the 'hypothetical monopolist' test, also known as the 'SSNIP' (small but significant non-transitory increase in price) test.

This test, which requires detailed quantitative analysis, asks whether the parties' customers would switch to readily available substitutes or to suppliers located elsewhere, in response to a hypothetical small (in the range 5–10 per cent), but permanent increase in the price of the products and in the areas being considered. If substitution would be enough to make the price increase unprofitable, because of the resulting loss of sales, additional substitutes and areas are included in the relevant market. The purpose of the test, therefore, is to allow the regulator, or parties engaging in self-assessment, to identify a set of products and a geographic area small enough to allow permanent increases in relative prices that would be profitable. This set of products or this geographic area will be what is considered the relevant market for competition purposes.[149] It would follow from this test that if there was a large difference in price between given products or services, they would be unlikely to be close substitutes or, therefore, included within the same relevant market.

As to the degree of substitutability, there is not a requirement for perfect substitutability, but there must be more than a limited degree. An example discussed below is scheduled passenger air transport, where relevant markets will be determined according to the customers' preferences (*see* Chapter 8 *Mergers and Alliances*).

Demand-side substitutability will similarly be applied to assess the boundaries of the relevant geographic market, focusing on whether businesses established elsewhere in fact constitute a real alternative source of supply for consumers.[150] Applying the SSNIP test, the assessment focuses on whether in response to a small but permanent increase in the price of the product or service, customers would switch to purchase that product or service from elsewhere.

3.7 'SUPPLY-SIDE' SUBSTITUTABILITY

The Commission may take account of 'supply-side' substitutability – the ability of potential competitors to enter the market, thus exercising a competitive constraint, within a relatively short period. This analysis will, as with demand-side substitutability involve the application of the SSNIP test to measure the extent to which producers or providers of a given product or service A would be likely to switch to producing or providing another product or service B, in response to a permanent increase of 5–10

149. Notice paras 15–19.
150. Notice para. 29.

per cent of product or service A. It requires that the supplier should be able to enter the market in the short term in response to small but permanent changes in prices. This must be possible without incurring significant additional costs or risks and must not entail a significant adjustment of existing tangible or intangible assets.[151]

There are few examples of supply-side substitutability having been found to be relevant in determining the relevant market in the case law of the Commission of the Court of Justice. The case which illustrates these principles is *Continental Can* (CC), where the Court of Justice overturned a finding of the Commission that CC was dominant in the market for the manufacture of cans used for meat and fish products. The Commission had focused on the absence of other possible choices of packaging available to meat and fish producers (applying demand-side substitutability), but had not considered whether manufacturers of metal cans used for other purposes could switch their production to adapt their products to meet their needs. If it would be profitable for such manufacturers to enter this market if CC were to raise prices significantly above costs, then such price rises would be profitable for a short time only, and this would act as a constraint on CC.[152]

The SSNIP test will be applied to measure the extent to which producers of different products or providers of different services, would switch to produce the product or service in question in response to a small but permanent increase in the price of the product or service in question. For supply-side substitutability to be relevant, the immediacy of the impact must be equivalent to the demand substitution effect and in practice, due to this requirement, this test will rarely be met. In *Aerospatiale-Alenia /de Havilland*, a three- to four-year period for manufacturers of 30-seat aircraft to switch their facilities to produce 50-seat aircraft was considered too long.[153]

The cases where supply-side substitutability has been found, thus widening the market definition are rare in practice, though there are cases where the argument has been raised and discussed.[154] Supply-side substitutability has been discussed in the context of airline mergers and alliances where arguments have been raised that markets for scheduled air transport services for passengers should be defined at the level of airlines' networks, which has not generally been accepted by the Commission (*see* Chapter 8 *Mergers and Alliances*)

3.8 COMMISSION APPROACH IN PRACTICE WHEN DEFINING THE MARKET

The Commission will have regard to case law of the Court of Justice and its own experience. The approach of the Commission (as well as national regulators) will be to invite the parties to submit their own definitions of the 'relevant market(s)' and will

151. Notice paras 20, 23.
152. Case 6/72 Europemballage v Commission (Continental Can) [1973] ECR 215 para. 33.
153. Aerospatiale-Alenia/de Havilland Case IV/M. 053, para. 14.
154. *Ibid.* Arguments on supply-side substitutability as regards 'network markets' have been made by airlines in relation passenger services discussed at Chapter 8.

seek detailed information in this regard. Given that market definition is based on the business realities in each case, it will also be a factual and empirical exercise, such as, in the case of air transport, numbers or types of passengers conveyed. The Commission or other regulator will rely on a variety of evidence when it comes to defining markets, and it will require sales data and other trade statistics, evidence of customers' purchasing patterns in particular recent past events such as customers switching to alternative products or services (product market), or diverting orders to other areas (geographic market) particularly where there have been changes in prices, or where new products or services have been launched. Quantitative tests (including with recourse to economists) will be applied to analyse such events or evidence submitted by the parties on whether, for examples, price increases would result in loss of customers in sufficient numbers such as to render them unprofitable.[155] The Commission will also 'market test' the parties' views by inviting views of customers and competitors, which views will carry greater weight if supported by evidence. The Commission will also rely on customer surveys, and this will often be the case with air transport cases.[156]

Barriers or costs if any associated with switching to alternative products or services would also be relevant.[157] As discussed above, substitute products or services would tend to be excluded if customers had to incur capital investment or other costs to switch to alternatives. Regulatory and other requirements, such as adherence to particular standards, access to distribution, or need for a physical presence, will also be taken into account.[158] In many areas of economic activity including air transport, previously national markets have become EU wide as a result of EU liberalisation, though regulatory barriers on a non-EU level may remain (discussed in Chapter 2 *Liberalisation of Air Transport*). Consumer or national preferences, if any, such as allegiance to a national carrier, will be taken into account. The extent to which the party(ies) take into account other products or services in their own price setting, for example, monitoring competitor products or services, will also be relevant. Temporal markets to the extent they exist, such as in the case of scheduled air transport services, peak and off- peak services, and distinctions based on distinct categories of customers such as time / non-time-sensitive passengers, may also be relevant (*see* Chapter 8 *Mergers and Alliances*).

In cases where it is not necessary to define markets due to competition issues not arising on alternative definitions applied, the Commission will leave market definition open.

155. In KLM/Martinair M.5141, the Commission scrutinised such 'critical loss' analysis on likely loss of passengers from the parties para. 295 et seq.
156. In KLM/Martinair M.5141, the Commission's in-depth investigation included a consumer survey carried out at Schiphol Airport (Amsterdam) which indicated that a significant proportion of passengers would either not travel at all or travel elsewhere if there were a sustained price increase for flights to Aruba or Curacao, thus limiting the potential for price increases.
157. Alpha Flight Services/Aéroports de Paris OJ 1998 L230/10 – if customers would incur material costs or only switch in the longer term that would not suffice to warrant inclusion in the relevant market.
158. Notice on market definition paras 30, 55.

CHAPTER 4

Elements of Article 101 TFEU

Article 101(1) TFEU provides:

> The following shall be prohibited as incompatible with the internal market: all agreements between undertakings, decisions by associations of undertakings and concerted practices which may affect trade between Member States and which have as their object or effect the prevention, restriction or distortion of competition within the internal market, and in particular those which:
>
> (a) directly or indirectly fix purchase or selling prices or any other trading conditions;
> (b) limit or control production, markets, technical development, or investment;
> (c) share markets or sources of supply;
> (d) apply dissimilar conditions to equivalent transactions with other trading parties, thereby placing them at a competitive disadvantage;
> (e) make the conclusion of contracts subject to acceptance by the other parties of supplementary obligations which, by their nature or according to commercial usage, have no connection with the subject of such contracts.

4.1 OVERVIEW

Agreements or concerted practices between undertakings which have as their object or effect the prevention, restriction or distortion of competition are contrary to Article 101(1) TFEU. The list of examples in Article 101(1)(a)–(e) is illustrative only. The key elements of Article 101(1) are discussed below. Agreements caught by Article 101(1) are void and unenforceable under Article 101(2) unless they satisfy the criteria for exemption under Article 101(3). It is the effect of agreements rather than their form which determines whether they will be caught by Article 101(1), and particular forms or wording of an agreement which are permitted if concluded between given parties in a given economic context, may not necessarily be permitted between different parties, or in a different economic context.

4.2 UNDERTAKINGS

The notion of 'undertaking' is the same for Articles 101, 102, the EU Merger Regulation 139/2004 and the State aid rules. The term 'undertaking' is not defined in the TFEU, but its meaning has been set out in case law of the Court of Justice, applying to a wide variety of entities. The key factor is whether the entity in question is engaged in economic activity, an 'undertaking' according to the ECJ being any natural or legal person engaged in economic activity, regardless of its legal status and the way in which it is financed.[159] The term 'undertaking' is broad, including companies, firms, businesses, partnerships, individuals operating as sole traders, associations of undertakings (e.g., trade associations), charities, non-profit making organisations and, in some circumstances, public entities that offer goods or services on a given market (discussed at section 4.2.3 below). Airlines, providing transport services to passengers, will, therefore, be 'undertakings'. Airports, which operate airports and manage infrastructure, will be also be 'undertakings' in so far as they carry out economic activities (*see* section 4.2.3 below).

4.2.1 Single Economic Entity: Related Companies

The Court has ruled that the term 'undertaking' must be understood as designating an economic unit for the purpose of the subject matter of the agreement in question, even if in law that unit consists of several legal entities.[160] The test is whether or not there is unity in their conduct on the market. Article 101 will not, therefore, apply to agreements between entities which form a single economic unit. In particular, an agreement between a parent and its subsidiary company, or between two companies which are under the control of a third, will not be agreements between undertakings if the subsidiary has no real freedom to determine its course of action on the market and, although having a separate legal personality, enjoys no economic independence.[161]

Factors relevant to this question will be the shareholding the parent has in the subsidiary, composition of the board of directors and the rights over the management of the company that the shareholding confers. When a company exercises decisive influence over another company, they will form a single economic entity and, therefore, are part of the same undertaking.[162] Where a subsidiary is wholly or majority owned by a parent, that parent is presumed to have control of it.[163] Where a minority shareholding enables the parent to determine the strategic commercial behaviour of the

159. Case C-41/90 Höfner and Elser v Macrotron [1991] ECR I-1979, Case T–319/99 Fenin v Commission, [2003] ECR I-357.
160. Case 170/83 Hydrotherm [1984] ECR 2999, para. 11, and Case T-234/95 DSG v Commission [2000] ECR II 2603, para. 124).
161. *See* Case 22/71 Beguelin Import v GL Import Export [1971] ECR 949; Case C-73/95P Viho Europe v Commission (Parker Pen) [1996] ECR-I 5457.
162. Communication from the Commission — Guidelines on the applicability of Article 101 of the Treaty on the Functioning of the European Union to horizontal cooperation agreements OJ C 11, 14.1.2011, p. 1 para. 11.
163. Viho v Commission Case C-73/95, Viho, *supra*.

subsidiary, where the parent can appoint more than half the board members, or where, due to remaining shares being widely dispersed (which can be the case with airlines), the parent and subsidiary may be a single economic entity. The rules on liability of a parent to pay fines of a subsidiary and calculation thereof are discussed in Chapter 9 *Enforcement.*

4.2.2 Single Economic Entity: Agents

Agreements between a principal and agent may also be found to be outside Article 101, if the agent is deemed a 'genuine' agent which forms a single undertaking with the principal. The question will depend on whether an agent may be considered 'independent' which in turn depends on the extent to which the agents accepts risks under the contract, an agreement with an agent who accepts little or no risk under the contract with the principal falling outside Article 101.[164]

4.2.3 Public Bodies, Undertakings Granted Exclusive Rights and Article 106 TFEU

Public bodies, such as State owned airports, may be subject to EU competition law depending on the nature of the functions they are carrying out. In so far as they are carrying out economic activities, they will be subject to the competition rules, but not when they are acting in the exercise of official authority. This will be the case where the activity in question is 'a task in the public interest which forms part of the essential functions of the State and where the activity is connected by its nature, its aims and rules to which it is subject with the exercise of powers... which are typically those of a public authority'.[165] The Court of Justice has held that powers relating to the control and supervision of airspace are typically those of a public authority[166] as are activities related to protection of the environment.[167] Eurocontrol, an entity created by Member States of the EU for the purpose of establishing navigational safety in the airspace of Europe, was found not to be engaging in economic activity for the purpose of the EU competition rules in so far as its activities related to the development of technical standards, procurement of prototypes and managing intellectual property rights, but was found to be engaging in an economic activity when providing technical assistance to national administrations. The fact that Eurocontrol was not directly remunerated by them, rather, being funded by contributions of Member States, did not alter this conclusion.[168] To the extent that a public authority engages in an economic activity which can be severed from those in which it engages as a public authority, such activity will be subject to competition law.

164. Commission Guidelines on Vertical Restraints 2010 OJ C 130 p.1 paras 18–22. *See* Chapter 6 *Article 101 TFEU: Vertical agreements.*
165. Case C-343/95 Diego Cali & Figli [1997] ECR 1547, paras 22–23.
166. Case C-364 Eurocontrol [1994] ECR I 43 at para. 17.
167. Diego Cali & Figli *supra* paras 22-23.
168. Case T-155/04, SELEX v Commission ECR [2006] II – 4803 paras 86-92.

Specifically, Article 106(1) TFEU requires that with regard to public undertakings and undertakings to which Member States grant exclusive rights, Member States must not enact any measure contrary the Treaty rules – notably Articles 101 and 102. In *Ahmed Saeed*, the ECJ held that for a Member State to give encouragement in any form whatsoever, to the adoption of agreements with regard to tariffs contrary to Article 101(1) or 102 would breach Article 106(1) (*see* Chapter 2 *Liberalisation Air Transport* section 2.6.5).[169]

In the *Aéroports de Paris* case, it was found that a public corporation placed under the authority of the Minister responsible for civil aviation was engaging in an economic activity for the purposes of Article 102 when it came to the provision of airport facilities to airlines and the various service providers and the management of those facilities – which were remunerated by commercial fees – and the fixing by ADP of the commercial fees and the conditions of the activities of groundhandlers, but not its purely administrative – in particular supervisory – activities (*See also* Chapter 7 *Abuse of a Dominant Position* section 7.4.5).[170]

As regards services of general economic interest, which are services which the State considers are essential for the general public and for which it is necessary to ensure that a quality service is provided at an affordable price, even where the market is not sufficiently profitable for the supply of such services, Article 106(2) provides that the competition rules shall apply to such services, but only in so far as they do not obstruct the performance, in law or fact, of the tasks that are assigned to those undertakings (*see* discussion in Chapter 10 *State Aid*).

4.3 AGREEMENTS, CONCERTED PRACTICES, DECISIONS

4.3.1 Agreement

4.3.1.1 Definition

Agreements take many forms. Within the air transport sector, resolutions adopted by IATA, have been considered to be agreements between undertakings, namely between the IATA member airlines.[171] 'Agreement' is broadly defined, it being sufficient for the purposes of Article 101(1) if the parties have expressed their joint intention to behave on the market in a certain way.[172] An agreement, therefore, can be said to exist when the parties adhere to a common plan which limits or tends to limit their individual

169. Case 66/86 Ahmed Saeed Flugreisen and Silver Line Reisebüro GmbH v Zentrale zur Bekämpfung unlauteren Wettbewerbs e.V. 1989 ECR 803.
170. Case T-128/98 Aéroports de Paris (ADP) v Commission ECR [2000] II 3929, para. 108, 130, upheld by the ECJ in case C-82/01, paras 74–83 – ADP was found to have abused a dominant position by charging discriminatory commercial fees from suppliers or users engaged in groundhandling or self-handling activities relating to catering. *See also* Chapter 7 *Abuse of a Dominant Position*.
171. *See* for example the Passenger and Cargo Agency Programmes, Decisions 91/480 and 91/481, discussed in Chapter 6 *Article 101 TFEU: Vertical agreements*.
172. Joined Cases T-305/94 etc Limburgse Vinyl Maatschappij NV and others v Commission (PVC II)13; Case T-41/96 Bayer AG v Commission [2000] ECR II 3383 para. 69.

commercial conduct by determining the lines of their behaviour in the market. It does not have to be made in writing, no formalities are necessary, and no contractual sanctions or enforcement measures are required. The agreement may be express or implicit in the behaviour of the parties.[173] The Commission will not make a distinction in applying the test of whether there is an 'agreement' whether the alleged infringement is horizontal or vertical.[174]

The fact that an undertaking does not conduct itself in the manner agreed, will not necessarily contradict the existence of an agreement.[175] It may also be the case that despite colluding with other undertakings, an undertaking which follows a different course may simply be trying to exploit the situation for its own benefit.[176]

4.3.1.2 'Agreement' in the Cartel Context: Attendance at a Meeting

The Court has held that if the Commission is able to establish attendance by a company at a meeting where cartel behaviour is discussed, that will of itself be sufficient to implicate the party attending, in the cartel unless the party can put forward evidence to establish that its participation was without any anticompetitive intention. This will be the case even if the company did not act on the outcome of discussions, as it will have been presumed to have given the others to believe it would subscribe to what was agreed. This presumption will be rebutted if the company publicly distanced itself from the cartel, by making clear to the other participants that it was not going to participate in the cartel.[177] The Court of Justice has stated that the company in question should write to the other participants recording its position or contacting the competition authorities denouncing the cartel.[178] (Cartels are discussed in more detail in Chapter 5 *Article 101 TFEU: Horizontal Agreements*).

4.3.2 Concerted Practice

'Concerted practice' denotes looser forms of collaboration and has been defined by the Court of Justice as 'a form of coordination between undertakings, which, without having been taken to the stage where an agreement properly so-called has been concluded, knowingly substitutes for the risks of competition, practical cooperation between them which leads to conditions of competition which do not correspond to the normal conditions of the market, having regard to the nature of the products, the

173. Bayer AG *supra*; Polypropylene OJ 1986 L230/1; Commission Case COMP/F/38.638 — Butadiene Rubber and Emulsion Styrene Butadiene Rubber para. 257.
174. Nintendo [2003] OJ L25553 para. 323.
175. Case T-89 Huls v Commission [1992] II 499 para. 127.
176. Case T-18/03 CD-Contact Data Gmbh v Commission [2009] ECR II 1021 para. 67.
177. Case C-199/92 Huls para. 155; Aalborg Portland v Commission Joined Cases C-204/00 P, C-205/00 P, C-211/00 P, C-213/00 P, C-217/00 P, General Court [2004] ECR I-123 para. 82.
178. *See* Case C-291/98 P Sarrió v Commission [2000] ECR I-9991, para. 50).

importance and number of the undertakings as well as the size and nature of the said market'.[179] The concepts of 'agreement' and 'concerted practice' are fluid and may overlap.

The Court has stated that while the concept of concerted practice implies the existence of reciprocal contacts, this condition is met where one competitor discloses its future intentions or conduct on the market to another when the latter requests it or, at the very least, accepts it (*see also* Information Exchange Chapter 5 *Article 101 TFEU: Horizontal Agreements*, section 5.2.9).[180]

4.3.3 Decisions of Associations of Undertakings

According to the Court, the concept of an association of undertakings plays a particular role in Article 101(1), seeking to prevent undertakings from being able to evade the rules on competition on account simply of the form in which they coordinate their conduct on the market. To ensure that this principle is effective, Article 101(1) covers not only direct methods of coordinating conduct between undertakings (agreements and concerted practices) but also institutionalised forms of cooperation, in which economic operators act through a collective structure or a common body.[181]

In the *Wouters* case, the Court held that rules of the association which restricted competition could nevertheless fall outside Article 101(1) if they were reasonably necessary to ensure the proper practice of the legal profession in the Netherlands.[182] Unreasonable regulatory rules which go beyond what is necessary to secure the objective sought would fall within Article 101(1) however.[183] The Court has similarly ruled that rules of a private cooperative purchasing association would fall outside Article 101(1) if they were necessary to ensure the proper functioning of the association.[184] These cases would suggest that some weighing of the anticompetitive against procompetitive effects and also public interest objectives may be possible under Article 101(1). The more conventional analysis would be for any procompetitive or other beneficial effects to be considered under Article 101(3). *See also* Commission guidelines on 101(3) and discussion on Article 101(3) at section 4.7 below.

'Association of undertakings' is broadly interpreted. The legal form of the association is irrelevant, associations without legal personality,[185] non-profit

179. Cases 40/73 etc. Suiker Unie v Commission [1975] ECR 1663, at para. 173 ('Suiker Unie'); Case C-199/92P Huls AG v Commission.
180. Joined Cases T-25/95 and others, Cimenteries CBE and others v Commission, [2000] ECR II 491 para. 1849.
181. Case C-309/99 Wouters and others v Algemene Raad van de Nederlandse Orde van Advocaten [2002] ECR I 1577 para. 62. The Dutch Bar Council was found to be an association of undertakings, the potentially restrictive rules could nevertheless be found to be outside Article 101(1).
182. *Ibid* para. 107.
183. Cases C-184/13 etc API v Ministero delle Infrastrutture e dei Trasporti, – measures fixing minimum tariffs for road transport in Italy not justifiable on road safety grounds.
184. Case C-250/92, Gøttrup-Klim e.a. Grovvareforeninger v Dansk Landbrugs Grovvareselskab AmbA. [1994] ECR I – 5641.
185. Hofner *supra*.

associations, associations with public law status or exercising statutory functions all being 'associations of undertakings' falling within the definition. In *Commission v Italy*, a national association of customs agents was found to be an association of undertakings.[186] Trade associations will be the most common form of association of undertakings.

'Decision' also has a wide meaning. It may include the membership rules, constitution, bylaws of the association, recommendations or other measures promulgated.[187] The legal status or binding / non-binding nature of a 'decision' is not relevant, rather any action by the association which seeks to coordinate the conduct of members or otherwise produces anticompetitive effects, will constitute a decision within the meaning of Article 101(1).[188]

4.4 EFFECT ON TRADE BETWEEN MEMBER STATES

Article 101 (and also Article 102) will only apply where trade between Member States of the EU is affected. An agreement may affect trade between Member States if it is 'possible to foresee with a sufficient degree of probability on the basis of a set of objective factors of law or of fact that the agreement in question may have an influence, direct or indirect, actual or potential, on the pattern of trade between member states, in such a way that it might hinder the realisation of the objectives of a single market between states'.[189]

The Court has ruled,[190] and the Commission has stated in Guidance discussed below, that agreements will normally fall outside Article 101 even where they have as their object or effect the prevention, restriction or distortion of competition, if they are not capable of appreciably affecting trade between Member States.[191]

The requirement for an effect on trade on trade between Member States does not mean that agreements between two enterprises situated in the same Member State will not be caught by Article 101, which may be the case where, for example, it makes it more difficult for other enterprises to penetrate the market or results in sales into the Member State being impeded.

The Commission has issued Guidelines on the effect of trade concept contained in Articles 101 and 102,[192] in which it quantifies which agreements are in principle not capable of appreciably affecting trade between Member States. It states that, in principle, agreements are not capable of appreciably affecting trade between Member States when the following cumulative conditions are met:

186. Case C-35/96 Commission v Italy [1998] ECR I 3851 para. 50.
187. National Sulphuric Acid Association Ltd OJ L260 1 October 1980 p24.
188. Case 45/85 Verband der Sachsversicherer v Commission – a recommendation requiring annual increases in premiums for fire insurance found to breach Article 101(1).
189. Case C-5/69 Völk v Vervaecke [1969] ECR 295 para. 5.
190. *Ibid.*
191. *De Minimis* Notice para. 8.
192. Commission Notice — Guidelines on the effect on trade concept contained in Articles [101] and [102] of the Treaty OJ C 101, 27.4.2004, pp. 81–96.

(i) the aggregate market share of the parties on any relevant market within the EU affected by the agreement does not exceed 5 per cent; and

(ii) in the case of horizontal agreements, the aggregate annual EU turnover of the undertakings concerned in the products covered by the agreement does not exceed EUR 40 million. In the case of agreements concerning the joint buying of products the relevant turnover shall be the parties' combined purchases of the products covered by the agreement. In the case of vertical agreements, the aggregate annual EU turnover of the supplier in the products covered by the agreement does not exceed EUR 40 million.[193]

The *De Minimis* Notice (discussed at section 4.5.3) also states that agreements between small and medium-sized undertakings are rarely capable of appreciably affecting trade between Member States. Small and medium-sized undertakings are currently defined as undertakings which have fewer than 250 employees and have either an annual turnover not exceeding EUR 50 million or an annual balance-sheet total not exceeding EUR 43 million.[194]

4.5 OBJECT OR EFFECT OF RESTRICTING COMPETITION

Agreements or concerted practices must have as their 'object or effect the prevention, restriction or distortion of competition' within the EU.

4.5.1 Appreciable Restriction of Competition

Similar to effect on trade, the prevention, restriction or distortion of competition must be 'appreciable'. The Court has held: 'an agreement falls outside the prohibition in Article [101] when it has only an insignificant effect on the markets, taking into account the weak position which the persons concerned have on the market of the product in question'.[195]

4.5.2 Restriction 'by Object'

Given that the conditions of 'object' or 'effect' are alternative, if it appears that an agreement has as its object the prevention, restriction or distortion of competition, there is no need to take account of the concrete effects of the agreement, hence to show that the agreement has in fact appreciably affected such trade.[196] In such a case, rather

193. Notice on effect on trade para. 52.

194. Commission Recommendation of 6 May 2003 concerning the definition of micro, small and medium-sized enterprises OJ L 124, 20.5.2003, pp. 36–41; *see* generally http://ec.europa.eu/growth/smes/business-friendly-environment/sme-definition/index_en.htm.

195. Volk v Vervaeke para. 7.

196. Consten and Grudig v Commission [1966] ECR 299; Case 19/77 Miller International Schallplatten GmbH v Commission 1978 ECR 131 para. 15 – the Court held that a detailed analysis of the effects would be required if the analysis of the clauses in question did not reveal the effect on competition to be sufficiently serious.

than the Commission having to conduct a detailed analysis showing anticompetitive effects on the market to prove the existence of an infringement, the burden instead shifts to the parties to demonstrate that the agreement satisfies the exemption criteria under Article 101(3). This is a task which is more onerous in the case of 'object' restrictions and may thus require the parties to make changes to agreements (in the form of commitments) in order to satisfy the Commission of their compatibility with Article 101.

Given these consequences, restrictions by object have generally been interpreted narrowly, as those which, based on their serious nature and on experience showing that they have such a high potential of negative effects on competition that it is unnecessary to demonstrate any actual effects on the market.[197] In practice, these have been 'hardcore' restrictions such as price fixing, market sharing and, in the vertical context, export bans.

There are nevertheless cases where agreements which have been restrictive 'by object' have benefited from exemption under Article 101(3). Joint ventures between airlines, where airlines cooperate on key parameters of competition including price, schedules and/or sharing of revenue, have been classified as restrictive by object, but the Commission has nevertheless examined the effects in detail and allowed them to proceed subject to commitments.[198]

As a result of cases of the European Court such as *Expedia* and *T-Mobile*, and Commission guidelines on restrictions by object which accompanied the *De Minimis* Notice 2014 (discussed at section 4.5.3 below), it appeared that the category of 'by object' restrictions to agreements was being expanded to cases where it was unclear whether there was a sufficient degree harm, it being suggested that it was sufficient if measures were capable of restricting, or had the potential to restrict, competition.[199]

A return to the more narrow approach was signalled by the judgment of the Court of Justice in the *Cartes Bancaires* case, where, in relation to a payment system which had legitimate aims, the Court of Justice held that the restriction 'by object' category should be interpreted narrowly, and found that the Commission and the General Court had failed to take into account the purpose of the system and whether the measures in themselves 'revealed a sufficient degree of harm to competition'.[200] Otherwise, the Commission would be exempted from the obligation to prove the actual effects on the market of agreements which were in no way established to be, by their very nature, harmful to competition.

197. Courts' approach summarised in Commission Guidelines on the application of Article [101(3)] of the Treaty OJ C 101, 27.4.2004, p97, para. 21.
198. *See* for example Case COMP/39.596 – BA /AA /IB; Case AT.39964 – Air France /KLM /Alitalia /Delta, 'SkyTeam alliance', Decision pursuant to Article 9 Regulation 1/2003 12 May 2015, para. 40; Alliances involving extensive cooperation are discussed in Chapter 8 *Mergers and Alliances*.
199. Case C-8/08 T-Mobile Netherlands and Others [2009] ECR I 4529; Case C-226/11 Expedia 13 December 2012.
200. 200 Case C-67/13 P Groupement des cartes bancaires v Commission 11 September 2014.

4.5.3 Notice on Agreements of Minor Importance

The Commission has issued guidance to assist companies to determine whether restrictions are likely to be 'appreciable'.[201] This provides that agreements which may affect trade between Member States and which may have as their effect the prevention, restriction or distortion of competition within the internal market, do not appreciably restrict competition within the meaning of Article 101(1) of the Treaty if:

(i) the aggregate market share held by the parties to the agreement does not exceed 10 per cent on any of the relevant markets affected by the agreement, where the agreement is made between undertakings which are actual or potential competitors on any of those markets (agreements between competitors); or

(ii) the market share held by each of the parties to the agreement does not exceed 15 per cent on any of the relevant markets affected by the agreement, where the agreement is made between undertakings which are not actual or potential competitors on any of those markets (agreements between non-competitors).

In cases where it is difficult to classify the agreement as either an agreement between competitors or an agreement between non-competitors, the 10 per cent threshold is applicable.[202]

The *De Minimis Notice* is not binding, and a difficulty in relying on the Notice is that it may not be clear, despite case law and Commission guidance on market definition, what the relevant market is. It is of use, however, and paragraph 5 of the Notice provides that in cases covered by the Notice, the Commission will not institute proceedings, either upon a complaint or on its own initiative. Further, where the Commission has instituted proceedings but undertakings can demonstrate that they have assumed in good faith that the market shares mentioned were not exceeded, the Commission will not impose fines. The Notice is also intended to give guidance to the courts and competition authorities of the Member States in their application of Article 101 of the Treaty (1), but is not binding.

The *De Minimis* Notice, as revised in 2014, has unfortunately, however, introduced uncertainty for companies. Under previous Notices, agreements could benefit from the market share presumptions provided they did not contain 'hardcore restrictions' namely price fixing, market sharing, agreements limiting output, and in the case of vertical agreements, notably, resale price maintenance and export bans. Following case law of the Court of Justice, however, in the *Expedia* judgment (*see* section 4.5.2 above), the reference to 'hardcore' restrictions was removed in the 2014 Notice and replaced by the much more uncertain notion of restrictions 'by object'. For reasons described in the preceding section, the scope of the guidance appears, therefore, to have become more narrow, making it more difficult for companies to rely on it.

201. Commission Notice on agreements of minor importance. The latest version is at: Official Journal of the European Union, C 291, 30 August 2014.

202. *De Minimis* Notice para. 8.

The Commission has also issued Guidelines accompanying the *De Minimis* Notice listing the restrictions of competition that are described as restrictions by object.[203] The Commission states that this document will be updated regularly so that the category of agreements by object is, therefore, not closed. While the judgment of the Court of Justice in the *Cartes Bancaires* case has scaled back the expansion of restriction 'by object', these new uncertainties, over and above the uncertainty of market definition, are another reason to treat apparently low market shares with caution.

4.6 NULLITY OF AGREEMENTS: ARTICLE 101(2) TFEU

Article 101(2) provides: 'Any agreements or decisions prohibited pursuant to [Article 101(1)] shall be automatically void.'

Agreements which infringe Article 101(1) are automatically void under Article 101(2) and are unenforceable both between the parties and cannot be enforced against third parties.[204] The nullity has a retrospective as well as prospective effect.[205]

4.6.1 Severance of Offending Clauses

Where an agreement has been found to infringe Article 101(1), it will only be the prohibited clauses in the agreement which will be void.[206] The Court has held that the automatic nullity under Article 101(2) applies only to those contractual provisions which are incompatible with Article 101(1) and that it would be inequitable if this were not the case. Enforceability of other parts of the agreement, such as orders and deliveries made and the resulting financial obligations, are not a matter for EU law, but rather, are to be determined by the national court under its own law.[207]

The question whether anticompetitive clauses can be severed, allowing the remainder of the agreement to remain enforceable is similarly, therefore, a matter for the national courts, and it would be expected that in such cases where Article 101(2) is found to apply by national courts (or by the Commission or other national competition authority (NCA)), the national court being asked to enforce such agreement would, applying the law applicable to the contract, seek to sever the offending clauses so as to uphold the remaining provisions of an agreement, if that is possible.

203. Guidance on restrictions of competition 'by object' for the purpose of defining which agreements may benefit from the *De Minimis* Notice accompanying the Commission Notice on agreements of minor importance which do not appreciably restrict competition under Article 101(1) TFEU (*De Minimis* Notice); Staff Working Document and the Notice are available at: http://ec.europa.eu/competition/antitrust/legislation/deminimis.html (revised version 3/06/2015 post Cartes Bancaires decision.).
204. Case 22/71 Béguelin Import v G.L. Import Export [1971] ECR 949 para. 29.
205. Case 48/72 Brasserie de Haecht v Oscar Wilkin and Marie Janssen (II) 1973 E.C.R. 77 paras 26-27.
206. Case 319/82 Société de Vente de Ciments et Bétons de l'Est SA v Kerpen & Kerpen GmbH und Co. KG [1983] ECR 4173.
207. *Ibid* para. 12.

4.6.2 Actions in National Courts Based on Article 101(2) TFEU

A finding of nullity whether by the Commission, national court or NCA, will mean that the agreement will be illegal under national law and could be subject to actions before national courts in damages. The right to bring an action for damages as a result of an agreement which breaches Article 101 is not limited to third parties, but also includes a party to the agreement, where it has suffered loss as a result of restrictions found to be anticompetitive.[208] Damages actions for breach of EU competition law are discussed in Chapter 9 *Enforcement*.

Article 101(2) could also be raised as a defence to an action based on contractual liability to pay by a defendant to the litigation who alleges that the contract is anticompetitive contract (known as the 'Euro-defence'). Given the direct applicability and primacy of Article 101 (and 102) as well as the principle of effectiveness (known as '*effet utlile*'), national courts would be obliged to recognise the right of a party to defend itself against an action which sought to give effect to anticompetitive conduct, contrary to EU law. Examples of parties avoiding contractual obligations by recourse to Article 101(2) are the exception rather than the rule.[209]

4.7 EXEMPTION 101(3) TFEU

Article 101(3) provides:

> The provisions of paragraph 1 may, however, be declared inapplicable in the case of:
>
> - any agreement or category of agreements between undertakings,
> - any decision or category of decisions by associations of undertakings,
> - any concerted practice or category of concerted practices,
>
> which contributes to improving the production or distribution of goods or to promoting technical or economic progress, while allowing consumers a fair share of the resulting benefit, and which does not:
>
> (a) impose on the undertakings concerned restrictions which are not indispensable to the attainment of these objectives;
> (b) afford such undertakings the possibility of eliminating competition in respect of a substantial part of the products in question.'

Many agreements which, strictly speaking, fall under 101(1), will qualify for exemption under Article 101(3), by satisfying the four cumulative conditions listed above. Agreements the object or effect of which is to restrict competition may qualify for exemption, although the onus is much higher when the object is to restrict competition (*see also* discussion at section 4.5 above on 'object or effect').

208. Case C-453/99 Courage Ltd v Bernard Crehan ECR 2001 I 6297. A tied tenant of a large chain could, to the extent that he had suffered loss as a result of long-term exclusivity obligations to purchase only from the chain, bring an action in the national courts in respect of such loss.
209. Ibid.

4.7.1 Abolition of Notification: Self-Assessment Regime

Until 1 May 2004, it was possible for the parties to an agreement to notify it to the Commission for exemption or negative clearance, and benefit from immunity from fines from the date of notification. It was also only possible for the Commission to grant exemption. From 1 May 2004 with the entry into force of Regulation 1/2003, it was no longer possible to notify agreements to the Commission.[210] Rather, whether the conditions of exemption were met became a matter of self-assessment by the parties and their advisers, by reference to Article 101(3) criteria and analysis thereunder. The duty of compliance is an ongoing duty and if conditions, such as market power of the parties and/or their competitors, change after the initial assessment of an agreement under Article 101(3), it is possible that the conditions of Article 101(3), such as indispensability, or competition not being eliminated in a substantial part of the market, may no longer be fulfilled. The criteria for exemption are discussed in turn below. There is also discussion in specific cases, such as airline alliances, at Chapter 8 *Mergers and Alliances*, and in relation to vertical agreements at Chapter 6 *Article 101 TFEU: Vertical Agreements*.

On 1 May 2004, application of EU competition law and Article 101(3) by NCAs and courts also became possible, enabling them to grant exemption to agreements.

4.7.2 Burden of Proof

In a case where a person challenges an agreement or practice before a national court or where the Commission or NCA challenges an agreement or practice, the burden is on that person or authority to prove that Article 101(1) is infringed. This will be a lower burden if the case involves a 'restriction by object' (*see* section 4.5 above). The burden is then on the parties to prove that the conditions of Article 101(3) are fulfilled.[211]

4.7.3 Exemption Criteria under Article 101(3) TFEU

4.7.3.1 Efficiency Gains

The agreement must contribute to improving the production of goods or to improving the production or distribution of goods or to improving technical or economic progress.

There are not clear distinctions between these efficiencies and the main distinction made will be cost efficiencies, for example, resulting from economies of scale, and qualitative efficiencies, whereby value is created in the form of new or improved products or services through research and development or other joint ventures or

210. Regulation 1/2003 Council Regulation (EC) No. 1/2003 of 16 December 2002 on the implementation of the rules on competition laid down in Articles 81 and 82 of the Treaty OJ L 1, 4.1.2003, p. 1.
211. Regulation 1/2003, Article 2.

alliances.[212] The focus of the Commission Guidelines on Article 101(3) is on economic efficiencies from the agreement, as opposed to non-economic considerations, though there may be scope for the inclusion of non-economic efficiencies, based on the fact that the Guidelines acknowledge that goals pursued by other Treaty provisions can be taken into account to the extent that they can be subsumed under the conditions of 101(3).[213] Further, the Guidelines on Article 101(3) state that types of efficiencies discussed are only examples, and not intended to be exhaustive.[214]

There is case law in various economic sectors where improvements in, for example, environmental protection have been taken into account[215] and in the context of agreements between competitors, the Commission has made clear in its memorandum accompanying the Horizontal Guidelines, that environmental agreements are to be assessed under the relevant chapter of the Horizontal Guidelines, whether it be it research and development, production, commercialisation or standardisation.[216]

4.7.3.2 Fair Share of the Benefits for Consumers

Consumers must receive a fair share of the efficiencies generated by the restrictive agreement.[217]

'Consumer' is a broad concept referring to all direct and indirect users of the products or services, which may be undertakings as well as final consumers.[218] Benefits should in principle be enjoyed by the consumers affected by the restrictions, but where markets are related and the group of consumers affected by the restriction and benefiting from the efficiency gains, are substantially the same, benefits may be taken into account.[219] In the context of air transport alliances, the Commission has accepted that efficiencies benefiting consumers on 'behind and beyond' routes could be taken into account where there was considerable commonality between the consumers on the different markets.[220]

'Fair share' means that benefits must at least compensate consumers for any likely negative impact caused by the restriction of competition under Article 101(1), so the net effect of the agreement must at least be neutral from the point of view of these consumers. A sliding scale will apply, so that the greater the negative impact of restrictions – such as an increase in market power and substantial reduction in competitive constraint faced by the parties – the greater the efficiencies and pass on of benefits must be.[221] The Commission views the pass on of benefits as being either cost

212. Commission Guidelines on the application of Article [101(3)] of the Treaty OJ C 101, 27.4.2004, p97 ('Guidelines on Article 101(3)') paras 59, 66, 70.
213. *Ibid* para. 42.
214. *Ibid* para. 63.
215. Ford /Volkswagen OJ 1993 L20/14 para. 26.
216. Commission Memo 10/676, 14 December 2010; *see also* discussion Bellamy & Child 7th Ed 3.048.
217. Guidelines on Article 101(3) para. 83.
218. *Ibid* para. 84.
219. Horizontal Guidelines para. 43.
220. Star Alliance 23 May 2013 paras 55 et seq (*See* Chapter 8 *Mergers and alliances*).
221. Guidelines on Article 101(3) paras 85, 90, 101.

efficiencies or, where prices will be higher, better quality products or services, in which case it must be considered whether they create sufficient value for consumers.[222]

4.7.3.3 Indispensability of the Restrictions

The restrictive agreement must be reasonably necessary to achieve the efficiencies, and the individual restrictions of competition that flow from the agreement must also be reasonably necessary for the attainment of the efficiencies.[223] This implies a proportionality test – that the efficiencies could not be realised by less restrictive means, and could not be achieved by the parties acting on their own.[224] It may be that a restriction may be indispensable for a certain period only, as where benefits cannot be achieved without considerable investment, in which case account will be taken of the period required for parties to ensure an adequate return on such investment.[225]

4.7.3.4 No Elimination of Competition in a Substantial Part of the Market

The agreement must not afford the parties the possibility of eliminating competition in respect of a substantial part of the products or services concerned. Whether this is the case depends on whether the market was competitive prior to the agreement and the reduction of competition as a result of the agreement. Market share of the parties and of their competitors, and the competitive constraint they impose, will be relevant.[226] The fact that a party to an agreement is dominant does not necessarily mean that the agreement may not merit exemption, but an analysis of efficiencies will be required. One potential example highlighted by the Commission would be where a dominant company enters into a joint venture that is a non-full function JV which restricts competition, but involves a substantial integration of assets (such as an airline alliance).[227]

4.7.4 Block Exemptions

The reference in Article 101(3) to 'categories of agreements' envisages what are known as 'block exemptions', under which categories of agreements which meet the terms of the applicable block exemption are considered automatically to satisfy Article 101(3) without the need for the detailed analysis of the individual conditions of Article 101(3). Agreements falling outside an applicable block exemption, which many agreements in practice will, will fall to be considered individually under Article 101(3).

There were a wide variety of Commission block exemptions applicable in the air transport sector, the last of which (tariff consultations) expired in 2007 (*see* Chapter 2

222. *Ibid* para. 102.
223. *Ibid* para. 73.
224. *Ibid* para. 76.
225. *Ibid* para. 81.
226. *Ibid* paras 107–109.
227. *Ibid* para. 106.

section 2.6.3). While there are no longer block exemptions in force which are specific to the air transport, Regulation 487/2009[228] empowers the Commission to adopt block exemptions for certain categories of agreement, namely: (a) joint planning and coordination of airline schedules; (b) consultations on tariffs for the carriage of passengers and baggage and of freight on scheduled air services; (c) joint operations on new less busy scheduled air services; (d) slot allocation at airports and airport scheduling (the Commission being under a duty to ensure consistency with Council Regulation 95/93 on common rules for the allocation of slots at Community airports (*see also* Chapter 7 section 7.4.5.4); and (e) common purchase, development and operation of CRSs relating to timetabling, reservations and ticketing by air transport undertakings.

There are other block exemptions which may be applicable to agreements between airlines and other entities, such as the Vertical Restraints Block Exemption 330/2010 in the case of supply and distribution agreements (discussed at Chapter 6 *Article 101 TFEU: Vertical Agreements*), the Technology Transfer Block Exemption in the relation to licensing agreements, and Research and Development and Specialisation Block Exemptions.[229]

228. Council Regulation (EC) No. 487/2009 of 25 May 2009 on the application of Article 81(3) of the Treaty to certain categories of agreements and concerted practices in the air transport sector.
229. Commission Regulations 316/2014 of 21 March 2014 on the application of Article 101(3) of the Treaty on the Functioning of the European Union to categories of technology transfer agreements; 1217/2010 of 14 December 2010 on the application of Article 101(3) of the Treaty on the Functioning of the European Union to certain categories of research and development agreements; 1218/2010 of 14 December 2010 on the application of Article 101(3) of the Treaty on the Functioning of the European Union to certain categories of specialisation agreements. A discussion of these block exemptions is beyond the scope of this work and readers are referred to competition texts such as Bellamy& Child 7th Edition 2013, Van Bael & Bellis 5th Edition 2010, and Whish & Bailey 8th Edition, 2015).

CHAPTER 5

Article 101 TFEU: Horizontal Agreements

Article 101(1) provides:

> The following shall be prohibited as incompatible with the internal market: all agreements between undertakings, decisions by associations of undertakings and concerted practices which may affect trade between Member States and which have as their object or effect the prevention, restriction or distortion of competition within the internal market, and in particular those which:
>
> (a) directly or indirectly fix purchase or selling prices or any other trading conditions;
> (b) limit or control production, markets, technical development, or investment;
> (c) share markets or sources of supply;
> (d) apply dissimilar conditions to equivalent transactions with other trading parties, thereby placing them at a competitive disadvantage;
> (e) make the conclusion of contracts subject to acceptance by the other parties of supplementary obligations which, by their nature or according to commercial usage, have no connection with the subject of such contracts.

5.1 OVERVIEW

Horizontal agreements are agreements entered into by companies operating at the same level of production or distribution in the market, in essence, actual or potential competitors. This chapter will deal with the most serious form of horizontal agreements, namely cartels, with focus on cartels between airlines. It will also deal with information exchange, trade associations and code-sharing agreements (CSAs). Forms of horizontal cooperation within alliances such as coordination of schedules, routes, pricing, and revenue and cost sharing are discussed in Chapter 8 *Mergers and Alliances*.

As a general principle, outside of cartels where market share has limited relevance, cooperation between competitors is most likely to lead to competition concerns if the parties have high market shares, with remaining competitors being unable to constrain the market power of the parties. Concerns will be more serious if there are high barriers to market entry, such as large investments required, regulatory barriers, or impossibility of access to infrastructure, such as airports or slots.

5.2 CARTELS

5.2.1 Overview

Cartels are agreements or concerted practices (definitions of 'agreement' and 'concerted practice' are discussed at section 4.3 above) between competitors aimed at coordinating their competitive behaviour and influencing competition through practices such as the fixing of prices or other trading conditions, the allocation of production or sales quotas, the sharing of markets or customers, bid rigging, restricting capacity, imports or exports and anticompetitive actions against other competitors, with the intention of limiting competition and increasing their own prices or profitability.[230] The likelihood of cartels tends to be the greatest in times of economic downturn when there may be temptation to coordinate activities, or they may arise where companies already cooperate in legitimate respects, but this leads them to compete less vigorously. Cartels are almost always found to have a negative effect on competition and to have no countervailing benefits which may merit exemption.

Cartels are punishable by fines on participating undertakings of up to 10 per cent of group worldwide turnover and may be the subject of damages actions by victims of the cartel in national courts (within and outside, the EU). In certain EU Member States such as France, Germany, Ireland and the UK, and in non-EU countries such as Australia, Canada, Japan, Russia and the US, cartels can also be a criminal offence punishable by imprisonment.[231]

There have been three decisions (strictly speaking four, including the 're-adoption' by the Commission of the *Airfreight cartel* decision) of the European Commission finding air carriers guilty of engaging in cartels: namely, price fixing in the case of the *Freightforwarders* and the *Airfreight* cartels, the latter of which was overturned on appeal by the General Court on procedural grounds then 're-adopted', and market sharing in the case of *SAS / Maersk* (*see* section 5.2.4 below).

5.2.2 Detection of Cartels and 'Whistleblowers': Commission Leniency Notice

Cartels are by their nature covert and parties take steps to preserve secrecy. Use of a designated email account for cartel communications, codenames for terms used, and

230. This corresponds to the general definitions of 'cartel' in the EU Directive 2014/104/EU on certain rules governing actions for damages under national law for infringements of the competition law provisions of the Member States and of the European Union (OJ L 349 of 5 December 2012, pages 1-19).
231. *See* http://www.internationalcompetitionnetwork.org/working-groups/current/cartel/templates.aspx.

storage of agreements off office premises have been employed, including in cartels in the air transport sector. The Commission enjoys extensive powers of investigation, having the power to conduct 'dawn raids', which are discussed in Chapter 9 *Enforcement*, but since 1996, it has also offered immunity from fines to a participant in a cartel who 'blows the whistle', and reductions of up to 50 per cent for other cartel members who cooperate with its investigation, depending on the 'added value' of the cooperation.[232] Individual EU Member State competition authorities operate similar schemes on a national level, as do many other jurisdictions worldwide.

The majority of cartels are now exposed as a result of leniency applications, which may be prompted by factors such as disagreements among cartelists if over time the cartel breaks down, change of management of a cartel member, acquisition of a cartelist during which infringements are discovered through due diligence, or general nervousness about investigations or customer complaints. Immunity from fines does not remove the liability of the whistleblower to damages actions by victims of the cartel, though the Commission has, in order not to discourage leniency applications, provided in the Damages Directive that leniency applications should be protected from disclosure in national court proceedings.[233]

As regards leniency procedures under national law, given the absence of a harmonised EU system on leniency, there is a risk that an applicant for leniency in one Member State may not qualify for leniency in other Member States. The Commission advises that leniency applicants should be granted favourable treatment and should apply for leniency to all national competition authorities (NCAs) which could act against the infringement in question.[234]

5.2.3 Third Party 'Facilitators'

It is possible for companies not active in the market to be guilty of a cartel.[235] The General Court upheld a finding of liability of a Swiss based consultancy firm which had amongst other things, organised cartel meetings at its premises, acted as a mediator in the case of disagreements and reimbursed travel expenses to avoid evidence of meetings (*see also* 'Trade Associations' at section 5.3.1 below).[236]

232. For guidance on immunity and cooperation *see* Commission Notice on Immunity from fines and reduction of fines in cartel cases (OJ C 298 of 8 December 2006, pages 17-22). Reductions reflect the timing of companies' cooperation and the extent to which the evidence they provide help the Commission to prove the respective cartels.
233. Damages Directive, *supra*, recital 26.
234. *See* European Competition Network Leniency (November 2012; Regulation 1/2003 Article 11.
235. Commission Decision COMP/E-2/37.857– Organic Peroxides.
236. Case T-99/04 Treuhand v Commission [2008] ECR II 1501 para. 122, the infringement related to coordination of a cartel in the market organic peroxides, used in the plastic and rubber industries. *See also* Commission Decision Case COMP/38589 — Heat Stabilisers, summarised in OJ 2010 C 307, imposing a fine, upheld by the General Court and ECJ in Case C-194/14 P, Treuhand v Commission, 22 October 2015.

5.2.4 Price Fixing or Fixing of Other Trading Conditions

Agreements or concerted practices whereby competitors agree to fix prices of products which they sell or buy are generally prohibited.[237] Joint purchasing agreements or price fixing may be permissible by virtue of Article 101(3) within alliances or other joint ventures or other wider agreements such as research or development agreements. It is not necessary that the agreement expressly or directly fixes the selling or purchasing price. Agreements on parameters of price, such as recommended minimum fees by a trade association, agreements on discounts, rebates, payment or credit terms, surcharges or other components of price, have all been prohibited.[238]

Agreements between competitors on standard trading conditions will often not to lead to any competition concerns. Where, however, they are directly relevant to pricing, such as agreements not to offer discounts or rebates or other special conditions to customers, or fixing uniform rates for overheads such as logistics services, or a component of price such as surcharges, they will infringe Article 101(1). Agreements on payment terms, guarantees and discouragement of global and long-term contracts have also been prohibited.[239]

5.2.4.1 Freightforwarders Cartel

The Commission, following a leniency application by Deutsche Post, investigated and fined 14 groups of freight forwarding companies EUR 169 million. It concluded that from 2007 to 2009 in four distinct cartels on Europe-US and China/Hong Kong–Europe lanes, the companies established and coordinated various surcharges and charging mechanisms, which were component elements of the final price billed to customers for these services.[240]

Two of these operated between Europe and the US and the rest of the world respectively, namely: (i) introducing a surcharge on a reporting service and to fix its amount according to the size of the customer, when the UK introduced an electronic

237. Article 101(1)(a), cases discussed below; *see* generally Revised Version of 03/06/2015 Commission Guidance on restrictions of competition 'by object' for the purpose of defining which agreements may benefit from the *De Minimis* Notice, SWD(2014) 198 final, and Chapter 8 *Mergers and Alliances*.

238. *See* for example Case 38549 Architectes Belges recommended minimum fees of a national association of architects; Joined Cases C-238/99 P, C-244/99 P, C-245/99 P, C-247/99 P, C-250/99 P to C-252/99 P and C-254/99 P ICI v Commission – target prices and target quotas were fixed, and initiatives to raise price levels and monitor the operation of the arrangements; Commission Decision Far East Trade Tariff Charges and Surcharges Agreement – agreement not to offer discounts; Commission Decision CASE AT.39462 – Freight forwarding 28 March 2012 – agreements on surcharges; Commission Decision in Airfreight alleging agreements between carriers on surcharges was annulled by the General Court (*see* below).

239. Commission Decision of 28 January 2009 relating to a proceeding under Article 101 Case COMP/39406 – Marine Hoses; upheld by General Court.

240. Commission Decision of 28 March 2012 relating to a proceeding under Article 101 TFEU and Article 53 of the EEA Agreement (Case COMP/39.462 — Freight forwarding; largely upheld on appeal by the General Court, Case T-267/12, Deutsche Bahn et ors v Commission 29 February 2016.

declaration for exports in 2003, the 'new export system' cartel; (ii) introducing a surcharge for administrative costs in respect of a requirement introduced by the US, to provide advance information on goods to be shipped to the US, and its level, the 'advanced manifest system'; and two operated in relation to trade lanes between China/ Hong Kong and Europe, namely: (iii) shifting contracts from USD to Renminbi (RMB) or, if this was not possible, introducing a currency adjustment factor and agreeing on its level. This followed the appreciation of the Chinese currency against the USD in 2005, local services at Chinese airports generally being paid for by forwarders in RMB, while the customers of forwarders were billed in USD which might have resulted in losses; and (iv) the introduction and timing of a peak season surcharge to be charged from September to December, the parties on occasions also discussing the level of the surcharge.

Participants and duration varied in each of the four cartels. Deutsche Post (including its subsidiaries DHL and Exel) received full immunity from fines under the Commission's 2006 leniency notice for all four cartels, as it was the first to reveal their existence the Commission. The fines were set on the basis of the Commission 2006 Guidelines on fines (*see* Chapter 9 *Enforcement*). Other members of the cartel, Deutsche Bahn (including Schenker and BAX), CEVA, Agility and Yusen received reductions of fines for cooperation ranging from 5 per cent to 50 per cent.

The parties brought appeals arguing that the Commission had made errors of fact and law in relation to the definition of the relevant market, the duration of the infringement and the calculation of the fines. The General Court rejected the majority of these. It held that the agreements on the surcharges and pricing mechanisms affected freight forwarding services as a 'package of services' on the trade lanes affected, and the Commission was entitled to base its fine calculations on the total value of these services.[241]

5.2.4.2 Airfreight Cartel Investigation

The most high profile decision on price fixing by the Commission in the air transport sector related to the fixing of a component of price, namely surcharges, principally on fuel prices. The decision and fines of EUR 799 million followed the largest cartel investigation in the air transport sector with dawn raids by the Commission – and investigations by authorities in other jurisdictions such as the US, Canada, South Korea, Japan and Australia. The European Commission's decision and fines were overturned on appeal in December 2015 by the General Court on grounds of internal inconsistencies which were found to infringe the parties' rights of defence, but the Commission subsequently adopted a new decision in respect of the cartel. The case is of interest in the respects discussed below:

241. T-264/12 UTi v Commission, General Court 29 February 2016. As regards one of the parties UTi Worldwide, the Court reduced the fine from EUR 3.07 million to EUR 2.97 million, on the basis that which its liability was solely derived from behaviour of its, subsidiaries and that the liability of the parent should not exceed that of its subsidiaries in such cases.

(1) *Background*

In February 2006, following a leniency application by Lufthansa and subsidiaries Lufthansa Cargo AG and Swiss, the Commission commenced an investigation of a number of carriers. Eleven carriers agreed to cooperate with the Commission and received fines, with reductions of between 10 per cent and 50 per cent.[242] Charges against 11 other carriers including a consultancy firm, were withdrawn for lack of evidence.

(2) *Conclusions of Commission Decision*

In November 2010, the Commission issued a decision imposing fines of EUR 799 million.[243] (This decision was 're-adopted' by the Commission, which stated that it was identical in terms of the behaviour targeted, but addressed the irregularities on the grounds of which its decision was annulled by the General Court (decision as yet unpublished, *see* section (4) below)). The 2010 decision concluded that from December 1999 until February 2006, airlines had colluded to introduce a fuel surcharge in respect of services to, from and within the EU, with the aim of ensuring that they imposed a flat rate surcharge per kilo of cargo, with coordination on increases or decreases to such charges. This was introduced in response to increasing oil prices globally. The decision also concluded that carriers had agreed to introduce a security surcharge, to address the costs of certain security measures imposed following the terrorist attacks of September 2001, and had reached agreement not to pay commission to freightforwarders on surcharges, thereby avoiding competing through negotiation of surcharges. The decision stated that contacts took place at head office and local office level, by means of bilateral and multilateral phone calls, and in some cases meetings of the local Board of Airline Representatives associations.[244]

There was no finding of an infringement, nor imposition of fines in respect of routes between the EEA and third countries prior to 1 May 2004 given the absence of enforcement powers on agreements with third country carriers until that date.[245] From

242. The criteria for determining the amount of the fine are set out in the Commission Guidelines on the method of setting fines imposed pursuant to Article 23(2)(a) of Regulation No. 1/2003 (OJ 2006 C 210 pages 2-5.
243. Commission Decision (Case COMP/39258 — Airfreight). A provisional non-confidential version of the Decision was published on 8 May 2015, available on the DG COMP website http://ec.europa.eu/competition/antitrust/cases/dec_docs/39258/39258_7008_7.pdf. Airlines fined were Air Canada, Air France-KLM, British Airways, Cathay Pacific, Cargolux, Japan Airlines, LAN Chile, Martinair, Qantas, SAS and Singapore Airlines.
244. There were also fines and settlements in other jurisdictions such as the US, with officers from some of the airlines concerned imprisoned in the US and Australia. In the passenger travel market, there was also a UK investigation of surcharges on transatlantic passenger travel, with a fine imposed on BA following a leniency application by Virgin: OFT decision 19 April 2012 imposing a fine of GBP 58.5 million, reduced from GBP 121 million imposed in August 2007.
245. These limited powers were under the 'transitional regime' that applied to the air transport sector then Articles 88 and 89 EEC Treaty (now, as amended, Articles 104 and 105 TFEU, discussed at Chapter 2 section 2.6.4). *See* for example para. 1123 on Commission Airfreight decision provisional non-confidential version, published on 08.05.2015.

1 May 2004, fines in respect of such routes were reduced by 50 per cent on the basis that part of the harm on such routes was likely to fall outside the EEA. The decision also concluded that carriers were authorised or encouraged to concert on prices on certain routes by the regulatory approach under bilateral ASAs with third countries, for which the Commission decided a reduction of 15 per cent in fines was appropriate. (For there to be no infringement by undertakings of competition law, there must be State compulsion to enter into anticompetitive arrangements, the legal framework eliminating any possibility of competitive activity on the part of the undertaking(s) concerned.[246]) Fines on SAS were increased by 50 per cent for recidivism, it having previously been fined for cartel involvement (*see* section 5.2.5.2 below).[247] The increase was not applied to the parent company SAS AB as it had not been in control of the infringing entity at the time of the previous infringement (discussed below).

The Commission decision gave rise to damages litigation in jurisdictions such as the UK, Germany, the Netherlands and in non-EU jurisdictions, by purchasers of air freight services (whether shippers or freightforwarders) claiming damages suffered as a result of being overcharged by the cartel.[248]

(3) Annulment of Airfreight Decision by General Court

On appeal by the majority of the airlines on a range of grounds, the General Court annulled the Commission's 2010 decision and fines on the procedural grounds of failure to state reasons, the Court finding inconsistency in the Commission's decision.[249]

On the one hand, in the grounds for its decision, the Commission referred to a single continuous infringement committed by all the addressees, for which they were all jointly and severally liable - irrespective of whether the airlines operated on the routes concerned. On the other, however, the articles of the decision, that is, the operative parts, referred to four infringements relating to different periods and different routes and committed by different carriers, with liability attributed only to the carriers which participated in the unlawful conduct referred to in those articles. The Court found that it was unclear, and that the Commission had not examined, the extent to which evidence set out in the grounds was liable to establish the existence of the separate infringements set out in the operative parts.

The Court emphasised that the principle of effective judicial protection required that the operative part of a decision adopted by the Commission, finding infringements

246. Case C-359/95 Commission v Ladbroke Racing ECR 1997 I 6265.
247. Commission Decision 2001/76 of 18 July 2001 (OJ L 265 5 October 2001 p. 15).
248. The actions within the EU jurisdictions are ongoing as at the date of publication so are not discussed, and actions or settlements in non-EU jurisdictions are beyond the scope of this work.
249. Judgments of 16 December 2015 in Cases T-9/11 Air Canada, T-28/11 Koninklijke Luchtvaart Maatschappij, T-36/11 Japan Airlines, T-38/11 Cathay Pacific Airways, T-39/11 Cargolux Airlines International, T-40/11 Latam Airlines Group and Others, T-43/11 Singapore Airlines and Others, T-46/11 Deutsche Lufthansa and Others, T-48/11 British Airways, T-56/11 SAS Cargo Group and Others, T-62/11 Air France-KLM, T-63/11 Société Air France and T-67/11 Martinair Holland v Commission.

of the competition rules, must be particularly clear and precise and that the undertakings held liable and penalised must be in a position to understand and to contest that imputation of liability and the imposition of those penalties, as set out in the wording of that operative part.

It also noted that national courts are bound by the decision adopted by the Commission, and that the meaning of the operative part of the decision must be unambiguous. In particular, the national courts must be in a position to understand the scope of that infringement and to identify the persons liable, in order to be able to rule on claims for damages brought by persons harmed by that infringement.

(4) Commission's 'Re-adopted' Decision

The European Commission did not appeal against the ruling of the General Court – which would be on points of law only – to the Court of Justice, but it issued a new decision (unpublished at the date of publication of this work) in which it stated that it addressed the Court's conclusions by bringing the operative part of its 2010 decision in line with the reasoning part, while remaining identical in terms of the behaviour targeted by the Commission. The fines remained unchanged, save for a reduction in the fine on Martinair, which had been capped at 10 per cent of the company's total turnover in 2009, but was reduced to reflect that its turnover in 2016 was lower than in the year preceding the adoption of the decision.[250] BA, in respect of which the General Court's annulment was partial, appealed against the ruling to the Court of Justice, in so far as it limited its annulment of the Commission Decision, rather than annulling it in unqualified terms.[251]

5.2.5 Market Sharing

5.2.5.1 Definition

Market sharing is any arrangement whereby competitors agree among themselves to allocate customers, territories/Member States, or types of products or services, thus ceasing to compete in each other's markets and exposing customers to higher prices. Cases of market sharing have included agreements whereby undertakings agreed to

250. European Commission – Press release_IP/17/661, 17 March 2017: 'Commission re-adopts decision and fines air cargo carriers €776 million for price-fixing cartel'.
251. Case C-122/16 P: Appeal brought on 26 February 2016 by British Airways plc against the judgment of the General Court delivered on 16 December 2015 in Case T-48/11: British Airways plc v European Commission OJ C 191, 30.5.2016, pp. 9–10. BA argued that the General Court wrongly found itself restricted by the 'ultra petita' principle according to which a court may not decide more than it has been asked by the parties. It argued this is on the basis that the General Court had of its own motion found there to be fundamental public policy defects which vitiated the European Commission's Decision entirely. Whether BA's appeal shall be continued given the Commission Decision of 17 March 2017 is not known.

retain their respective domestic markets and fix prices and quotas for the export of products[252] and concerted action on market sharing with a view to protecting markets from parallel imports.[253]

5.2.5.2 SAS/Maersk Decision

The Commission found there to be a market sharing cartel - in the form of a non-compete agreement in respect of routes - in the case of *SAS/Maersk*.[254] The parties had notified a code-share agreement under which SAS could market Maersk Air's flights as SAS flights on domestic routes within, and on international routes to/from Denmark, and extended SAS's frequent flyer programme to Maersk's clients, to the Commission for approval in 1999 under the competition regime then applicable to agreements between airlines, Regulation 3975/87.[255] Previously, a competitor had complained to the Commission that there was greater coordination between the parties than had been announced publicly.

The Commission conducted on-site investigations and found that the actual cooperation on these routes was broader than what had been notified, given that at the same time, the parties had withdrawn from certain routes where they had until then been in competition. The withdrawal by Maersk from Copenhagen-Stockholm which was the busiest route in question, had also resulted in the exit of the other competitor on the route, Finnair, as the two airlines previously had a code-sharing agreement (CSA), thus giving SAS a monopoly. There was also an agreement by Maersk not to launch any new international routes from Copenhagen without approval from SAS, and the withdrawal by SAS from other routes to be served only by Maersk.

The Commission concluded that these withdrawals had been agreed, as opposed to being unilateral decisions. In assessing the fine, the Commission considered that this was a very serious infringement which had a significant impact, due to the volume of passengers affected notably on the Stockholm–Copenhagen route, the large number of other routes affected, the scope of the geographic markets affected, with the isolation of national markets and given that it extended the market power of SAS. The duration was just under two and a half years. The Commission also had regard to the disparity in size of the parties and the cooperation offered after on-site inspections. The fines imposed on SAS and Maersk were EUR 35 million and EUR 14 million respectively.[256]

---

252. Case C-41/96 ACF Chemie farma NV v Commission (relating to quinine).
253. Joined cases 29/83 and 30/83 CRAM v Commission (relating to zinc).
254. Commission Decision 2001/716/EC of 18 July 2001 relating to a proceeding pursuant to Article 101 (COMP.D.2 37.444 — SAS/Maersk Air and COMP.D.2 37.386 — Sun-Air versus SAS and Maersk Air) (OJ 2001 L 265, p. 15).
255. The procedures under Regulation 3975/87 are discussed in Chapter 2.
256. An appeal against the level of fines was upheld by the General Court Case T-241/01 [2005] ECR 2005 II 2917; *see also* summary on weblink http://eur-lex.europa.eu/legal-content/EN/SUM/?uri=CELEX:62001TJ0241.

5.2.6 Bid Rigging

Bid rigging, or collusive tendering, is most likely to occur in industries where firms compete for very large contracts and where there are tendering procedures. It is a practice whereby bidders in a tender procedure coordinate their bids in order to determine who wins the tender and at what price, losing bidders putting in a higher price. As with cartel offences generally, bid rigging may form part of broader arrangements including price fixing, market sharing and agreements on quotas. In the *Marine Hoses* case, the cartel comprised market sharing, price fixing and the rigging of bids for contracts tendered by purchasers of marine hoses used for the transport of oil (major oil companies). This led to a fine of EUR 131 million, prison sentences of a number of individuals and damages litigation with customers such as oil companies, bringing claims.[257] An example of bid rigging in the insurance sector was the 'Spitzer inquiry' in the US, where there were cases of insurers being invited to submit higher quotes ('phony bids') by brokers placing insurance on behalf of clients, so inflating premiums and commission.[258]

The practice whereby a bidder which does not want to win the tender but wishes to submit a bid so as to remain on the purchaser's tender list, and engages in discussions with other bidders so that it may submit a bid which is unsuccessful (known as 'cover pricing'), is also prohibited and punishable by fines.[259]

5.2.7 Agreements Limiting Production

Limiting supply to a market will result in upward pressure in prices. Agreements setting quotas may form a part of wider arrangements fixing prices, or sharing markets, with quotas enabling the cartelists to monitor the market share, particularly where there would be the possibility of cartel members offering secret deals on pricing, or improvements in service.[260] Agreements limiting production may also arise in industries suffering from overcapacity and will generally be prohibited.[261]

5.2.8 Collective Boycott, Standards

A collective boycott occurs when competitors agree to take steps to exclude an actual or potential competitor. Such steps could include an agreement by competitors to

257. Marine Hoses *supra*.
258. Related practices were demands by brokers for additional payments from insurers over and above ordinary broker commission, based on volumes of business they placed. *See also* European Commission Staff Working Document – Sector Inquiry under Article 17 of Regulation (EC) No. 1/2003 on business insurance (Final Report) – (COM(2007) 556 final.
259. *See* UK Decision of the Office of Fair Trading CA98/02/2009 Bid rigging in the construction industry in England 21 September 2009; fines in relation to 'cover pricing' significantly reduced on appeal by the Competition Appeal Tribunal Case Nos: 1117/1/1/09 et ors.
260. Market share was a criterion for market sharing agreements in Marine Hoses *supra*.
261. Case C-209/07 Beef Industry Development Society v Barry Brothers (Carrigmore) Meats [2008] ECR I 8637.

terminate contracts with a competitor whose activities are causing them to suffer reduced profits.[262] Indirect steps may also be employed, such as the setting of standards, with the goal of excluding competitors or delaying the introduction of new technologies.[263]

Collective steps taken against customers would also be prohibited. This would be by virtue of amongst other things, the prohibition of price fixing and/or other agreements on trading conditions (discussed at section 5.2.4 above).

5.2.9 Information Exchange

5.2.9.1 Prohibition of Exchange of 'Strategic' Information

EU competition law prohibits the exchange of commercially sensitive - or the term more recently used in case law and the Commission Horizontal Guidelines, 'strategic' - information, such as competitors' intended market behaviour. The Commission has summarised the case law of the European Courts in relation to information exchanges in its Guidelines on the applicability of Article 101 of the TFEU to horizontal cooperation agreements (the 'Horizontal Guidelines').[264]

The EU's position on information exchange is particularly strict. The premise is that each company must determine independently the policy which it intends to adopt on the market and the conditions which it intends to offer to its customers - it cannot coordinate its behaviour with competitors.[265] The Court of Justice has also held: 'Although it is correct to say that this requirement of independence does not deprive economic operators of the right to adapt themselves intelligently to the existing and anticipated conduct of their competitors, it does however strictly preclude any direct or indirect contact between such operators, the object or effect whereof is either to influence the conduct on the market of an actual or potential competitor or to disclose to such a competitor the course of conduct which they themselves have decided to adopt or contemplate adopting on the market.[266]

Information exchange can of itself breach Article 101(1), therefore, if the information exchanged reduces strategic uncertainty, facilitating collusion and reducing incentives to compete, thereby reducing the independence of competitors' conduct on the market, and diminishes their incentives to compete.[267] Further, where information has been exchanged or received, there is a presumption - which a firm under investigation must adduce evidence to rebut - that any recipient will have accepted the

262. case C-68/12 Judgment in Case C-68/12 Protimonopolný úrad Slovenskej republiky v Slovenská sporitel'ňa a.s.- preliminary ruling on a reference from Slovakian court, Slovak banks having been condemned by the national competition authority of coordination of contracts with a non-bank financial institution offering cashless foreign exchange transactions.
263. Case IV/35.691 Pre-insulated pipes REF.
264. OJ C 11/1 14/01/2011.
265. Commission Horizontal Guidelines 2011 para. 60.
266. Joined Cases 40/73 and others, Suiker Unie v Commission [1975] ECR para. 174; Case C-8/08, T-Mobile, para. 35.
267. Horizontal Guidelines para. 61.

information and adapted its market conduct accordingly, unless it responds with a clear statement that it does not wish to receive such data.[268]

This is also the case where disclosure is unilateral, one undertaking alone revealing to its competitors, strategic information concerning its future commercial policy, given it reduces strategic uncertainty as to the future operation of the market for all the competitors involved, and increases the risk of limiting competition and of collusive behaviour. Further, mere attendance at a single meeting where one or more companies exchange such information may be sufficient for it to be caught by Article 101, even in the absence of an explicit agreement to raise prices, if it affords them the opportunity to take account of the information exchanged with their competitors, in order to determine their conduct on the market.[269]

Strategic information can be related to prices (e.g., actual prices, discounts, increases, reductions or rebates), customer lists, production costs, quantities, turnovers, sales, capacities, qualities, marketing plans, risks, investments, technologies and R&D programmes and their results. Generally, information related to prices and quantities is the most strategic, followed by information about costs and demand.[270] In particular, information on parties' intentions concerning future conduct regarding prices or quantities will generally be considered to have the object of fixing prices or quantities.[271]

Other relevant factors may be the frequency, and as discussed below (section 5.2.9.3), the recency of information exchanged. Frequent exchange of specific information on quantities sold by individual competitors can facilitate coordination, particularly where there are few competitors and they account for a large part of the relevant market.[272]

5.2.9.2 Pre-merger/Joint Venture Discussions

There are commercial scenarios, notably pre-merger / joint venture discussions, where there will be exchange of information between the parties. In such cases, it would be a minimum requirement that information exchanged should be strictly limited to what is necessary for the purposes of the discussion and restricted to individuals involved who are subject to confidentiality obligations.

5.2.9.3 Permissible Information Exchange

Information exchange may nevertheless be procompetitive, being useful for benchmarking of prices or for analysis of market trends or technologies, and subject to

268. *See* Case C-199/92 P, Hüls, [1999] ECR I-4287, para. 162; Case C-49/92 P, Anic Partezipazioni, [1999] ECR I-4125, para. 121.*See also* Chapter 4 section 4.3.1.2
269. T-Mobile *supra* para. 59.
270. Horizontal Guidelines para. 86.
271. Horizontal Guidelines para. 74.
272. UK Agricultural Tractor Registration Exchange, OJ 1992 L68/19, upheld on appeal Case C-7/95 P, John Deere v Commission [1998] ECR I 3111, para. 67.

safeguards this is permissible – such as individual company information being anonymised, aggregated, collated by an independent body such as a trade association, and individualised information disseminated after a certain amount of time such as a year.[273] There has been a block exemption in the insurance industry which exempts, subject to safeguards, the exchange of information between insurers on the costs of insuring risks.[274]

Information which is freely available in the public domain should not give rise to competition concerns.

If strategic or commercially sensitive information is exchanged, trade associations or other bodies such as consultancies, which coordinate the exchange may also be guilty of an infringement (*see* sections 5.2.3 and 5.3.1.)

5.2.10 'Price Signalling': Announcements on Price Increases

Where a company makes a unilateral announcement that is also genuinely public, this generally does not constitute a concerted practice within the meaning of Article 101(1). As a result of recent Commission commitments decisions in the shipping sector, there could potentially be an infringement, however, where such an announcement was followed by public announcements by other competitors which enabled readjustments of their own earlier announcements, thus enabling them to reach a common understanding about the terms of coordination.[275] In the *Wood Pulp* case (1993), the Court of Justice had found that a system of quarterly price announcements by wood pulp producers to customers in the EU did not breach Article 101 or constitute evidence of collusion.[276]

In a new development, the Commission investigated whether regular announcements by container shipping companies on their websites or via specialised press, of their intentions to apply future price increases on similar routes and on similar dates (General Rate Increases announcements) breached Article 101. It considered that the announcements may be anticompetitive on the basis that they were non-binding, 'testing the water' and allowed the shipping companies to postpone increases or modify prices before they came into effect, and possibly align them with those announced by other carriers. There was no finding of an infringement, but the Commission accepted commitments from the companies requiring greater

273. *Ibid.* It may be that depending on the characteristics of the market a lesser period may be permissible – six months was accepted by the UK authorities in 'What If?' case – Private motor insurance: exchange of data 2 December 2011.
274. Commission Regulation (EU) No. 267/2010 of 24 March 2010 on the application of Article 101(3) of the Treaty on the Functioning of the European Union to certain categories of agreements, decisions and concerted practices in the insurance sector OJ L 83, 30.3.2010, p. 1. This Regulation expired on 31 March 2017.
275. Horizontal Guidelines para. 63.
276. Case C-85/89, Ahlström osakeyhtiö and others v Commission.

transparency as to price to be charged and a shorter period in advance of increases, to remove the possibility of coordination.[277] (Commitment decisions generally are discussed in Chapter 9 *Enforcement.*)

5.3 COOPERATION AGREEMENTS BETWEEN AIRLINES

There is a wide spectrum of cooperation that can take place between airlines which may be low level cooperation on interlining, frequent flyer programmes and lounge access, or expanded cooperation such as code-sharing, joint venture type alliances involving coordination of prices, schedules, and merger-like cooperation with sharing of revenues and costs.[278] Many types of cooperation, such as IATA tariff consultations, have benefited from the sector specific exemptions which were in force in the air transport sector until they were finally abolished in 2007 (*see* Chapter 2 *Liberalisation of Air Transport*). There are also cases where resolutions adopted by IATA have been reviewed under Article 101, on the basis they constitute agreements between IATA member airlines, notably the Passenger and Cargo Agency Programme exemption decisions of 1991 (discussed in Chapter 6 *Article 101 TFEU: Vertical Agreements*, due to the vertical issues raised).

The majority of cases under Article 101 have concerned joint operation and cooperation between airlines, whether applications for exemption under Article 101(3) under the notification regime which applied before 1 May 2004, or commitment decisions after that date. These are discussed within the context of alliances in Chapter 8 *Mergers and Alliances* and generally in Chapter 9 *Enforcement.*

Stand-alone agreements which may take place and where competition issues arise are discussed below, notably agreements within trade associations, code-sharing agreements and cooperation on computer reservation system.

5.3.1 Trade Associations

Trade associations serve legitimate purposes promoting the interests of a particular industry, whether setting standards, liaising with other associations at different levels of trade, and lobbying. However, they can also be a forum for anticompetitive activity by providing competitors with an opportunity to meet, or by coordinating the exchange of market sensitive information, such as detailed data on sales, production capacities or market intentions on pricing or capacity. They can, therefore, be a forum for cartel activity. In the case of a cartel in the steel sector, information was found to have been

277. European Commission - Press release Commission accepts commitments by container liner shipping companies on price transparency 7 July 2016; Decisions available at http://ec.europa.eu/competition/elojade/isef/case_details.cfm?proc_code = 1_39850.

278. 'Block exemptions' which formerly applied to categories of cooperation agreements between airlines are summarised in Chapter 2.

exchanged through the trade association Eurofer, which was found guilty of infringing Article 101(1).[279]

Further, where trade associations develop standards these should be objective, non-discriminatory and not exclude competitors from the market.[280]

5.3.2 Code-Sharing Agreements

5.3.2.1 Definition of Code-Sharing

A code-sharing agreement (CSA) is an agreement whereby one airline (the 'marketing carrier') markets services on flights operated by another airline (the 'operating carrier') under its own code and flight number. The marketing carrier sells and issues tickets on the flight as if it was operating the flight itself. There is in principle no limit to the number of marketing carriers on a given flight. CSAs are very widespread and may take various forms, such as 'free-flow' or 'blocked space' agreements, with variations thereon. They may be stand-alone agreements between independent airlines, or may form part of wider agreements within more integrated alliances.

5.3.2.2 Benefits of Code-Sharing

Code-sharing enables airlines to extend their network, achieve better connectivity, facilitating wider presence in the market or greater frequencies, without the need to invest in new aircraft, thus spreading risk, and increasing load factors, which should lead to lower prices. Other benefits would be greater choice, faster and more reliable transfers and uncomplicated itineraries, and if 'double marginalisation' is eliminated, potentially lower fares.[281] Full service carriers will often have a high proportion of their capacity sold by other carriers through code-shares.

5.3.2.3 Types of Code-Sharing

CSAs may be *'free-flow'* CSAs – these offer free access to the operating carrier's inventory. These are versatile, can deal with small loads, and offer virtually last seat

279. Commission Decision 94/215/ECSC of 16 February 1994 relating to a proceeding pursuant to Article 65 of the ECSC Treaty concerning agreements and concerted practices engaged in by European producers of beams OJ 1994 L 116, p. 1, upheld by the General Court and ultimately ECJ Case C-179/99 P, Eurofer v Commission, ECR [2003] I - 10740 More recent case law has involved the imposition of fines on third party facilitators. *See* section 5.2.3 above.
280. *See* generally Communication from the Commission — Guidelines on the applicability of Article 101 of the Treaty on the Functioning of the European Union to horizontal cooperation agreements OJ C 11, 14.1.2011, p. 1–72, paras 257 et seq.
281. Double marginalisation arises when both operators in a supply relationship mark up the prices they charge their respective partner above their respective marginal costs, which leads to deadweight loss. In CSAs where these mark-ups are substantially reduced or eliminated, this may lead to lower prices. *See* generally CASE COMP/AT.39595 - Continental/United/Lufthansa/Air Canada 23 May 2013 (Star Alliance A++) para. 64.

availability, and are generally preferred by airlines. They require investment in IT, including a mapping facility between the booking classes in the two carriers' revenue management systems.[282] If the code-share partners are competitors, free-flow CSAs may give rise to concerns given they may result in a reduction of competition.

'Blocked space' CSAs are more rigid, determining the number of seats to be sold in advance by the marketing carrier and at a price agreed. Such agreements may be appropriate for large numbers of passengers travelling together, where one or more of the airlines have poor IT systems, or there is a stipulation in an ASA compelling the carriers to enter into a blocked space agreement.[283]

Blocked space agreements fall into two categories. Under a *'hard' blocked space* agreement, the marketing carrier pays the operating carrier the agreed price for the block of seats reserved, irrespective of whether it sells the seats, so such agreements would tend to be less restrictive of competition. The marketing carrier and the operating carrier each bear the commercial risk of unsold seats, and both parties are responsible for the sale of their allocated number of seats. Blocked space agreements have been used as a remedy by the Commission in mergers or alliances where concerns are raised on certain routes, the Commission having required, in certain cases, the parties to agree to enter into blocked space agreements on request by a new entrant to facilitate market entry by other carriers.[284]

Under *'soft' blocked space* agreements, which account for the majority of blocked space agreements, it is possible for the marketing carrier to return unused capacity to the operating carrier, according to terms agreed between the carriers, with or without penalty up to a given time before departure.[285]

5.3.2.4 Competition Assessment of CSAs

There is as yet limited EU case law or guidelines, nor reference to code-sharing in former block exemption Regulations. There have been two studies on CSAs at EU level – a Report prepared by Steer Davies Gleave and Clyde & Co for the European Commission 'Competition impact of airline code-share agreements' in 2007 ('SDG / Clyde Report') and a study published in 2006 by the ECA (European Competition Authorities) 'Code-sharing agreements in scheduled passenger air transport' (in which national case law has been discussed) – some discussion of CSAs in merger decisions, and two Commission investigations with Article 101 proceedings brought in one case (discussed below). The competition treatment of CSAs, whether stand-alone or within the context of alliances, will be governed by Article 101 TFEU. The principles of assessment of alliances under Article 101 will also be relevant to CSAs (*see* Chapter 8

282. *See* generally Report prepared by Steer Davies Gleave and Clyde & Co for the European Commission 'Competition impact of airline code-share agreements' in 2007 ('SDG /Clyde Report'): ec.europa.eu/competition/sectors/transport/reports/airlinecodeshare.pdf.
283. *See* SDG / Clyde Report 2007 – para. 5.13.
284. *See* for example Case No. COMP/M.3770 – Lufthansa/Swiss, para. 197.
285. The SDG / Clyde Report found that this may frequently be without penalty up to 72 hours in advance of the flight para. 5.14.

Mergers and Alliances). Within the context of mergers, they would be considered within the merger analysis under the EU Merger Regulation 139/2004 (or merger control regimes at national level).[286]

In the competition assessment of CSAs, a key factor is whether the parties are competitors. In the case of *unilateral* or non-overlapping CSAs, the carriers do not compete on the same routes, but use the CSA on a route on which they do not operate, for example, the marketing carrier using the CSA to widen its offer of destinations from its home market and increase eligibility for FFP points. In the case of complementary CSAs which concern *behind and beyond* routes, the marketing carrier can secure connections with its own services. This type of CSA will be the least restrictive and offer the greatest benefits for consumers.[287] An issue to consider may be whether the parties may be potential competitors, such that the existence of the agreement may deter the marketing carrier from entering into competition with the operating carrier on the route in question. For this to be the case, there would have to be a real commercial possibility of entry by the non-operating carrier.[288]

In the case of *parallel* or overlapping CSAs, where the airlines operate services on the same route, this may lead to a decrease of competition, with a risk of alignment of pricing or reduction in capacity, such that Article 101(1) would apply and the agreement would have to satisfy the criteria for exemption under Article 101(3).

Given CSAs involve the sale by one carrier of another's capacity, they would also give rise to a distribution or 'vertical' relationship, so that restrictions on the marketing carrier's ability to sell, such as resale price maintenance, could fall within the prohibition of hardcore restrictions in vertical agreements. Competition issues could also potentially be raised by exclusivity provisions preventing a code-share partner from entering into CSAs with other airlines, due to the potential foreclosure effect, as could revenue allocation between the parties if terms favoured a particular carrier over others. In the case of CSAs within the context of metal neutral alliances, there would be sharing of revenues, which would require assessment under Article 101(3) (*see* Chapter 8 *Mergers and Alliances*).

The analysis of CSAs will also depend on the features of the agreement in question (terms, duration), whether the parties are competitors on the routes in question and/or on other routes outside of the agreement, and on other factors such as the broader context of agreements if any between the parties, the competitiveness of the market, barriers to entry (e.g., slot congestion), the market power of the parties (also having regards to '*de minimis*' rules, *see* Chapter 4, section 4.5 above) on the routes affected, applying the origin and destination approach. Market definition in the case of cooperation between airlines and the O&D approach are discussed in Chapter 8 *Mergers and Alliances*.

---

286. *See* for example Case No COMP/M.7270 - Cesky Aeroholding/ Travel Service / Ceske Aeroline 18 December 2014.
287. An example would be BA selling a journey from London to Albuquerque, BA operating London to Dallas, American Airlines operating Dallas to Albuquerque SDG / Clyde Report para. 3.7.
288. ECA Report *supra*, para. 30; *see also* T-374/94 – European Night Services, ECR 1998, II 3141, para. 137.

The parties' freedom to set prices will be a relevant factor. Further, in a free flow code-share, the commission received from the marketing carrier is normally a percentage of the fare it charges for the tickets it sells. Therefore, the higher the price at which the marketing carrier sells tickets, the greater its commission will be.[289] The likelihood of the marketing carrier representing a material competitive constraint for the operating carrier would further be limited if, for example, the operating carrier was entitled to terminate the code-share agreement if the marketing carrier started to offer fares that were substantially lower than those of the operating carrier, thus depriving the marketing carrier of any benefit of an aggressive pricing policy.[290]

Benefits of code-sharing have been outlined above and the existence of such benefits will have to be demonstrated to merit exemption under Article 101(3) where CSAs are caught by Article 101(1). Other factors to consider will include the indispensability of the restrictions within the CSA to achieving the efficiencies created by the agreement, such as it being impossible for the marketing carrier to operate the route in question, due perhaps to investments required or to the route being thin, and the requirement that the route remains competitive notwithstanding the CSA, such that competition is not eliminated in a substantial part of the market. Article 101(3) criteria are discussed in Chapter 4 section 4.7.

CSAs may, similar to other agreements between airlines, restrict competition within the EU even if one of the partners is based outside the EU. An investigation was commenced by the Commission in 2011, in respect of a suspected free-flow CSA on hub-to-hub routes between Lufthansa and Turkish Airlines (Munich-Istanbul and Frankfurt-Istanbul), on which Lufthansa and Turkish Airlines were the major operators. A parallel investigation was launched in respect of a CSA between Brussels Airlines and TAP Portugal (Brussels – Lisbon). The Commission stated that this form of free-flow, parallel, hub-to-hub code share agreement might distort competition, leading to higher prices and less service quality for customers on the routes in question.[291]

The Commission closed its investigation of Lufthansa / Turkish Airlines on the grounds that the parties did not have full marketing rights to each other's seat inventory, that they applied differing pricing strategies, and that the codeshare accounted for only a marginal share of the parties' sales on the routes of concern. In respect of the CSA between Brussels Airlines and TAP Portugal, proceedings were commenced on the basis of Commission concerns that the parties might be reaching agreement to reduce capacity and aligning their fare structures and prices on the route.[292]

If code-sharing takes place between competing carriers, information exchange between the parties should be limited to what is strictly necessary, to avoid the risk of coordination of market behaviour leading to cartels. Code-sharing which takes place

289. Cesky Aeroholding/ Travel Service / Ceske Aeroline supra, para. 105.
290. *Ibid* para. 106.
291. Commission Press Release IP/11/147, 11 February 2011. Cases COMP/39794 Lufthansa/ Turkish Airlines and COMP/39860 Brussels Airlines/TAP Air Portugal. Lufthansa's CSA came to an end in the course of 2014.
292. Commission Press Release 16/3653, 27 October 2016 (proceedings ongoing).

within a wider context involving a cartel, or which facilitates a cartel, will always be prohibited. In *SAS / Maersk* (discussed above), the Commission found that agreements between the parties who had notified a CSA, were broader than the notified agreement and involved market sharing.[293] In December 2011, the Commission conducted dawn raids at the premises of Brussels Airlines and TAP Portugal in Belgium and Portugal, having concerns that the agreements between the parties may be wider than the code-sharing.[294]

5.3.3 Cooperation on CRSs/GDSs

Historically, airlines operated computer reservations systems (CRSs) - also commonly known as Global Distribution Systems or GDSs - computerised systems containing information about their schedules, availability and fares which were made available to subscribers (travel agents) and through which reservations could be made and tickets issued. This system eliminated the need for travel agents to telephone the company concerned for each booking. Reservations would be made directly by the agency on the basis of data provided by the system. In the 1980s, airlines in the EU set up CRSs Amadeus and Galileo, amongst others, and an EU Code of Conduct was adopted to remove discrimination against other airlines.[295]

A further development was the approval by the Commission in 1991 of a cooperation agreement between two major CRS providers, Amadeus and its US counterpart Sabre (then owned by American Airlines), whereby they would offer travel agents and other subscribers a joint product, users of the two systems paying a single fee. It was found that the cooperation would reduce price competition between the two systems who could not market independently in the EU, and thus fall within Article 101(1), but it would improve distribution in the EU and worldwide. Remedies to ensure airlines' willingness to deal with other CRSs on equivalent terms, and to ensure that Amadeus and Sabre would not impede non-associated carriers from distributing their tickets through other CRSs were agreed.[296] (The application of the rules on vertical agreements and abuse of a dominant position to CRSs are discussed in Chapter 6 section 6.7 and Chapter 7 section 7.4.4.2 respectively.)

293. SAS / Maersk *supra*.
294. Commission Press Release MEMO 11/926 19 December 2011.
295. *See also* Chapter 2 and Chapter 6 *Article 101 TFEU: Vertical Agreements* and Chapter 7 *Abuse of a Dominant Position*.
296. Commission Press Release IP/00/835; Comp Rep EC 1991 p. 73.

CHAPTER 6

Article 101 TFEU: Vertical Agreements

6.1 OVERVIEW

Article 101(1) TFEU applies to 'vertical' agreements - between undertakings at different levels of trade - as well as 'horizontal' agreements (*see* discussion in Chapters 4 *Elements of Article 101 TFEU and* 5 *Article 101 TFEU: Horizontal Agreements*).[297] Vertical agreements setting out the terms of sale or purchase, such as price, quantity and other commercial terms related to the contract products or services, do not raise competition issues, but restrictions on the parties, such as exclusivity obligations, or pricing or territorial restrictions which may foreclose competitors from the market or affect prices may be caught by Article 101(1).

Article 102 which prohibits abuse of a dominant position, also applies to vertical agreements where one of the parties occupies a 'dominant position' in a substantial part of the EU, such as agreements imposing exclusivity obligations or, potentially, granting rebates to travel agents.[298]

As with horizontal agreements, EU competition law adopts an effects-based approach in determining whether a vertical agreement falls within Article 101(1) and/or merits exemption under Article 101(3). There is also a block exemption in respect of vertical agreements - the Vertical Restraints Block Exemption Regulation 330/2010 (VBER) and often this will be the first point of reference in the case of vertical agreements.[299] This obviates the need for a detailed assessment, offering a safe harbour to agreements where the respective shares of the parties do not exceed 30 per cent and which do not contain certain severe types of restrictions - 'hardcore' restrictions set out

297. For a detailed discussion of vertical agreements generally *see* competition texts referred to in the Introduction and Vertical Agreements in EU Competition Law, Wijckmans and Tuytschaever.
298. Discussed in Chapter 7 *Abuse of a Dominant Position*.
299. Commission Regulation 330/2010 of 20 April 2010 on the application of Article 101(3) TFEU to categories of vertical agreements and concerted practices 2010 OJ L 102 page 1; accompanied by European Commission guidelines on vertical restraints ('Vertical Guidelines') 2010 OJ C 130/1.

in VBER Article 4 - on the basis that such agreements are presumed to give rise to efficiencies and consumer benefits.[300] Vertical agreements where the shares of the parties do not exceed 15 per cent will, further, be deemed '*de minimis*' and therefore outside Article 101(1) altogether, provided they do not contain hardcore restrictions or restrictions by object.[301]

The possibility of notifying agreements to the Commission for negative clearance or exemption and immunity from fines from the date of filing was abolished from 1 May 2004. In cases where an agreement does not fulfil the criteria of the VBER, therefore, parties must conduct their own assessment of the compatibility of agreements with competition law.

6.2 DEFINITION OF VERTICAL AGREEMENT AND EXAMPLES

A vertical agreement is an agreement entered into by two or more companies that, for the purposes of the agreement, operate at different levels of the production or distribution chain.[302] For the purposes of the VBER, the supplier or manufacturer is described as the 'supplier' and the distributor, agent or customer as the 'buyer'.

The most common vertical agreements will be arrangements where a supplier appoints a distributor or distributors across territories of the EU (possibly with ancillary IP rights such as trademarks), or distributors or customers undertake to source their supplies from a single supplier. The categories of vertical agreements are not limited. Examples would include an agreement between an airline with its distributors (or agents or other intermediaries such as computer reservation systems(CRSs) / global distribution systems (GDSs) connecting airlines with agents for the sale of tickets), or between an airline and its customers (passengers or tour operators); a supply agreement between a manufacturer and a customer, for example, an airline manufacturer or maintenance company with an airline; or more generally, a distribution agreement whereby a supplier sells goods to a distributor who resells the goods in its own name. Other agreements which would be classified as vertical would be where an airline (or other company or airport authority) provides services such as groundhandling to another airline, or an airline offers the sale of another airline's capacity, such as code-sharing, the horizontal aspects of which are discussed in Chapter 5 *Article 101 TFEU: Horizontal Agreements*.

In vertical agreements, as with other dealings between competitors, information exchange should always be limited to what is necessary for the transaction so as to ensure no disclosure of market sensitive information which could give rise to coordination between competitors (*see* Chapter 5 section 5.2.9).

300. VBER recital 8.
301. *See* Chapter 4.5 for discussion of *De minimis*.
302. VBER Article 1(a).

6.3 VERTICAL RESTRAINTS BLOCK EXEMPTION REGULATION

The VBER applies to all vertical agreements concerning the sale of goods or services, with the exception of motor vehicles which have their own specific block exemption. The VBER does not apply to agreements for the licensing of IP such as patents or copyright, save where they are ancillary to a vertical agreement. Most commonly, this would be the licensing of a trademark to a distributor selling the supplier's products.

6.3.1 'Safe Harbour'

The VBER grants an automatic exemption to many vertical agreements, most commonly agreements containing exclusivity or non-compete obligations, provided they do not contain any 'hardcore' restrictions and provided the market shares of the supplier for the supply of the products in question, and of the buyer in the market for the purchase of the products in question, do not exceed 30 per cent. In the case of small- and medium-sized enterprises (SMEs), market share is not generally relevant.[303]

Market share may be calculated by reference to national geographic markets where distribution takes place on primarily a national basis, such as airline ticket distribution by travel agents.[304] Market definition should be examined on a case-by-case basis.[305]

6.3.2 Hardcore Restrictions

The VBER lists hardcore restrictions, the inclusion of which will exclude the whole agreement from the VBER, irrespective of the market shares of the parties, although the application of Article 101(3) is not necessarily excluded in such a case.[306]

6.3.2.1 Resale Price Maintenance

The first hardcore restriction is resale price maintenance – the fixing of the price or minimum price at which distributors can resell products, or in the case of an agent which is an 'independent agent', an obligation preventing or restricting the agent from

303. Vertical Guidelines paras 23, 87. Small and medium-sized undertakings are currently defined as undertakings which have fewer than 250 employees and have either an annual turnover not exceeding EUR 50 million or an annual balance-sheet total not exceeding EUR 43 million (Commission Recommendation of 6 May 2003 concerning the definition of micro, small and medium-sized enterprises OJ L 124, 20.5.2003, pp. 36–41).
304. *See* generally Case T-219/99 British Airways v Commission.
305. *see* Chapter 3 on 'Market definition' and Chapter 8.4.1 on market definition in the case of mergers and alliances between airlines; *see also* Article 7 VBER on application of the market share threshold).
306. In individual cases it may exceptionally be possible for hardcore restrictions to qualify for exemption under Article 101(3). Limited cases by way of example are provided by the Vertical Guidelines paras 60-64 which also refer to the Commission Guidelines on the application of Article 101(3) more generally OJ C 101, 27.4.2004, p. 97 para. 18.

sharing its commission with the customer (*see* generally section 6.4 Agency below).[307] The Vertical Guidelines leave open the possibility that where the parties' market shares are very low, the restriction of competition may not be appreciable, so that Article 101(1) may not apply.[308]

The imposition of maximum resale prices is generally permitted, as are recommended prices, provided they are indeed recommended only and not accompanied by threats or incentives.[309]

6.3.2.2 Territorial (Including Online) and Customer Restrictions

The second hardcore restriction is any restriction on the territory into which, or customers to whom, the buyer may sell.[310] This seeks to prevent market partitioning by territory or customer.

A supplier may appoint an exclusive distributor (or agent) for a territory (with or without limits on the customers to whom it may sell), such that the distributor cannot actively market the goods or services into other territories or to customers which have been exclusively allocated to another distributor, or reserved to the supplier. The distributor could, therefore, be restricted from actively approaching individual customers by direct mail, including the sending of unsolicited e-mails, or visits, or actively approaching a specific customer group or customers in a specific territory, through advertisement in the media, on the internet, or other promotions specifically targeted at that customer group or targeted at customers in that territory.[311]

'Passive sales' i.e., sales in response to unsolicited orders, including online sales (which are deemed passive sales, including if the website content is translated into different languages) and sales realised through advertising by internet or otherwise, must always remain possible for the distributor. Action to prevent passive sales such as threats of termination, discontinuance of orders or disincentives on a distributor to make such sales, will equally be prohibited.

As regards online sales more generally, the Vertical Guidelines make clear that every distributor must be allowed to use the internet to sell products and set out guidance on permissible restrictions as regards online sales.[312] The Commission has noted that there has been a large increase in trade in goods and services over the internet, but more limited growth of cross-border online sales within the EU, which prompted the Commission to launch an e-commerce inquiry in May 2015. In an interim report of March 2016, it suggests that the practice of 'geo-blocking' – re-routing internet users to websites in their own territory thus preventing them making purchases from

307. VBER Article 4(a); Vertical Guidelines paras 48-49.
308. Vertical Guidelines para. 10, referring to ECJ case law including Case 5/69 Volk v Vervaeke [1969] ECR 295.
309. Vertical Guidelines para. 226.
310. VBER Article 4(b) and (c).
311. Vertical Guidelines para. 51.
312. *Ibid* paras 51-54.

other EU territories – is widespread, and the Commission shall be considering whether intervention on competition grounds may be justified.[313]

In 1993, the Commission took the view that an IATA resolution within its Tariff Coordination Conferences, which restricted the freedom of passengers to purchase tickets outside the country of travel origin breached Article 101(1), and following discussions with IATA, the restriction was modified so as to be no longer applicable to travel within the EU, Norway and Sweden (now a full EU member).[314]

6.3.2.3 *Restrictions on the Sale of Spare Parts*

The third hardcore restriction concerns agreements that prevent or restrict end users, independent repairers and service providers from obtaining spare parts directly from the manufacturer of those spare parts. It requires that a supplier of components to a buyer, such as an original equipment manufacturer (OEM) cannot be prevented from supplying those parts to end users or independent repairers, but may be prevented from supplying them to repairers entrusted by the OEM to service or repair its products, such that the OEM may require its repairers to buy the spare parts from it.[315]

6.3.2.4 *Selective Distribution: IATA Agency Programmes*

The VBER contains provisions on selective distribution agreements, a restricted form of distribution whereby only distributors admitted to a network of authorised distributors may resell the goods in question – used in the case of high tech or luxury goods, where qualification of personnel and after sales service are important.[316]

In 1991, the Commission exempted IATA resolutions – which for Article 101 purposes were considered to be agreements between member airlines of IATA, formalised through resolutions – establishing a collective selective distribution system for agents to be accredited as passenger or cargo agents of IATA member airlines, and laying down a formula for the calculation of commission.[317] A prohibition on agents rebating part of commission to customers was removed at the Commission's

313. The Commission stated geo-blocking is partly due to unilateral decisions by companies not to sell abroad but also contractual barriers set up by companies preventing consumers from shopping online across EU borders. *See* Commission Staff Working Document Geo-blocking practices in e-commerce Issues paper presenting initial findings of the e-commerce sector inquiry conducted by the Directorate-General for Competition 18.3.2016 SWD(2016) 70 final; *See also* Commission press release 18 March 2016 at http://europa.eu/rapid/press-release_IP-16-922_en.htm;
314. Comp Rep EC 1993 p155.
315. VBER Article 4(e), Vertical Guidelines para. 59; *see also* Chapter 7 *Abuse of a Dominant Position* section 7.4.4.
316. VBER Article 4(c) and (d).
317. 91/480/EEC: Commission Decision of 30 July 1991 relating to a proceeding pursuant to Article [101] (case No. IV/32.659 IATA Passenger Agency Programme) J L 258, 16.9.1991, p. 18; 91/481/EEC: Commission Decision of 30 July 1991 relating to a proceeding pursuant to Article 101 (case No. IV/32.792 – IATA Cargo Agency Programme) OJ L 258, 16.9.1991, p. 29.

insistence, so as to encourage competition between agents. Quantitative requirements on minimum turnover and higher than necessary staff requirements were removed, as were exclusivity restrictions preventing agents acting for non-IATA members and on another basis than the IATA resolutions. Airlines also had to be free to set their own levels of remuneration to agents.

The system was found to restrict competition contrary to Article 101(1) given that it was applied by the majority of airlines worldwide, creating a rigid structure and leaving little room for individual airlines to use forms of distribution based on a different type of policy. The Commission also found that some limitation of competition was inherent in any collective distribution system in which the criteria for selection were homogeneous, such that competition between agents would be more limited than would otherwise be the case.

Given the amendments which were made to the resolutions, exemption under Article 101(3) was merited on the basis of improving the quality of agents, creating a network allowing airlines worldwide to distribute their services widely through suitably accredited sales outlets, with reduced costs of administering their agents and agents representing a large number of airlines.

6.3.3 Agreements Between Competitors

The VBER does not generally apply to agreements containing restrictions between competitors unless they are non-reciprocal - one distributes another's goods but not vice versa - and, in summary, provided the level at which they compete is at the distribution level.[318]

6.3.4 Restrictions Excluded from the VBER

The following restrictions, if present, would not be covered by the VBER. However, they are not hardcore restrictions, so the rest of the agreement may benefit from the VBER. In relation to such restrictions, it will be a matter for individual assessment whether Article 101(1) applies so as to render them unenforceable, and if so, whether they would merit exemption under Article 101(3).

6.3.4.1 Non-compete Restriction in Excess of Five Years

The first excluded restriction is a 'non-compete' restriction for a period exceeding five years. This may be either an exclusive purchase obligation whereby the buyer undertakes to purchase from the supplier all or more than 80 per cent of its total requirements, or an obligation whereby the buyer agrees not to manufacture, purchase, sell or resell goods or services which compete with the contract goods or services, which is for an indefinite duration or for more than five years.[319]

318. VBER Article 2(4).
319. VBER Article 1(d).

Non-compete obligations which are tacitly renewable beyond a period of five years are also excluded from the VBER.[320] When renewal beyond five years requires the express consent of both parties and no obstacles exist to prevent the buyer from terminating the non-compete obligation at the end of the five-year period, they shall be within the VBER, however.

6.3.4.2 Post-Termination Restriction

The second restriction excluded from the VBER is any non-compete restriction on the buyer post-termination. This could be direct, or indirect – such as, for example, an obligation on the buyer to give the supplier the opportunity to match or beat competing offers to supply goods and to order from the supplier where it can match the offer made by a competitor (known as an 'English clause').[321] There is a limited exception to this exclusion where the buyer sells from premises owned by the buyer, the restriction is necessary for the protection of knowhow transferred by the supplier to the buyer, and is limited to one year.[322]

Non-compete agreements beyond five years (or post-termination) are not necessarily anticompetitive but will require good justification. As an example, the Commission has stated that where relationship specific investments are made by a supplier, a greater commitment than five years may be permitted.[323]

6.3.5 Assessment of Agreements Outside the VBER

The VBER obviously does not apply where the market share of any of the parties exceeds 30 per cent, to certain agreements between competitors, or to the non-compete restrictions excluded from the VBER, discussed above. There is, however, no presumption that an agreement is contrary to Article 101 simply because the threshold is exceeded (with many large manufacturers or buyers it will be) or because excluded restrictions are present in an agreement. Rather, they will fall to be considered under Article 101(1) and 101(3). The Commission's Vertical Guidelines offer guidance on the interpretation of the VBER and criteria for assessment of such cases. A detailed discussion of these is beyond the scope of this work.

In summary, however, as regards non-compete or other exclusivity obligations discussed above, the question to consider will be whether they foreclose competitors from the market to such an extent that competition is restricted. The Article 101(3) analysis will focus on the benefits resulting from the agreement, including the proportionality of the restrictions (as where one party has incurred significant

320. VBER Article 5(1)(a).
321. VBER Article 5(1)(b) and Vertical Guidelines para. 129; *see also* section 6.6 below and Chapter 7 section 7.4.2
322. VBER Article 5(1)(b) and 5(3).
323. Vertical Guidelines para. 146; case law has permitted long-term supply agreements with minimum purchase obligations in the region of 15 years in specific cases e.g., Shotton / Maybank (OJ 1990 C106/3).

expenditure to provide goods or services to a given customer, which may justify a longer duration), and whether there is a competitive market such that competition is not eliminated in a substantial part of the market. Exclusivity obligations imposed by dominant undertakings will require specific justification.

Restrictions on suppliers are not prohibited, or addressed, by the VBER and are thus a matter for individual assessment under Article 101(3). By way of guidance, obligations on suppliers to supply only one buyer in the EU are not expected to raise concerns where the market shares of the parties do not exceed 30 per cent, though factors such as duration and nature of products are relevant.[324]

6.3.6 Withdrawal of the Benefit of the VBER

While the VBER creates a presumption of legality, it is possible for the Commission (or national competition authority (NCA) if only its territory is affected), to issue a decision withdrawing the benefit of the VBER where it finds in a particular case that an agreement to which the exemption provided for in this Regulation applies, nevertheless has effects which are incompatible with Article 101(3).[325]

6.4 APPLICATION OF THE VBER TO AGENCY AGREEMENTS

6.4.1 Overview

An agent is a legal or physical person vested with the power to negotiate and/or conclude contracts on behalf of another person (the principal), either in the agent's own name or in the name of the principal, for the sale of goods supplied by the principal, or the purchase of goods by the principal.[326]

The competition rules which apply to agency agreements will depend on whether the agent is 'independent' or 'genuine'. In the case of an agent who is independent, the competition analysis will be the same as that applied to vertical agreements generally, albeit that the principal will have greater freedom as regards the setting of prices. With 'genuine' agents, however, who form a single economic unit with the principal, all restrictions, such as limits on the territories into which, customers to whom, or prices at which the agents must sell the goods or services, will fall outside Article 101 (*see* the following section and also Chapter 4 section 4.2.2 above).

6.4.2 'Genuine Agency'

The Vertical Guidelines set out criteria for the assessment of agency agreements.[327] If an agent is 'genuine', Article 101 will not apply. The General Court has held that a

324. Vertical Guidelines paras 192 et seq.
325. VBER recitals 13-15.
326. Vertical Guidelines para. 12.
327. *See* Vertical Guidelines paras 12-21.

genuine agent working for the benefit of his principal may, in principle, be treated 'as an auxiliary organ forming an integral part of the latter's undertaking, who must carry out his principal's instructions and thus, like a commercial employee, forms an economic unit with his undertaking'.[328] There would not, therefore, be an agreement between undertakings for the purposes of Article 101(1) TFEU.

In this regard, the Vertical Guidelines provide that an agency agreement will fall outside Article 101 if the agent bears no, or only insignificant risks in relation to the sales contracts it negotiates or concludes. The Commission divides risks into three categories, any of which will result in the agent being an independent undertaking. These are: first, if the agent accepts risks under the contract with the customer, such as non-payment by the customer, or liability to customers, such as loss under the contract, for example, resulting from the air travel services, or obligations to finance stocks / ownership of goods, such as proprietary interest in inventory; second, market-specific investments required to carry out its functions, such as equipment or staff training costs or marketing costs. Risks related to the cost of providing agency services in general, such as costs of premises or personnel, or the agent's income being dependent on the principal's success, will not prevent the agent from being deemed a genuine agent; or third, if the agent is required to perform other activities, not as an agent, but for its own risk.[329]

Where an agent acts for more than one principal, that does not of itself make Article 101(1) applicable[330] but it may do so.[331] Even in cases where an agent would be a genuine agent, Article 101 could be infringed, if for example, a number of principals use the same agents to collude on marketing strategy or exchange commercially sensitive information between the principals.[332]

6.4.3 Agent Discounting of Commission

A ban by a principal on an agent discounting commission will be considered to be the agency equivalent of resale price maintenance, which is a hardcore restriction (*see* section 6.3.2 above).[333] The Court of Justice has held that agreements, (or national legislation per the *Vlaamse Reisbureaus* case above) which prohibited agents from deciding, on their own initiative, to pass on to their customers some portion of the commission they received, restricted competition between travel agents by preventing them from competing on prices and, therefore, infringed Article 101.[334] In the

328. Case T-325/01 DaimlerChrysler AG v Commission [2005] ECR II 3319, the General Court quashing a fine by the Commission of EUR 71.85 million, on the grounds that there was no agreement between undertakings.
329. Vertical guidelines para. 15, *see* generally section 2.1 paras 12–17.
330. *Ibid* para. 13.
331. Case C-311/85 VZW Vereniging van Vlaamse Reisbureaus v Sociale Dienst [1987] ECR 3801, para. 19. Agent was to be regarded as independent where it sold travel organised by a large number of different tour operators and tour operator sold travel through a very large number of agents.
332. Vertical Guidelines para. 20.
333. Vertical Guidelines para. 49.
334. *Ibid* paras 17-20.

Commission decisions granting exemptions to the IATA Passenger and Cargo Agency Programmes (1991) respectively (*see* section 6.3.2 above), IATA were required to remove a ban on agents rebating part of commission to customers.

In the online platforms context, this position could be less clear in the light of NCA investigations in which the importance of transparency of pricing has been emphasised (*see* section 6.5 below). Further, in an appeal brought by Skyscanner against commitments given to the UK competition authorities by Expedia, Booking.com and Intercontinental Hotel Group, which required that discounting of commission could not be prohibited, the Competition Appeal Tribunal overturned the commitments decision and remitted the matter to the UK competition authority for reconsideration.[335]

6.5 NATIONAL CASE LAW ON MOST FAVOURED NATION CLAUSES AND ONLINE PLATFORMS

Most favoured nation (MFN) clauses, or more precisely, most favoured customer clauses, are clauses whereby the supplier undertakes to the buyer or customer that it will not offer better terms to any other buyer or customer. There is no EU case law on MFN clauses and the position has generally been liberal under competition law. The Vertical Guidelines provide, under the section on resale price maintenance, that such clauses may have anticompetitive effects if they are used to support minimum resale prices by reducing the supplier's incentives to reduce prices.[336] Issues surrounding MFNs are arising more frequently in the case of online platforms which may be used for, amongst other things, the reservation of travel or hotels (*see* preceding section). Online travel agents (OTAs) such as Expedia or Opodo, provide flight search and flight booking facilities. Their revenues are generated primarily through booking fees, supplemented by advertising revenue.

In parallel cases involving Booking.com, the French, Swedish and Italian competition authorities objected to clauses whereby Booking.com obliged hotels to offer it the same or better room prices as they offered to other OTAs or distribution channels, on the basis that they could restrict competition between Booking.com and other online travel agencies, and hinder new platforms from entering the market. As a result, Booking.com committed to abandon such clauses throughout the EEA. The authorities found that an MFN clause whereby the hotel could not offer lower prices on its own website or offline than it offered to Booking.com, was compatible with EU (and national) competition law, on the basis that it ensured transparency of prices, which would not otherwise be provided by such platforms.[337] The German competition

335. Case 1226/2/12/14 Skyscanner v CMA, Booking.com, Expedia, IHG and Skoosh International [2014] CAT 16.
336. Vertical Guidelines para. 48.
337. European Commission press release IP-14-2661, 15 December 2014.

authority, however, reached a different position and found that the latter clause restricted the hotel's freedom to set its own prices, reducing its incentive to offer lower prices.[338]

There have been other investigations ongoing at national level in other EU Member States. It may be that, as a result of the e-commerce sector inquiry launched by the Commission in May 2015, which is due to be concluded in the first quarter of 2017, a unified EU position on this issue will be established.[339]

6.6 'ENGLISH CLAUSES' IN VERTICAL AGREEMENTS

Clauses whereby a customer undertakes to inform its supplier of any better offers it receives from other suppliers, in order to allow the supplier to match such terms, known as 'English' clauses, are considered as similar in effect to exclusive purchase obligations, which may have the effect of foreclosing competing suppliers, and more so when the buyer has to reveal who makes the better offer (*see also* section 6.3.4.2 above).[340]

6.7 DISTRIBUTION OF AIR TICKETS THROUGH COMPUTER RESERVATION SYSTEMS (CRSs)/GLOBAL DISTRIBUTION SYSTEMS (GDSs)

CRSs (more commonly known as Global Distribution Systems (GDSs)) are defined as 'a computerised system containing information about, *inter alia*, schedules, availability and fares, of more than one air carrier, with or without facilities to make reservations or issue tickets, to the extent that some or all of these services are made available to subscribers'.[341] They provide a single interface between airlines and travel agents, providing travel agents with instantaneous information about the availability of air transport services and the fares for such services, permitting them to make immediate confirmed reservations on behalf of the consumer. They were originally owned by airlines – 'parent carriers' – and the CRS Code of Conduct imposed obligations of non-discrimination on parent carriers, including discrimination against other carriers in terms of content.[342] Volumes of distribution offered by CRSs have been reduced by the increase in direct sales by airlines to customers, predominantly due to growth of online sales and low cost carriers (LCCs) using their own websites, and to a

338. FCO Press release Bundeskartellamt issues statement of objections regarding Booking.com's 'best price' clauses 2 April 2015.
339. *See* DG comp webpage http://ec.europa.eu/competition/antitrust/sector_inquiries_e_commerce.html.
340. *See* Vertical Guidelines para. 129.
341. Regulation 80/2009 on a Code of Conduct for computerised reservation systems and repealing Council Regulation (EEC) No. 2299/89 OJ 2009 L 35/47, Article 2(4). CRSs are also discussed in Chapter 2, 5 and Chapter 7.).
342. Regulation 80/2009 on a Code of Conduct for computerised reservation systems and repealing Council Regulation (EEC) No. 2299/89 OJ 2009 L 35/47.

lesser degree, network carriers, depending on booking classes, and airlines have now generally divested their controlling shares in CRS providers.[343]

Restrictions between airlines and CRSs are vertical agreements, and restrictions in them, such as exclusivity or MFN clauses, would fall to be considered according to the principles described above. There is no case law at EU level on vertical agreements between airlines and CRSs, though there have been decisions under Article 102 and under the Code of Conduct (discussed in Chapter 7 section 7.4.3).[344]

343. *See* generally Mid-term evaluation of Regulation 80/2009 on a code of conduct for computerised reservation systems and repealing Council Regulation 2299/89, Final Report September 2012, prepared for European Commission DG MOVE 27, by Steer Davies Gleave, available on; http://ec.europa.eu/transport/modes/air/studies/doc/internal_market/crs_fitness_check_report_final.pdf.

344. It was reported in 2015 by travel bodies representing CRSs and travel agents (European Technology and Travel Services Association) that a complaint to the European Commission was brought against Lufthansa in respect of a booking fee it charges on fares booked through websites using CRSs, arguing that it breached the Code of Conduct for CRSs.

CHAPTER 7

Article 102: TFEU Abuse of a Dominant Position

Article 102 provides:

> Any abuse by one or more undertakings of a dominant position within the internal market or in a substantial part of it shall be prohibited as incompatible with the internal market in so far as it may affect trade between Member States.
> Such abuse may, in particular, consist in:
>
> (a) directly or indirectly imposing unfair purchase or selling prices or other unfair trading conditions;
> (b) limiting production, markets or technical development to the prejudice of consumers;
> (c) applying dissimilar conditions to equivalent transactions with other trading parties, thereby placing them at a competitive disadvantage;
> (d) making the conclusion of contracts subject to acceptance by the other parties of supplementary obligations which, by their nature or according to commercial usage, have no connection with the subject of such contracts.

7.1 OVERVIEW

Article 102 TFEU prohibits the abuse of a dominant position by an undertaking (or undertakings where 'collective dominance' is found) within the EU or a substantial part (a single Member State, region or indeed an airport, may suffice), in so far as it may affect trade between Member States. Article 102 applies to unilateral conduct in the market, though this could also include terms in agreements between a dominant firm and other trading partners such as, potentially, exclusivity or similar obligations, such terms being unenforceable by the dominant firm.

Abuses fall into two broad categories – 'exclusionary' abuses, which exclude competitors from the market, such as refusal to deal or allow access to essential infrastructure (such as airports, or computer reservation systems (CRSs), tying or loyalty rebates, and 'exploitative' abuses, where the dominant company such as an airport, exploits its market power by, for example, charging excessive prices, discriminating without good reasons, or imposing other unfair conditions on trading partners. Article 102 TFEU does not contain an equivalent exemption for anticompetitive agreements as set out in Article 101(3) TFEU, whereby a company's conduct may be permitted because of procompetitive benefits. However, a dominant company may be able to show that conduct, which on the face it may appear abusive, is objectively justified and proportionate.

7.2 DOMINANT POSITION

7.2.1 Definition

Dominance has been defined as 'a position of economic strength enjoyed by an undertaking, which enables it to prevent effective competition being maintained on a relevant market, by affording it the power to behave to an appreciable extent independently of its competitors, its customers and ultimately of consumers'.[345] It is possible for groups of companies to be held to be collectively dominant, though such cases are rare and have not arisen in the air transport sector.[346]

7.2.2 Assessment of Dominance

Commission guidelines on its enforcement priorities in applying Article 102 to abusive exclusionary conduct by dominant undertakings (Guidelines on exclusionary abuses) provide that the assessment of dominance will take into account the competitive structure of the market, and in particular, constraints imposed by: (i) existing supplies from actual competitors and their position on the market; (ii) the credible threat of future expansion by actual competitors or entry by potential competitors; and (iii) the bargaining strength of the undertaking's customers (countervailing buyer power).[347]

Market shares and the number and relative size of competitors are the primary indicators of dominance. Dominance is not generally likely if the undertaking's market share is below 40 per cent in the 'relevant market', unless competitors are much smaller. In *Virgin/British Airways*, a market share of 39.7 per cent of the market - for UK sales through travel agents - was sufficient to establish dominance, taken in

345. Case 27/76, United Brands [1978] ECR 207; Case 85/76 Hoffmann-La Roche & Co. *v.* Commission [1979] ECR 461, para. 38.
346. An agreement between the parties, adoption of a common market strategy, common trading terms and an oligopolistic market conducive to parallel behaviour could establish collective dominance. Members of liner conferences have been found to be collectively dominant e.g., Cases T-19198 and others Atlantic Container Line v. Commission ('TACA') [2003] ECR II 3275.). For a detailed discussion generally *see* Bellamy & Child 7th Edition 10.047 et seq.
347. Communication from the Commission — Guidance on the Commission's enforcement priorities in applying Article [102] of the EC Treaty to abusive exclusionary conduct by dominant undertakings, ('Guidelines on exclusionary abuses') OJ C 45, 24.2.2009, pp. 7–20, para. 12.

combination with the much smaller size of competitors suggesting a lack of competition, and the several years' duration of BA's market power.[348] The higher the market share and the longer the period over which it is held, the more likely it is that there will be dominance. A market share of above 50 per cent gives rise to a presumption of dominance.[349] A market share of 40–45 per cent would not of itself permit a finding of dominance, which would also depend on the strength and number of the competitors.[350] The trend or development of market shares over time may also be taken into account. A high market share on a given route would not necessarily indicate dominance, if the route is such that it could only support one carrier, which may be the case with remote areas.[351] Holding a high share of slots at an airport could also potentially give rise to a dominant position, albeit issues have not thus far arisen in this regard. In the merger context, the Commission found that an increase of share of slots held by IAG at Heathrow from 53 per cent to 56–57 per cent did not give rise to concerns, due to the neutral impact given the airport was already heavily congested.[352]

Other factors relevant to dominance would be countervailing buyer power (this tends not to be the case with airlines' customers), barriers to entry, economic strength and scale of activities of the potentially dominant company, such as existence of a network, strong brand name, access to capital and technological lead over competitors.

7.2.3 Relevant Market: Calculation of Market Share

Abuse of dominance and calculation of the market share of the allegedly dominant undertaking must be assessed on the market affected by the abuse or practice, known as the 'relevant market'. This comprises the 'product' market and 'geographic' market. The product market comprises those products or services that compete with those provided by the firm alleged to be dominant, and depends on the extent to which demand for the product or service in question can be satisfied by products or services which are sufficiently similar as to be reasonable substitutes by consumers. The geographic market is generally defined as the area in which effective competition takes place. In the case of scheduled passenger services, the origin and destination (O&D) approach is used. In the case of *Ahmed Saeed*, the Court stated that scheduled flights on a particular route could constitute the relevant market, and the economic strength of an airline on that route would depend on the competitive position of other carriers operating on the same route, on a route capable of serving as a substitute, or by operators of other means of transport such as charter flights, railways and road

348. Commission Decision 2000/74/EC, Virgin/British Airways, OJ L 30, 4.2.2000, pp. 1–24. The Commission found that BA's market share was over 2.2 times the combined share of its four largest rivals in 1998. Case T-219/99, British Airways plc v Commission [2003] ECR II 5917, upheld by Court of Justice Case C-95/04 P, British Airways v Commission [2007] ECR I-2331.
349. Case C-62/86, Akzo *v.* Commission, [1991] ECR I 3439, para. 60. The ECJ stated that this was in itself, absent exceptional circumstances, adequate evidence of a dominant position.
350. United Brands *supra* paras 109–110.
351. Services to remote areas may qualify for State aid under the EU State aid rules under the public services obligation exception, *see* Chapter 10.
352. IAG/Aer Lingus Case No. M.7541.

transport.[353] The principles of market definition are discussed in greater detail in Chapter 3, and in relation to agreements and mergers between airlines, in Chapter 8, section 8.4.

7.3 SUBSTANTIAL PART OF THE INTERNAL MARKET

Dominance must be established within the internal market as a whole, or at least a substantial part of it. The extent of the market will depend on the nature of the product or service, its availability and consumers'/customers' readiness to switch to alternative products or services. A single Member State may constitute a substantial part of the internal market,[354] as may a region or indeed a port or an airport.[355]

7.4 ABUSE

7.4.1 Definition

Article 102 does not define 'abuse', but provides a non-exhaustive list of abusive conduct in (a)–(d) above. Abuse has been described by the Court of Justice as: 'An objective concept relating to the behaviour of an undertaking in a dominant position which is such as to influence the structure of a market ... and which, through recourse to methods different from those which condition normal competition ... has the effect of hindering the maintenance of the degree of competition still existing in the market or the growth of that competition.'[356]

While to hold a dominant position is not prohibited, abuse is. Further, a dominant company has 'a special responsibility not to allow its conduct to impair genuine undistorted competition'.[357] The focus of the Commission's enforcement under Article 102 is on 'exclusionary abuse' – whereby dominant companies exclude their competitors by practices other than competing on the merits.[358] Absence of competition in a market may not necessarily be the result of exclusionary practices by a dominant undertaking, such as 'thin' routes, which may sustain only one carrier. 'Exploitative' abuses such as excessive prices, are prohibited, but in recent years, tend to be dealt with by national competition authorities (NCAs) applying EU competition and/or national law. The following are examples of abuses.

353. Case C-66/86 Ahmed Saeed Flugreisen and Silver Line Reisebüro GmbH *v.* Zentrale zur Bekämpfung unlauteren Wettbewerbs e.V. 1989 ECR 803 paras 39–41.
354. BA *v.* Commission *supra* – UK market for sales of tickets through travel agents.
355. Commission Decision 95/364/EC of 28 June 1995 relating to a proceeding pursuant to Article 90(3) [now 106(3)] of the Treaty OJ L 216, 12.9.1995, pp. 8–14 – Brussels Airport found to constitute a substantial part of the internal market, in line with case law findings in the Port of Genoa case, Case C-179/90 Merci convenzionali porto di Genova SpA *v.* Siderurgica Gabrielli SpA [1991] ECR I-5889.
356. Hoffmann-La Roche *supra* para. 91.
357. Case 322/81 Michelin *v.* Commission [1983] ECR 3461.), such that an abuse may occur, even irrespective of any fault.
358. Guidelines on exclusionary abuses, *supra*.

7.4.2 Rebates, Exclusivity Obligations, 'English Clauses'

Article 102 generally prohibits agreements obliging a customer to obtain all or most of its supplies from a dominant undertaking, or schemes involving rebates or discounts, which achieve similar results. If rebates are expressly conditional on customers buying all or most of their purchases from the dominant undertaking - whether expressed as a target or a percentage of total purchases, they are likely to be prohibited. These are known as 'loyalty' or 'fidelity' rebates.[359] The granting of quantitative rebates, however, linked solely to the size of the order or volume of purchases, fixed objectively and applicable to all possible purchasers - as opposed to being based on estimates made for each customer according to its presumed capacity of absorption - would be presumed not to be abusive.[360]

Rebates will also generally infringe Article 102 if they have 'loyalty inducing' effects, deterring the customer from making purchases from rival suppliers. This could be the case with loyalty schemes, such as frequent flyer schemes (FFPs) or corporate discounts, if they cause barriers to entry. There is some case law at national level on FFPs and corporate discounts, but not thus far at EU level.[361] Rebates to travel agents, dependent on meeting growth targets have been condemned at EU level, however.

In *Virgin/British Airways*, the Commission imposed a fine of EUR 6.8 million on BA for entering into loyalty schemes with travel agents.[362] BA offered a performance reward calculated on a sliding scale, based on the extent to which a travel agent increased the value of its sales of BA tickets, and subject to the agents increasing their sales of such tickets from one year to the next. Meeting a target led to an increase in the commission paid on all BA tickets sold by the agent during the relevant reference period, and not just on the tickets sold after the target was reached ('retroactive rebates'). Such commissions were considered to be similar to a loyalty discount, based not on cost savings, but simply on customers' loyalty. As a result, competitors could be excluded from the market because agents had an incentive to maintain or increase their sales of BA tickets, to the detriment of sales of tickets of rival airlines, so making it more difficult for other airlines to compete with BA on the UK market.

The Commission (upheld by the General Court and the Court of Justice) stated that rebates could be permitted where they reflected extra services provided and cost savings, but not for incentives for customers to remain loyal, which foreclose the market from its competitors.[363] The Commission and the General Court took a broad approach to the question whether the rebates produced exclusionary effects - there had been modest increases in competitors' market shares - noting the pressure exerted on

359. Hoffmann-La Roche, *supra* para. 89.
360. *Ibid.para 90*
361. *See* for example Swedish Competition Authority, SAS 12 November 1999; Lufthansa corporate discounts http://www.bundeskartellamt.de/SharedDocs/Meldung/EN/Pressemitteilungen/2012/20_12_2012_Lufthansa.html.
362. Commission Decision 2000/74/EC of 14 July 1999 relating to a proceeding under Article [102] of the EC Treaty (IV/D-2/34.780 – Virgin/British Airways) OJ L 30, 4.2.2000, p. 1, upheld by General Court in Case T-219/99, British Airways plc v Commission [2003] ECR II 5917 para. 100; upheld by ECJ Case C-95/04 P, British Airways v Commission [2007] ECR I-2331.
363. *Ibid.*, paras 98–102.

agents making it particularly difficult for competitors to outbid BA in the face of discounts or bonuses based on overall sales volume.

Rather than being based on likely exclusionary effects, the finding of abuse was based on the fact that the rebates tended to remove or restrict the agents' freedom to sell their services to the airlines of their choice, and thereby hinder the access of BA's competitor airlines to the UK market for air travel agency services.[364] It also found that they resulted in discrimination between travel agents, applying different commission rates to travel agents operating in the UK, according to whether or not they had achieved their sales objectives by comparison with the reference period, contrary to Article 102(c).

EU competition law has remained strict in the area of the application of Article 102 to rebates.[365] There is a possibility that this may change, following an Opinion by the Advocate General on an appeal by Intel against a Commission decision, upheld by the General Court, imposing a record fine of EUR 1.06 billion, which concluded that the Commission's and General Court's characterisation of abuse in the context of rebates was too broad. The Opinion is not binding on the Court of Justice, which is yet to hand down a decision. [366]

7.4.2.1 *Investigations of Other Carriers: Rebates Principles*

At the same time as the BA decision, the Commission set out its policy on commissions paid by airlines to agents. These included requirements that commissions could only be differentiated or increased if they reflected costs of distribution through different agents, or the value of services provided by the agents; nor must they relate to previous reference periods exceeding six months, set targets by reference to sales in a previous period i.e., not be dependent on growth in sales, and must increase in a straight line above any base stated in the agreement.[367]

After the BA decision, the Commission launched investigations into eight other EU carriers offering incentive schemes to travel agents which resulted in changes made to certain airlines' schemes, without formal decisions or fines.[368]

7.4.2.2 *'English Clauses'*

Similar to exclusivity obligations imposed on customers, these are clauses whereby a customer agrees to inform a dominant supplier of any better offers it receives from other suppliers, and is obliged to allow the supplier to match such terms, if it wishes to

364. British Airways *v.* Commission *supra* para. 21.
365. Case T-286/09 – Intel *v.* Commission, 12 June 2014.
366. Advocat General Opinion on an appeal by Intel to the Court of Justice, 20 October 2016 in Case C-413/14 P Intel Corporation Inc. v Commission.
367. Commission Press Release IP/99/504, 14 July 1999.
368. *See* Competition Policy Newsletter No. 2, 2003, p. 65.

do so. These will be likely to infringe Article 102. They may also raise issues under Article 101 (*see* Chapter 6 *Article 101 TFEU: Vertical Agreements* section 6.6).

7.4.3 Predatory Pricing and Similar Practices

7.4.3.1 Predation Generally

It is normal for a competitor to undercut its competitors' prices to attract new business. However, where that company is in a dominant position, the EU competition rules may, in certain cases, prohibit this. There will generally be an infringement of Article 102 if there is evidence showing that a dominant undertaking engages in predatory conduct by deliberately incurring losses, or foregoing profits in the short term, so as to foreclose or be likely to foreclose one or more of its actual or potential competitors, with a view to strengthening or maintaining its market power.[369]

According to EU case law, pricing below average variable costs (costs that vary depending on the quantities produced) is presumed to be abusive in the case of dominant firms, and pricing below average total costs (average fixed costs plus average variable costs) will be abusive if there is evidence of an intention to eliminate a competitor.[370] In *Akzo v. Commission*, the Court held that, in relation to pricing below average variable cost: 'A dominant undertaking has no interest in applying such prices except that of eliminating competitors so as to enable it subsequently to raise its price by taking advantage of its monopolistic position, since each sale generates a loss . . .'.[371] The question of determining the cost assessment may not be straightforward, generally, or in the case of airlines. The Court has also held that there is no absolute right for a dominant company to meet competition by matching the prices of competitors, if it results in predatory prices.[372] In the air transport sector, the Commission has conceded that price-matching by a high-cost incumbent could nevertheless be a non-predatory competitive response to the entry of low-cost firms when there are high exit costs and/or sunk re-entry costs.[373]

Where prices charged are below average variable costs or where prices are below average total costs but above average variable costs, the Commission is not required to show that the dominant company would have a realistic possibility of recouping losses sustained once the predation came to an end. This is on the basis that that a dominant company could still strengthen its position by eliminating competitors.[374]

Predation will not be straightforward to prove, and the Commission will rely on documentary evidence of any of intent to eliminate a competitor, such as threats to drive a competitor out of the market. In *Akzo v. Commission*, the Court accepted that there was clear evidence of Akzo threatening a competitor in two meetings with below

369. Guidelines on exclusionary abuses, *supra* para. 63.
370. Case T-83/91 Tetra Pak *v.* Commission, ECR [1994] II-755 para. 148; Case 62/86 Akzo Chemie *v.* Commission [1991] ECR I-3359.
371. Akzo *v.* Commission, *supra*, para. 71.
372. *Ibid.*, paras 182, 185–186.
373. EC Report on Competition 1990 para. 387.
374. Case T-340/03 France Télécom *v.* Commission [2007] ECR II-107, para. 228.

cost pricing if it did not withdraw from the organic peroxides market, as well as a detailed plan, with figures, describing the measures that it would put into effect if the competitor would not withdraw from the market.[375]

7.4.3.2 Predation in the Air Transport Sector

According to the Commission, predation in the air transport sector could take the form of action to increase capacity by scheduling more services ('capacity dumping'), to reschedule flights to reduce the demand for entrants' services, as well as action in cutting prices. It states that an increase of capacity by the incumbent after entry, is a strong signal that predation may be taking place, as would a price increase once (and if) exit takes place. It states that predation can take place in markets other than the one in which entry takes place (or is planned), since predation might occur in other markets where the incumbent and entrant already compete.[376]

There has been no case law at EU level in the air transport sector, though the issue has arisen, when a complaint was brought by easyJet to the Commission against KLM in 1997, alleging that it was trying to price it out of routes from Amsterdam. This led to a dawn raid by Commission officials at KLM's offices, and the case closed without a formal decision.

7.4.4 Refusal to Supply/Deal

Competition problems relating to refusal to supply tend to arise when the dominant undertaking competes on the same market with a buyer (usually on a downstream market which is needed to provide the service in question) whom the dominant undertaking refuses to supply, or offers the product or service on unreasonable terms.[377] This is an issue which could also arise with original equipment manufacturers which produce equipment (the primary market) but are vertically integrated and operate in aftermarkets or secondary markets for the supply of spare parts, highly technical tools, or services, if they refuse such products to other downstream operators. In such cases, there will be no abuse if there is objective justification for the refusal.[378]

A refusal to grant access to an essential facility or a network are examples.[379] Refusal to supply an existing customer which abides by normal commercial practice, and in certain circumstances, a new customer, may infringe Article 102 in the absence of objective justification. Examples from air transport case law are discussed below.

375. Akzo *v.* Commission, *supra*, paras 76 to 82, 115, and 131 to 140.
376. EC Report on Competition 1990 para. 387.
377. Commercial Solvents *v.* Commission Joined cases 6 and 7–73 ecr [1974] 223.
378. *See also* discussion at Chapter 6, section 6.3.2 *Vertical Agreements:* Restrictions on the Sale of Spare Parts - and discussion of Regulation 330/2010.
379. Commission Decision 94/19/EC of 21 December 1993 in Case IV/34.689 Sea Containers *v.* Stena Sealink — Interim Measures (OJ L 15, 18.1.1994, p. 8) and Commission Decision 92/213/EEC of 26 February 1992 in Case IV/33.544 British Midland *v.* Aer Lingus OJ L 96, 10.4.1992, p. 34.

7.4.4.1 *Refusal to Interline*

In 1992, acting on a complaint by British Midland (BM), the Commission found that Aer Lingus had abused its dominant position (it held 75 per cent, British Airways 25 per cent) on the London/Dublin route, one of the busiest routes in the EU, by cancelling an interlining agreement with BM once it started its own service to Dublin, and imposed a fine of EUR 750,000.[380] 'Interlining' is the procedure, based on an IATA Agreement signed up to by most world airlines, whereby other signatories can sell their services, so that a travel agent can offer a single ticket offering transport by different carriers and can change reservations after the ticket is booked.

As a result of Aer Lingus terminating its interlining agreement with BM, passengers with BM tickets could no longer change flights onto Aer Lingus services and travel agents could no longer issue tickets combining flights by both airlines. This made BM's flights less attractive, in particular to business travellers who preferred higher priced, fully flexible tickets, and to travel agents. This made it more difficult for BM to compete. The Commission also found that refusal to interline for reasons other than, for example, creditworthiness, was not normal competition on the merits, noting that Aer Lingus did not cancel its interline agreement with the other airline operating on the route, BA.

The Commission nevertheless conceded that if a dominant airline has been able to develop a high frequency, that is a legitimate competitive advantage which it need not necessarily share with rivals. Therefore, new entrants should not be able to rely forever on their competitors' frequencies and networks, but had to be encouraged to build up extensive networks and high frequencies by themselves to gain commercial standing and attract sufficient interest from travel agents and passengers. The Commission, therefore, limited the duty to interline to a duration which was necessary for BM to develop its service. Having regard to Aer Lingus's very high share of passengers and frequencies and the scarcity of available slots at Heathrow, such that BM could not increase the frequency of its Dublin service rapidly without lowering the frequency of some of its other services, it considered a two-year period sufficient for it build up commercial strength and an adequate schedule.

7.4.4.2 *Computer Reservation Systems Denial of Access, Discrimination*

One of the first cases and fines imposed by the Commission in the air transport sector was against Sabena in 1988, which was fined EUR 100,000 for refusing a competitor, London European Airways (LEA), access to its CRS – Saphir.[381] A CRS is the system that travel agencies use to make airline bookings, with information on schedules, fares and availability.

380. Commission Decision IV/33.544, British Midland *v.* Aer Lingus OJ L 96, 10.4.1992, pp. 34–45.
381. Commission Decision 88/589/EEC IV/32.318, London European – Sabena, OJ L 317, 24.11.1988, pp. 47–54.

The Commission found that Sabena had a dominant position on the market for computer reservation services in Belgium and that this refusal was designed to drive a competitor, offering lower fares, out of the Belgian market. Sabena's refusal had been on the grounds that LEA's low fares policy represented a potential threat, and it had agreed to admit LEA to its CRS if it changed its pricing policy or reached a commercial arrangement related to using Sabena groundhandling. The Commission found that this aimed to artificially increase prices, to limit production and markets to the prejudice of consumers, since Sabena's refusal could result in LEA abandoning its plan to open a route between Brussels and Luton, and that Sabena had made the conclusion of a Saphir contract subject to the conclusion by LEA of a groundhandling contract which was not related to the subject matter of the first contract, all of which were abuses under Article 102.[382]

In defining the market, the Commission had found that the advantages of a computerised system (speed, quantity of data, immediate reservation and issue of ticket, constantly updated information) were such that this could not be regarded as equivalent to other means of making reservations, so the ability to offer customers a computerised reservation service was an important feature of an airline's marketing policy. CRSs thus constituted the relevant product market, and the territory in which bookings were made through it, Belgium, was the relevant geographic market.[383]

Shortly after the commencement of proceedings, Sabena accepted LEA into the Saphir reservation system on normal non-discriminatory commercial terms to be agreed between the companies.

The Sabena case pre-dated the Regulation and Code of Conduct on the operation of CRSs which was originally adopted in 1989 (Regulation 2299/89 *see* Chapter 2 *Liberalisation of Air Transport*).[384] This required that an airline, which owned or controlled a CRS must not discriminate against a competing CRS, in particular by refusing to provide the same data with equal timelines as that which it provided to its own CRS, and it sought to prevent owner carriers from distorting competition by granting incentives to travel agents to use their own CRS.

In the first decision under that Code, the Commission fined Lufthansa EUR 10,000 for introducing incentives to travel agencies for the issue of electronic tickets in Germany. Lufthansa part owned the CRS Start Amadeus – and refused to make its ticketing function available to Start's competitor – Sabre, so incentives could only be earned by Start subscribers.[385] Proceedings were also brought by the Commission against Air France for possible abuse of Article 102, for favouring Amadeus (part-owned by Air France), by providing it with more accurate and prompt information on

382. Article 102 includes the prohibition of tying: 'making the conclusion of contracts subject to acceptance by the other parties of supplementary obligations which, by their nature or according to commercial usage, have no connection with the subject of such contracts'.
383. *Ibid.*, para. 14–16.
384. Now Regulation (EC) No. 80/2009 of the European Parliament and of the Council of 14 January 2009 on a Code of Conduct for computerised reservation systems and repealing Council Regulation (EEC) No. 2299/89.
385. 1999/618/EC: Commission Decision of 20 July 1999 on a procedure relating to the application of Council Regulation (EEC) No. 2299/89 (Electronic ticketing) (notified under document number OJ L 244, 16.9.1999, p. 56.

certain domestic and international tariffs than it did to Sabre, a CRS owned by American Airlines, thereby putting the latter at a competitive disadvantage. The case closed after Air France agreed to offer equivalent terms as to Amadeus, and reciprocal terms agreed between Sabre and Amadeus.[386]

7.4.5 Airports, Access, Discrimination, and Article 106 TFEU

7.4.5.1 Access to Airports

Access to infrastructure is an essential condition of engaging in transport activity. The main issues here are discrimination between airport users in the granting or refusal of access, in charges for access and the quality of service offered. These issues are more serious with the increasing difficulty of capacity constraints.

Individual airports may occupy a dominant position such that operators may commit an abuse in cases of denial of access to airlines or groundhandlers, or if they discriminate in charges or the quality of service they themselves offer. In the case of Brussels Airport[387] and subsequent cases on airports, the relevant market was defined as the market in services linked to access to airport infrastructures such as the exploitation of runways, taxiways and aprons and approach guidance, and the levels of traffic were such that it was a substantial part of the EU. In these cases, the Commission referred to case law on port installations, whereby the ECJ had found that the organisation of such facilities for third parties might constitute a relevant market on the basis that access to such installations at either end of the route was essential to the provision of the service. On the basis that there was no genuine alternative offering for the services provided, which was the case with Brussels Airport, this was the relevant market.[388]

In cases where the airport is publicly owned or operating on the basis of special or exclusive rights granted by the State, Article 106 requires that Member States may not enact nor maintain in force any measure contrary to the competition rules (*see also* Chapter 4 section 4.2.3). In such cases, the Commission has brought actions on the basis of Article 102 in conjunction with Article 106, where they have engaged in discriminatory or other abusive practices.

The general principle is that every user should pay the same price for access to infrastructure, unless there is objective justification for differentials, such as economies of scale.

386. Commission Press Releases IP/99/171 15th March 1999, IP/00/835 25 July 2000. The case was referred to the Commission by the US Department of Justice under the Positive Comity provisions of the 1991 EU/US cooperation Agreement in the field of competition.
387. 95/364/EC: Commission Decision of 28 June 1995 relating to a proceeding pursuant to Article 90(3) [now 106(3)] of the Treaty OJ L 216, 12.9.1995, pp. 8–14.
388. *Ibid.*, para. 8, referring to Case C-179/90 Porto di Genova SpA *v.* Siderurgica Gabrielli SpA [1991] ECR I-5889.

7.4.5.2 Discrimination in Landing Charges

In 1995, the Commission adopted a decision requiring the Belgian State to bring to an end a system of discounts on landing fees charged at Zaventem Airport.[389] It concluded that the system constituted a State measure within the meaning of Article 106(1) (ex Article 90(1)) which had the effect of applying to airlines, unequal conditions for equivalent services (associated with landing and take-off), thereby placing some of them at a competitive disadvantage. The system therefore infringed Article 106(1), read in conjunction with Article 102.

Given the fees were set by the State by legislation, as opposed to by Brussels Airport, the Commission confirmed that a Member State infringes Articles 106 and 102 TFEU when it requires an undertaking to abuse its dominant position (or reduces the room for manoeuvre of undertakings, through which the Member State exerts an influence on competition).[390]

British Midland had complained to the Commission that Brussels National Airport operated a system of rebates on landing charges, based on numbers of movements and the weight of aircraft, but which set the targets to qualify for rebates at such a high level that only Sabena, the Belgian national carrier, could benefit. This resulted in Sabena paying 18 per cent less on take-off and landing fees for an equivalent service. The Commission found that this placed British Midland, which was operating in competition on the London-Brussels route, at a competitive disadvantage and that there was no objective justification, such as savings from economies from scale.

While in most cases, pricing abuses by dominant undertakings seek to maximise their profits, the Commission confirmed that there was no need for the dominant undertaking to be acting in its own interest, if its action sought to give preferential treatment to another undertaking such as a national carrier. The discounts here were in fact contrary to the interests of the airport since they reduced the revenue which it might obtain from landing the fees.[391]

Proceedings were initiated with regard to other systems in other Member States where volume discounts on landing fees were differentiated according to the domestic or international origin of flights. In Portugal and Finland, landing charges for domestic flights benefited from 60 per cent and 50 per cent lower fees respectively, as compared with intra-EU flights. There was no objective justification, such as cost differences, and the Commission required the airports to end the system of linking charges to the origin of flights.[392]

On appeal to the Court of Justice by Portugal, raising arguments that the rebates were quantity rebates, the Court held that there were no reductions in unit costs resulting in savings to justify the rebates, given that aircraft required the same landing and take-off services, regardless of how many aircraft belonged to the same company.

389. Commission Decision Brussels Airport, *supra*.
390. *Ibid.*, paras 14–15, referring also to Case 30/87, Bodson *v.* Pompes funèbres [1988] ECR 479.
391. *Ibid.*, para. 17.
392. Commission Decisions 1999/199/EC (IV/35.703 — Portuguese airports, OJ 1999 L 69 p. 31; 1999/198/EC: IV/35.767 – Ilmailulaitos/Luftfartsverket, OJ 1999 L 69, p. 24.

It held that the rebates, which benefited Portuguese airlines, conferred an economic advantage which was not justified, and led to the application of dissimilar conditions to equivalent transactions.[393]

7.4.5.3 Denial of Access to Groundhandling

Groundhandling is a significant part of operating costs of airlines, which often did not have a choice of provider. Such additional costs are passed on to consumers in the form of higher fares.[394] Directive 96/67/EC increased competition for groundhandling services (services provided to airlines at airports such as passenger and baggage handling, fuelling and cleaning of aircraft).

Following a complaint by airlines that Frankfurt Airport was abusing its dominant position by not granting them the right to provide groundhandling services themselves (self-handling), nor giving access to other companies to provide such services (third party handling), the Commission found that it has abused its dominant position, reserving the provision of such services to itself. Arguments that this would cause congestion were rejected, save in respect of part of a terminal which had been allowed a temporary derogation under the Groundling Directive. The Commission also stated that that Frankfurt Airport could not conclude long-term contracts with its major customers, which effectively would have prolonged its groundhandling monopoly.[395]

A Commission proposal from 2011 to further open up this market was not approved by the Council and was withdrawn by the Commission in 2014. In addition, Directive 2009/12/EC lays down the basic principles for the levying of airport charges paid by air carriers for the use of airport facilities and services.[396] This, however, has not prevented disputes between airports and airlines from continuing.

7.4.5.4 Access to Slots: EU Regulation on Slots at Airports

Fair access to slots at airports has not been the subject of case law at EU competition level and is regulated by Regulation 95/93.[397] This sought to ensure fair access to airports and airport services, requiring that airport 'slots' – defined as permission to

393. Case C-163/99 Portugal *v.* Commission ECR [2001] I-2613 paras 48–54.
394. A Groundhandling Directive Council Directive 96/67/EEC which provided, under certain conditions, for the gradual opening up, from 1 January 1998 until 31 December 2002, of access to the groundhandling market in Community airports.
395. Commission Decision 98/190/EC relating to a proceeding under Article 86 of the EC Treaty (IV/34.801 FAG – Flughafen Frankfurt/Main AG) OJ L 72 p. 30; Commission Decision 98/387/EC on the application of Article 9 of Council Directive 96/67/EC to Frankfurt Airport (Flughafen Frankfurt/Main AG) OJ L 173, 18.6.1998, pp. 32–44. The Decision referred to Council Directive 96/67/EC on access to the groundhandling market at Community airports OJ L 272, 25.10.1996, pp. 36–45.
396. Directive 2009/12/EC of the European Parliament and of the Council of 11 March 2009 on airport charges OJ L 70, 14.3.2009, p. 11.
397. Council Regulation No. 95/93 of 18 January 1993 on common rules for the allocation of slots at Community airports (OJ L 14, 22.1.1993, as amended by Regulations 894/2002, 1554/2003 and 793/2004.

land or take off on a specific date and at a specific time – at congested airports be allocated to airlines in an equitable, non-discriminatory and transparent way by an independent 'slot coordinator'. This slot allocation system has been found by the Commission to prevent the optimal use of airport capacity at busy airports, airlines being able to underuse their slots to avoid returning them to the 'slot pool' for reallocation to competitors and proposals for reform have been made.[398]

7.4.5.5 Discriminatory Charges

In 1997, following a complaint brought against the Paris airports operator by an independent provider of catering services to airlines that competed with a subsidiary of Air France at Orly airport, the Commission found that it had charged much lower commercial and occupancy fees to the subsidiary of Air France than to the complainant, which was an independent supplier of catering services to airlines at various EU airports.[399] The Commission found there was no objective justification for the differences, which distorted competition not only between groundhandling service suppliers but also between air carriers, which benefited in terms of cost, and ordered that they be brought to an end.

Directive 2009/12/EC on airport charges[400] lays down the basic principles for the levying of airport charges paid by air carriers for the use of airport facilities and services. Charges remain a contentious issue between airports and airlines, however.

7.4.5.6 Discrimination in Quality of Service

The general principle is that every user should be offered the same quality of service, save where there is objective justification, as where there are limits on capacity. This does not necessarily require all users to have the same treatment, or that all airlines should be handled at the same terminal, but they should receive equivalent treatment so far as possible.

Following complaints from airline users of Orly airport, the Commission found that the operator, Aéroports de Paris (AdP) had discriminated against competitors of Air France in its management of passenger terminals, distributing traffic so as to benefit Air France, which had exclusive use of a modern terminal with excess capacity, with competitors grouped together in a terminal which was older and did not have enough capacity to handle all the traffic. AdP agreed to re-distribute traffic and carry out works

398. In 2011, the Commission proposed amendments to the Regulation. Thus far, there has been no agreement *See* generally DG Comp website: http://ec.europa.eu/transport/modes/air/airports/slots_en.htm; *see* 'Better Airports Package' December 2011, Press release IP/11/1484. *See also* Chapter 2 section 2.6.3.4.

399. 98/513/EC: Commission Decision of 11 June 1998 relating to a proceeding under Article 86 of the EC Treaty (IV/35.613 – Alpha Flight Services/Aéroports de Paris. OJ L 230 pp. 10–27. Decision upheld by General Court. Aéroports de Paris *v.* Commission Case C-82/01 P.

400. Directive 2009/12 *supra*.

to improve the older terminal and to provide regular reports on the quality of service at each terminal, without proceedings being brought.[401]

7.4.5.7 Poor Quality Service

Poor quality of service may also be an abuse. The Commission brought proceedings under Articles 106 and 102 TFEU following complaints from airlines about the groundhandling services supplied on a monopoly basis by Olympic Airways at Athens Airport (such as registration, baggage handling, cleaning and catering) and the lack of transparency in the charges. As a result, works were carried out and publication of tariffs which would be closer to the actual cost of supply. Olympic Airways also agreed to end its monopoly of groundhandling, from 1 January 1998, (the date laid down by the Council Directive on access to the groundhandling market) when a new operator, selected by tender, would start to compete.[402]

7.4.6 Excessive Pricing

It is an abuse for a dominant undertaking to charge excessive or unfair prices.

EU Directive 2009/12/EC[403] lays down principles for the levying of airport charges paid by air carriers for the use of airport facilities and services, but disputes arise. There is no case law on excessive pricing per se (cases also involving discriminatory pricing) at EU level in the air transport sector, though there have been cases where Member State competition authorities have condemned airport authorities for abuse of a dominant position by levying charges which are discriminatory or excessive.

Proving excessive pricing may be a complex exercise. EU competition law does not act as a pricing regulator, but if it is established amongst other things, that the price bears no reasonable relation to the economic value of the service being provided, an abuse may be established.[404]

401. Annual Report on the application of the competition rules in the European Union 1996 p. 142.
402. Commission Press Release IP/97/876, 15 October 1997.
403. Directive 2009/12 *supra*.
404. United Brands [1978] ECR 207; Commission Decision Scandlines Svergie AB *v.* Port of Helsingborg COMP/A.36.568.– a 'cost-plus approach' – assessing economic value of a product/service by adding to the costs incurred in the provision of this product/service a reasonable profit which would be a predetermined percentage of the production costs was rejected.

Chapter 8
Mergers and Alliances

8.1 OVERVIEW

The European Commission is generally supportive of consolidation in the European air transport sector. If an airline wishes to significantly expand its network or offer greater frequencies, it will be very difficult for it to do this on its own, given also the capital intensive nature of the industry, with low margins and increased pressure on pricing, with the transparency of online sale of tickets. If carriers combine their operations with carriers in different geographic regions, it is likely that synergies will create efficiencies and benefits for consumers, but if the parties compete on given routes, competition may also be restricted, or eliminated if they are the only operators and barriers to market entry are high. The vast majority of air transport mergers and all alliances have been approved, albeit subject to conditions.

In its 2015 Competition Annual Report, the Commission stated: 'The air transport sector is still very fragmented. In the EU there are more than 150 airlines offering scheduled air passenger transport. The five largest airlines in the EU (i.e. Lufthansa, Air France/KLM and International Consolidated Airlines Group (IAG, the holding company of British Airways and Iberia [and Vueling Airlines], Ryanair and easyJet) account for only 50 % of the EU market. In contrast, in the United States, the three legacy carrier groups American Airlines, Delta and United together with low cost carrier Southwest jointly control more than 80 % of the United States market.'[405]

Mergers involving structural changes, and alliances where parties engage in cooperation under which they may be closely aligned, are subject to different enforcement regimes under EU competition law. The EU regime for the assessment of mergers is one of compulsory pre-notification to the Commission under the European Merger Regulation 139/2004 (EUMR).[406] There is no regime for the notification of alliances,

405. Commission Report on Competition Policy 2015 (COM (2016) 393 final) 15 June 2016 p. 73.
406. Council Regulation (EC) No. 139/2004 of 20 January 2004 on the control of concentrations between undertakings OJ 2004 L 24/1).

which, rather, are subject to a self-assessment regime, whereby the parties must determine whether the alliance falls within Article 101(1) (the prohibition of anticompetitive agreements) and if so, whether it would merit exemption on the basis of efficiencies and consumer benefits under Article 101(3).

The respective regimes for the control of mergers and alliances and criteria for determining whether given arrangements fall within the EUMR or Article 101 are discussed separately below (sections 8.2 and 8.3 below). The substantive application of the EUMR and Article 101, including market definition, assessment of effects on competition and remedies applicable, are similar under both regimes and are discussed together (sections 8.4 and 8.5). Code-sharing agreements(CSAs) were discussed in Chapter 5 section 5.3.2, but the more integrated forms of cooperation are discussed in this chapter.

8.2 MERGERS

8.2.1 Merger Control Regime: EU Merger Regulation

The EU Merger Regulation 139/2004 (EUMR) is the European framework for the control of mergers, requiring pre-notification of mergers, or 'concentrations' per the EUMR, if certain turnover thresholds are met. A 'concentration' will be created where there is a change of control on a lasting basis which results from an acquisition, merger or joint venture. The Commission assesses the notified concentration on the basis of its effect on the structure of competition in the EU.[407] The test under Article 2(2) and (3) of the EUMR is whether or not a concentration would 'significantly impede effective competition in the EU or a substantial part of it, in particular as a result of the creation or strengthening of a dominant position'. A concentration that significantly impedes effective competition must be prohibited.

Mergers, or 'concentrations', involve structural changes in the market whereby control is acquired over an undertaking, thus integrating two or more companies into a single entity. Within the EU, the Commission has exclusive jurisdiction over concentrations with an 'EU dimension'. Where transactions are subject to notification and clearance by the Commission under the EUMR, they are not subject to parallel merger inquiries under the national merger control provisions of Member States, notification under the EUMR thus offering a 'one-stop shop'. Like the rest of EU competition law, the EUMR gives the Commission jurisdiction over mergers affecting the whole of the EEA (the EU plus Iceland, Liechtenstein and Norway). If the EUMR turnover thresholds are not met, national competition authorities (NCAs) of the Member States may review the merger. In some cases, Member States or the parties may, however, request that the European Commission review the merger.

Notwithstanding the limitation of the Commission's enforcement powers under Article 101 (and 102) prior to 1 May 2004, to routes within the EU only, in the case of

407. EUMR Recital 20.

mergers, the Commission enjoyed full powers to vet mergers involving between non-EU and/or EU airlines since the entry into force of the EUMR in 1990.[408]

8.2.2 Definition of 'Concentration'

A 'concentration' is an operation where a change of control in the undertakings concerned occurs on a lasting basis, and which brings about a lasting change in the structure of the market.[409] Article 3(1) EUMR provides that a 'concentration' arises in the case of:

- the merger of two or more previously independent undertakings; or
- the acquisition of direct or indirect control, by contract conferring rights over management, or any other means such as purchase of assets or shares, of all or part of an undertaking. The majority of mergers between airlines fall within this category; or
- the establishment of a 'full-function' joint venture, namely an undertaking under the control of two or more undertakings which performs on a lasting basis all the functions of an autonomous economic entity.[410] If such control is not established, the joint venture will instead be subject to Article 101.

8.2.2.1 Control

'Control' is widely defined – it may be de facto or legal control – and may be acquired by means of shares, contracts or other means – which confer the possibility of exercising a decisive influence over an undertaking.[411] 'Decisive influence' will be established if the acquirer can determine the strategic decisions in the controlled undertaking, or in the case of joint control, the power to block actions which determine the strategic commercial behaviour of an undertaking.[412] The key decisions which will confer control will be decisions relating to the strategic operation, as opposed to day-to-day running, of the merged entity, such as business plan, appointment of senior management and annual budget. Control may be sole or joint control.

Sole control may be acquired through the purchase of an undertaking or the majority of its voting shares, or potentially even a minority shareholding if it enables the acquiring company to solely determine the strategic commercial behaviour of the undertaking. Whether sole control is established, will depend on the percentage of votes required to adopt key decisions or on whether there are preferential shares to

408. Council Regulation (EEC) No. 4064/89 of 21 December 1989 on the control of concentrations between undertakings OJ L 395 of 30 December 1989, now replaced by Regulation 139/2004.
409. Commission Consolidated Jurisdictional Notice, 2008 OJ C95/1, para. 12; EUMR Recital 20.
410. EUMR Article 3(1) in combination with 3(4).
411. EUMR Article 3(2); Commission Consolidated Jurisdictional Notice under Council Regulation (EC) No. 139/2004 on the control of concentrations between undertakings, OJ 2008 C 95/1 ('Consolidated Jurisdictional Notice') para. 16.
412. Consolidated Jurisdictional Notice para. 65.

which rights of management are attached. Even if the voting rights attached to shares are not sufficient to impose decisions, if they confer a blocking right so that the shareholder can on its own produce deadlock, that can constitute sole control, known as 'negative sole control'. This could be the case where a higher percentage, or 'supermajority', is required for strategic decisions, and a veto right is conferred on only one shareholder, irrespective of whether it is a majority or minority shareholder.[413]

Joint control will be created where two or more undertakings acquire the ability to exercise decisive influence. In the case of mergers where none of the shareholders have sole control, a shareholder will be considered to have joint control if it has the power to exercise a decisive influence over the most important strategic decisions of the undertaking.[414] Joint control will be clearly established where there are only two parent companies which share equally the voting rights in the joint venture. Equally, however, where a minority shareholder has veto rights over key decisions relating to the running of the merged entity, such as business plan, appointment of senior management and annual budget, it will be considered to exercise joint control.[415] Shareholdings of less than 50 per cent will frequently confer joint control (and in the situations described in the previous paragraph may even confer sole control).[416]

Where a minority shareholding does not confer control, it will be outside the scope of the EUMR, but may be subject to Article 101 and/or 102 TFEU. Minority shareholdings are discussed further below.

8.2.2.2 Full-Function Joint Ventures

The creation of a 'full-function' joint venture also constitutes a 'concentration' for the purposes of the EUMR. A joint venture will generally be 'full-function' where first, joint control is established (*see* the preceding section) and second, it has sufficient resources to operate independently on a market, performing on a lasting basis all the functions normally carried out by undertakings operating in the same market, with its own management and access to resources such as staff (they do not necessarily have to be employed by the joint venture, but any arrangements with the parents must be on an arm's-length basis), assets and capital.[417] It must, therefore, not operate merely as an auxiliary part of one or both parent companies; it must have staff dedicated to its

413. *Ibid.*, paras 56 and 58.
414. *Ibid.*, paras 62, 63.
415. *Ibid.*, paras 67–68.
416. In Singapore Airlines/Virgin Atlantic, the Commission found that although the Virgin Group controlled a majority of shares in Virgin and nominated the majority of the members on the board, Singapore Airlines had joint control of Virgin through its veto rights and procedure cases of disagreement over strategic business decisions. (COMP/M.1855 Singapore Airlines/Virgin Atlantic; *see also* Case No. COMP/M.6828 – Delta Air Lines/Virgin Group/Virgin Atlantic; Alitalia/Etihad *supra*. In Case No. COMP/M.1626 – Sair Group/SAA, 20 percent was sufficient to establish joint control.
417. EUMR Article 3(4).

day-to-day operations and sufficient capital for its long-term sustainability.[418] An example of a full-function JV between airlines was KLM/Alitalia.[419]

Where joint ventures are not 'full-function', they are subject to Articles 101 and 102 TFEU. This will be the case where the joint venture does not conduct its business autonomously and at arm's length from its parent undertakings, rather, being directly managed by the parent undertakings and using their assets and marketing channels. Joint ventures within the Global alliances fall within this category.[420] Joint ventures which are not full-function may also be subject to national merger control rules to the extent they apply, a matter of the laws of the individual countries. Similarly, joint ventures which are full-function but which fall short of the EUMR turnover thresholds will be subject to Articles 101 and 102 and possibly also to national merger and/or other competition laws.

8.2.2.3 Non-controlling Minority Shareholdings

It is possible that the acquisition of a non-controlling minority interest in an undertaking could have the potential to restrict competition, but this falls outside the EUMR, due to the lack of requisite 'control'. In 2007, the Commission had prohibited the proposed acquisition by Ryanair of the whole of Aer Lingus.[421] Ryanair already held 25 per cent of shares in Aer Lingus, who requested the Commission to direct Ryanair to divest its shares on the grounds that they were restricting its ability to enter into other alliances with airlines, but the Commission refused to do so on the basis it had no such power under the EUMR. The rights conferred on Ryanair, in particular the right to block 'special resolutions' were associated exclusively with rights related to the protection of minority shareholders and did not amount to control.[422]

The minority shareholding was, however, reviewed by the UK competition authorities under the UK merger control regime, which also applies to mergers which confer a 'material influence' on the acquirer over the target, a lower threshold than 'control'. The UK authorities concluded that the minority shareholding could result in a substantial lessening of competition in the UK, affecting Aer Lingus's commercial strategy, in particular its ability to combine with another airline and to optimise its portfolio of slots, and ordered Ryanair to reduce its shareholding to 5 per cent.[423]

Minority stakes which do not confer control, fall outside the EUMR and would fall to be assessed under Article 101 and/or 102 TFEU.

---

418. Consolidated Jurisdictional Notice para. 94.
419. Commission Decision Case No. COMP/JV.19, KLM/Alitalia of 11 August 1999.
420. *See* most recently the transatlantic joint venture agreement ('SkyTeam alliance') in Commission Decision Case AT.39964 – Air France/KLM/Alitalia/Delta, 12 May 2015.
421. Ryanair/Aer Lingus I Case No. COMP/M.4439.
422. Case T-411/07, Aer Lingus Group *v.* Commission Case T-411/07 Aer Lingus Group plc *v.* Commission [2010] ECR II-3691; *see also* Case T-411/07 R, unsuccessful application for interim measures to prevent Ryanair exercising voting rights.
423. Decision 28 Aug 2013 confirmed on appeal by the English Court of Appeal, Ryanair *v.* CMA [2015] EWCA Civ 83.

8.2.2.4 Potential 'Enforcement Gap' and Review of the EUMR

The Commission has considered that there is a potential 'enforcement gap' in the EUMR due to its failure to include within its scope, anticompetitive effects caused by non-controlling minority interests. It therefore issued a consultation to explore extending its scope to such interests.[424] The White Paper includes among issues to be addressed, the possible use by an acquirer of a significant minority shareholding falling short of control, to limit the competitive strategies available to the target, by influencing decisions on approving significant investments, raising capital, changing the product or geographic scope of the business, or engaging in mergers and acquisitions. Depending on the outcome of the consultation this may result in changes to the EUMR and/or to guidance on the Regulation issued by the Commission.

8.2.3 'EU Dimension'

8.2.3.1 EU Merger Thresholds

A concentration has an EU, or in the EUMR terminology, a 'Community' dimension, if:

- the combined aggregate worldwide turnover (from ordinary activities and after turnover taxes) of all the undertakings concerned (in the case of the acquisition of parts of undertakings, only the turnover relating to the parts which are the subject of the concentration shall be taken into account with regard to the seller(s)) is more than EUR 5 billion; and
- the aggregate EEA-wide turnover of each of at least two of the undertakings concerned is more than EUR 250 million; unless
- each of the undertakings concerned achieves more than two-thirds of its aggregate EEA-wide turnover within one and the same Member State.

Alternatively, if these thresholds are not met, a concentration will nevertheless have an EU dimension, if:

- the combined aggregate worldwide turnover of all the undertakings concerned is more than EUR 2.5 billion;
- in each of at least three Member States, the combined aggregate turnover of all the undertakings concerned is more than EUR 100 million;
- in each of at least three Member States included for the purpose of the second point above, the aggregate turnover of each of at least two of the undertakings concerned is more than EUR 25 million; and
- the aggregate EEA-wide turnover of each of at least two of the undertakings concerned is more than EUR 100 million; unless

424. White Paper: Towards more effective EU merger control, COM/2014/0449 final (July 2014).

- each of the undertakings concerned achieves more than two-thirds of its aggregate EEA-wide turnover within one and the same Member State.[425]

8.2.3.2 *Calculation of Turnover: 'Undertakings Concerned'*

For the purposes of calculating turnover, the 'undertakings concerned' are generally the undertakings acquiring sole or joint control, and the undertaking over which control is acquired. Where only part of an undertaking is acquired, only the turnover of the part being acquired is taken into account, that of the vendor not being relevant. In calculating the acquirer's turnover, total group turnover across all business sectors must be included, including the turnover of all the undertakings that control or are controlled by it.[426]

8.2.3.3 *Geographic Allocation of Turnover*

Turnover is calculated in accordance with Article 5(1) of the EUMR and the Commission Consolidated Jurisdictional Notice.[427] In airline mergers, three methodologies are accepted by the Commission for calculation of turnover, namely, the Point of Sale methodology, whereby turnover is allocated to the country where the ticket was sold, the Point of Departure methodology, whereby turnover is allocated to the country from which the passenger departed, and the 50/50 methodology whereby turnover on each route is allocated on a 50/50 basis to the country of origin and country of final destination.[428] In the case of the Point of Departure approach, the Commission has stated that it will determine whether the entire turnover from round trip journeys should be allocated to the point of departure, as opposed to a 50/50 split, on a case-by-case basis. Where both parties sell point to point as opposed to bundled round trip tickets, it decided that it was appropriate to split turnover equally between the territories of origin and departure.[429] The location of the customer approach is increasingly difficult to apply in practice, with the increase in online sales.[430]

8.2.3.4 *Concentrations Lacking an EU Dimension*

Subject to possible exceptions discussed in the following section, concentrations where the above thresholds are not met will lack an EU dimension and will be subject to national merger control regimes, to the extent they may be applicable, a question

425. EUMR Article 1.
426. EUMR Recital 10, Article 5; Consolidated Jurisdictional Notice 129–131.
427. Consolidated Jurisdictional Notice *supra*, paras 196–198).
428. Swissair/Sabena II M.616 and subsequent cases.
429. Ryanair/Aer Lingus M.4439 paras 28–29.
430. In IAG/Aer Lingus, Aer Lingus only used the Point of Departure and the 50/50 methodologies as it proved very difficult for it to accurately calculate its turnover under the Point of Sale methodology due to the vast majority of Aer Lingus' sales being made online. The thresholds were met whatever methodology was used. IAG/Aer Lingus Case No. M.7541 para. 12.

which will depend on national laws. There is neither harmonisation of national merger control regimes, nor time limits for assessing and clearing mergers, so each Member State where any of the parties realise turnover should be considered. Most non-EU countries also have merger control regimes, many of which, such as the US, Australia, Canada, require notification of mergers.

8.2.4 EU Merger Regulation: Notification and Procedure

8.2.4.1 Notification to the Commission

Under the EU Regulation 139/2004, where parties propose to enter into a merger (known as a 'concentration'), which has an EU dimension, they must notify the European Commission for approval and the merger may not be completed until the Commission has given its authorisation.[431] To be able to notify, the parties must be able to demonstrate a good faith intention to conclude an agreement, such as a signed memorandum of understanding or a heads of terms document, or in the case of a public bid, a public announcement of an intention to make such a bid.[432] Notification is normally undertaken by the acquirer, or in the case of an acquisition resulting in joint control, by the parties acquiring joint control. Notification must be submitted using the Form CO, which is annexed to Regulation 802/2004, implementing the EUMR.[433] The notification requires large amounts of information relating to the parties, and data and discussion of 'affected markets' - markets on which the parties have a combined market share of 20 per cent or more.[434]

The time limits for a Commission decision are very short (25 working days in Phase I cases - discussed below). However, there will be 'pre-notification' discussions between the parties and the Commission, dealing with the content of notifications, information required, potential competition issues arising, and these will involve the submission of a draft notification (potentially more than one, or with amendments required, depending on the complexity), before the notification is formally submitted. A summary of the transaction will be published in the Official Journal of the EU and competitors and customers (including large corporate customers, travel agents, consumer associations) and potentially, airports and/or slot coordinators, will be sent questions by the Commission seeking information and their views. The Commission may also look at statements the parties have made in responses to requests for information in previous mergers or alliances, and compare them to the parties' notification submissions.

A 'simplified procedure' under which less detailed information is required, is possible in the case of non-problematic transactions, which will be mergers where first, the combined market share on markets in which two merging companies compete

431. EUMR Article 7.
432. Article 4(2).
433. Commission Regulation 802/2004 of 21 April 2004 implementing Council Regulation (EC) No. 139/2004 on the control of concentrations between undertakings OJ L 133/1, as amended (available in consolidated form on the DGCOMP website.)
434. Regulation 802/2004, *supra* Article 6(3); *see also* section on 'Market Definition' below.

(horizontal overlap markets) is no more than 20 per cent and second, in the case of vertically related markets, where one of the merging companies sells an input to a market in which the other company is active is no more than 30 per cent; and thirdly, in cases where the parties' combined market shares are between 20 per cent and 50 per cent, the increase in market share after the combination of their activities is very low.[435]

The information required to notify a merger has been reduced following amendments to the Implementing Regulation 802/2004 as part of a 'Simplification Package' introduced with effect from 1 January 2014[436] also making it simpler for the merging companies to ask the Commission to waive their obligation to provide certain information in their notification and to request a referral of a case from the Commission to a Member State or vice versa has also been reduced.

Member States can request the referral of a concentration within 15 working days of notification, or the parties may, by way of a Reasoned Submission, request that the Commission refer the merger to the competition authority of a Member State, if the merger threatens to significantly affect competition within that Member State which presents the characteristics of being a distinct market.[437] One or more Member States may also request that the Commission examine a merger lacking an EU dimension but which threatens to significantly affect competition within the territory of the Member State or States making the request. Such a referral was made by the Greek authorities to the Commission in Aegean/Olympic II.[438] Finally, parties to a merger lacking an EU dimension may request the Commission to review the merger if notifications would be required in three or more Member States.[439]

8.2.4.2 *Types of Merger Decision: Phase I and II Decisions*

If the proposed merger would be likely to significantly impede effective competition, in the EU or in a substantial part of it, in particular by the creation or strengthening of a dominant position, the Commission must declare it 'incompatible with the common market'.[440] The procedure can comprise two phases.

Phase I decisions clearing the merger account for the vast majority of merger control procedures. Phase I decisions are subject to a time limit of 25 working days.[441]

435. Commission Notice of 5 December 2013 on a simplified procedure for treatment of certain concentrations under Council Regulation (EC) No. 139/2004, OJ C366/5.
436. Commission Implementing Regulation (EU) No. 1269/2013, 2013 OJ L 336/1. The information required to notify a merger has been reduced following amendments to the Implementing Regulation 802/2004 as part of a 'Simplification Package' introduced with effect from 1 January 2014 also making it simpler for the merging companies to ask the Commission to waive their obligation to provide certain information in their notification and to request a referral of a case from the Commission to a Member State or vice versa has also been reduced – *see also* Commission Press Release IP/13/1214 5 December 2013.
437. EUMR Arts Arts 9, 4(4)
438. EUMR Art 22; Case No. COMP/M.6796 – Aegean/Olympic II, 9 October 2013. The EUMR thresholds had been met in the Aegean/Olympic I merger notification, prohibited in Case No. COMP/M.5830 – Olympic/Aegean Airlines I, 26 January 2011.
439. EUMR Article 4(5).
440. EUMR Article 2(3).
441. *See* section 8.5 below.

The three types of decision which the Commission may issue in Phase I cases, other than referrals to Member State competition authorities are: Article 6(1)(a) – the concentration does not fall within the scope of the EUMR; Article 6(1)(b) – the concentration does not raise serious doubts as to its compatibility with the common market, namely, approval; and Article 6(1)(c) – the concentration raises serious doubts as to its compatibility with the common market, thus requiring a Phase II procedure.

Under Article 6(2) EUMR, the Commission may attach to its decision clearing a merger, conditions to address competition concerns. The majority of mergers between airlines, where overlaps between the parties on routes may give rise to significant market shares, will be subject to conditions or commitments (also known as remedies). These commitments will be 'market tested', being published for third party comment, before they will be made final.

A *Phase II* in-depth investigation will be commenced in cases where there are serious concerns which cannot be dealt with by means of remedies agreed with the Commission.[442] This may take up to a further 90 working days and may be extended to 105 working days if the notifying parties offer commitments later than 55 working days from initiation of proceedings. There may also be an extension of up to 20 working days upon request by, or with the agreement of, the notifying parties, up to a maximum, therefore, of 125 working days. Decisions may similarly result in remedies, pursuant to Article 8 EUMR.[443] The types of decisions at the end of a Phase II procedure may, therefore, be: Article 8(1) – approval in the case of compatibility with the common market; Article 8(2) – approval with conditions and obligations, rendering the concentration compatible with the common market; and Article 8(3) –prohibition, in the case of incompatibility with the common market.[444]

Thus far, there have been three prohibition decisions in the case of mergers between airlines, each of which involved mergers between airlines based in the same Member State and operating from the same hub, namely Ryanair/Aer Lingus I and III and Aegean/Olympic I (subsequently approved in Aegean/Olympic II).

8.3 ALLIANCES

The term 'alliance' in this chapter refers to joint ventures to develop joint networks with coordination on prices, capacity and schedules, and merger-like integration comprising revenue and cost sharing. The term 'alliance' is also commonly used to describe the three Global Alliances (oneworld, SkyTeam, Star) established in the late 1990s, within which a wider variety of lower degrees of cooperation take place between alliance members.

---

442. EUMR Article 6(1)(c).

443. Examples of Phase II decisions in the air transport sector are Lufthansa/Austrian Airlines, CASE COMP/M.5440 – 31 July 2009 a clearance decision with commitments and prohibition decisions in Aegean/Olympic I *supra*, Ryanair/Aer Lingus I and III, *supra*.

444. Other decisions, which have not arisen in the air transport sector are: Article 8(4) – dissolution of the merger in case of premature implementation or implementation in breach of a condition for clearance, Article 8(5) – interim measures and Article 8(6) – revocation of a clearance decision in case of incorrect information or breach of obligation.

The most common forms of cooperation, and listed in the order of intensity of cooperation and likelihood of competition issues arising, include low level cooperation such as: *interlining*, whereby an airline can issue tickets including a segment that it operates itself, as well as a segment operated by the another airline, with the party(ies) who operate the segment charging the issuing airline for the segment that they operate – the passenger using a single ticket for a journey, with two or more flight legs and different carriers, without having to collect luggage or check in at the transit airport(s); sharing of *frequent flyer programmes* (FFPs) – loyalty programmes offered by airlines under which customers enrolled in the programme accrue points for travel on that airline that can be redeemed for free air travel and increased benefits, such as airport lounge access, priority bookings and now increasingly wide benefits such as hotel accommodation and other benefits; and *airport arrangements* such as lounge access and ticketing.

Intermediate forms of cooperation include *blocked space CSAs* (where one carrier purchases a number of seats on another carrier's services and bears the risk of not selling them), then *free flow CSAs*, where one airline can freely sell seats on another's services. CSAs are discussed in Chapter 5 section 5.3.2.

High-level merger-like cooperation is discussed in the sections below.

8.3.1 Regulatory Barriers

Alliances are more common in air transport than in other sectors, often being used as a 'second best' means of achieving close integration similar to mergers and thus avoiding regulatory barriers to cross-border mergers. The European Commission – US DoT report of November 2010 stated: 'This form of cooperation is effectively a close substitute to a merger because it typically involves full coordination of the major airline functions on the affected routes, including scheduling, pricing, revenue management, marketing and sales.'[445] Before the 'Open Skies' judgment of the Court of Justice in 2002, mergers between airlines in different Member States of the EU were rare.[446] This was because air-traffic rights held by a merging airline(s) that ceased to be majority owned and controlled by nationals of the Member State in which it was based, could be lost, due to nationality clauses in bilateral Air Services Agreements(ASAs) between EU Member States and third countries requiring that the airline in question be majority owned and controlled by nationals of the country in question. Following the 'Open Skies' case, in many, but not all cases, the nationality clause in third country 'ASAs' was replaced by a 'Community clause' whereby any carrier in the EU would equally

445. Transatlantic Airline Alliances: Competitive Issues and Regulatory Approaches, A Report by the European Commission and the United States Department of Transportation, 16 November 2010 para. 24.

446. 'Open Skies' Judgements of the Court of Justice in Case C-466/98 Commission *v.* United Kingdom [2002] ECR I-9427; Case C-467/98 Commission *v.* Denmark [2002] ECR 9519; Case C-468/98 Commission *v.* Sweden [2002] ECR 9575; Case C-469/98 Commission *v.* Finland [2002] ECR 9627; Case C-471/98 Commission *v.* Belgium [2002] ECR 9681; Case C-472/98 Commission *v.* Luxemburg [2002] ECR 9741; Case C-475/98 Commission *v.* Austria [2002] ECR 9797; Case C-476/98 Commission *v.* Germany [2002] ECR 9855. *See* Chapter 2.

benefit from the traffic rights granted to a carrier based in another Member State under a third country ASA. The Open Skies case and related issues are discussed in more detail in Chapter 2 section 2.7.

Mergers between EU carriers and carriers based outside the EU, however, continue to be restricted as a result of national ownership and control restrictions. In the US, for example, foreign ownership and control of airlines must not exceed 49 per cent 25 per cent respectively, and in the EU, non-EU nationals cannot own more than 49.9 per cent of an EU airline and must not effectively control it.[447]

8.3.2 Features of Alliances

Alliances do not involve structural changes, such as transfers of shares or assets which would be such as to confer 'control' within the meaning of the EUMR. The parties' cooperation is far-reaching and may be akin to a merger, however, with coordination of pricing, frequency, route schedules, capacity, and may involve merger like integration with the sharing of revenues and costs. Cooperation may also involve joint purchasing, joint distribution of tickets, and sharing of common airport facilities including groundhandling and IT. In the case of such alliances, the parties will largely act as a single entity on the routes on which they are cooperating, thus removing competition between them.

Alliances where incentives between the airlines are aligned, such that it will be neutral to each carrier whether tickets are sold on its airline or the joint venture partner – the incentive being to maximise the alliance revenue as opposed to their own revenue – are known as 'metal [aircraft] neutral'. Although the parties remain independent carriers and retain their own corporate identity, the cooperation is intended to achieve the benefits associated with a merger.

Being cooperation agreements as opposed to involving structural changes, alliances operate under corporate structures different from mergers, and as with any commercial arrangement, they may be terminated,[448] airlines may exit or switch to another alliance,[449] or changes may take place, for example, required by the Commission or other competition authority to avoid or remedy breaches of competition law. Mergers are, however, irreversible, subject only to fundamental changes such as 'demerger' of the corporate structure taking place.

It may not always be clear whether a joint venture should be considered as cooperative and, therefore, subject to Article 101. As discussed above, a joint venture will be subject to the EU Merger Regulation if it is 'full-function' (*see* section 8.2.2 above).

---

447. 49 U.S. Code § 40102 15C; Council Regulation 1008/2008 of 24 September 2008 on common rules for the operation of air services in the Community (Recast) OJ L 293/3, Article 4(f). *See* generally Chapter 2.
448. An example of an alliance which terminated is Delta/Swissair/Singapore Airlines.
449. Aer Lingus exited the one world Alliance in 2007, and was later acquired by IAG, a member of one world.

8.3.3 Control Regime: Alliances

Alliances are subject to Article 101 unless they result in the creation of a 'full-function' joint venture, which will be caught by the EUMR (discussed at section 8.2.2 above). In accordance with Article 101(1), where cooperation agreements are entered into between actual or potential competitors, they will be prohibited by Article 101(1) if they prevent, restrict or distort competition, unless they create efficiencies and consumer benefits, satisfying the criteria for exemption under Article 101(3). Article 101(3) is discussed generally at Chapter 4 *Elements of Article 101 TFEU* and at section 8.4.2 below.

Prior to 1 May 2004, it was possible to notify alliances and other cooperation agreements to the Commission for exemption under Article 101(3).[450] Unlike mergers, however, there is now no procedure for notifying alliances for clearance. Rather, the parties must conduct their own assessment of compatibility with the competition rules, subject to the possibility of enforcement by the Commission. Since 2004, the circumstances and procedure by which decisions on alliances are reached, are that the Commission opens proceedings under Regulation 1/2003 and sends requests for information to the parties and interested third parties such as their main corporate customers, travel agents, competitors on routes of concern, airports and/or slot coordinators.[451] If it proposes to adopt a decision finding an infringement, it sends a Statement of Objections (SO) to the parties, to which they may respond.

Decisions in recent years on alliances in the air transport sector have been 'commitment decisions' in which commitments were offered by the parties, as a condition of proceeding with the cooperation.[452] The procedure is discussed in Chapter 9 section 9.6. In summary, if the Commission is satisfied with commitments offered, it market tests the commitments, publishing a non-confidential summary of the case and the main commitments or other proposed course of action, in the Official Journal of the European Union, so that interested third parties may submit comments.[453] Depending on the results, it may require the parties to amend the commitments before the Commission makes them binding through a commitment decision.

Prior to 1 May 2004, the Commission had very limited enforcement powers in relation to agreements between carriers which related to services between the EU and

450. Examples of exemption decisions following notifications in the air transport sector under the then regime of Regulation 3975/87 OJ L 374/1 (Regulation 3975/87 is discussed in Chapter 2) include *COMP/37.730 — Lufthansa/Austrian Airlines, 5 July 2002*; CASE COMP/A.38.477/D2: British Airways/SN Brussels Airlines) 10 March 2003, CASE COMP/D2/38.479: British Airways/Iberia/GB Airways, 10 December 2003; Case COMP/38.284/D2 Société Air France/ Alitalia Linee Aeree Italiane S.p.A. 7 April 2004.

451. Council Regulation 1/2003 of 16 December 2002 on the implementation of the rules on competition laid down in Articles 81 and 82 of the Treaty OJ 2003 L 1/1. Enforcement and Regulation 1/2003 generally is discussed in Chapter 9.

452. Regulation 1/2003, Article 9(1); joint ventures within the three Global Alliances are Commission Decisions in Case COMP/39.596 - British Airways, American Airlines, Iberia of 14 July 2010; CASE COMP/AT.39595 - Continental/United/Lufthansa/Air Canada of 23 May 2013; and CASE AT.39964 - Air France/KLM/Alitalia/Delta of 12 May 2015.

453. Regulation 1/2003, Article 27(4).

third countries.[454] The EU competition rules nevertheless impacted on alliances. Proposed alliances between British Airways and American Airlines were withdrawn in 1998 and 2002 due to large slot releases at Heathrow required by the competition authorities.[455] Regulation 411/2004 brought air transport within the application of Regulation 1/2003, giving the Commission full power from 1 May 2004 to apply the EU competition rules to alliances relating to services to or from non-EU countries.[456] These cases are discussed below.

8.4 COMPETITION ANALYSIS OF MERGERS AND ALLIANCES

8.4.1 Market Definition of Air Transport Services

8.4.1.1 Overview

The basic principles applicable to market definition are discussed in Chapter 3. On the basis of these, specific principles have developed in the air transport sector and are discussed below. In summary, the 'point of origin/point of destination' (O&D) city-pair approach is the primary reference point for defining the relevant product and geographic markets for scheduled passenger air transport services. As a result, every combination of a point of origin and a point of destination is considered a separate market. With case law, this approach has evolved, with distinctions between time-sensitive and non-time-sensitive passengers, direct *v.* indirect fights, airport substitutability, and including other modes of transport notably rail. Competition on the basis of networks has been considered in the competition assessment, as opposed to within market definition.

8.4.1.2 O&D Approach: Demand-Side Substitutability

For the purposes of defining the relevant market, the Commission carries out an analysis of, primarily, demand-side substitution. The approach which has been applied was first set out in the *Ahmed Saeed* case, where the Court held that in defining the relevant market for air transport services, the test to be employed was whether the scheduled flight on a particular route, could be distinguished from the possible alternatives such as charter flights, railways and road transport, as well as scheduled

454. These limited powers were under the 'transitional regime' that applied to the air transport sector then Articles 88 and 89 EEC Treaty (now, as amended, Articles 104 and 105 TFEU, discussed at Chapter 2). This limitation was acknowledged by the Commission in the Airfreight cartel decision (CASE AT.39258 – Airfreight, 09/11/2010; provisional non-confidential version, published on 08.05.2015, in which no fines were imposed in respect of alleged cartel activity on EU-third country routes prior to 1 May 2004 (*see* generally Chapter 5.2.4 above).

455. *See* summary in Commission Memo 10/330, 14 July 2010.

456. Council Regulation 411/2004 of 26 February 2004 repealing Regulation 3975/87 and amending Regulations 3976/87 and 1/2003, in connection with air transport between the Community and third countries (OJ 2004 L 68/1.)

flights on other routes which might serve as substitutes. It stated that the economic strength of an airline on a route served by scheduled flights may depend on the competitive position of other carriers operating on the same route or on a route capable of serving as a substitute.[457]

The Commission and the Court have since then developed the origin and destination approach according to which the relevant market for scheduled passenger air transport services is defined on the basis of the 'point of origin/point of destination' (O&D) city-pair approach. This reflects the demand-side perspective, whereby passengers consider all possible alternatives of travelling from a city of origin to a city of destination, which they do not consider substitutable for a different city pair. As a result, every combination of a point of origin and a point of destination would be considered to be a separate market.[458]

In the case of certain leisure travellers, it has been considered whether the point of destination may not necessarily be determinative, namely for those who might consider flying to different city or holiday airports without having a clear preference for one destination ('destination insensitive customers') but it has not been found to constitute a separate market. The Commission found it unrealistic to assume that a significant proportion of passengers would not care whether they flew to Rome, Faro, Riga or Turin.[459]

8.4.1.3 Supply-Side Substitutability and Network Effects

The possible application of supply-side substitutability to market definition, by reference to 'network competition', has been raised in cases before the Commission and the Court of Justice – whether by the parties or by respondents to market investigations in the case of alliances or mergers, or by low cost carriers (LCCs) arguing in favour of network markets when challenging mergers. The Commission has cited its Notice on market definition and decisional practice, whereby it has given pre-eminence to demand-side substitution, on the basis that customers still need transportation from one point to another, and that competition takes place on an O&D city-pair basis.[460] The General Court has also confirmed that demand substitution justified the O&D approach in defining the relevant market in *Niki Luftfahrt GmbH v. Commission.*[461]

The Commission has, however, recognised the relevance of network effects. In the *Air France/KLM* merger, it stated that given that network competition represented a supply-side perspective and followed the business model of network carriers, it was

457. Case 66/86 Ahmed Saeed Flugreisen and Others [1989] ECR 803, paras 39–41.
458. Cases of the ECJ confirming the conformity of the O&D approach with the EU principles of market definition include Air France *v.* Commission, easyJet *v.* Commission and T-162/10 – Niki Luftfahrt GmbH *v.* European Commission, paras 140 and following.
459. Ryanair/Aer Lingus I para. 63.
460. Commission Notice on the Definition of the Relevant Market for the purposes of Community law 1997 OJ C 372/3.
461. Case T-162/10 Niki Luftfahrt GmbH *v.* Commission paras 140 et seq.

'arguably of little relevance' to an individual consumer, confronted with high prices due to a monopoly on a particular O&D pair, that the airlines competed worldwide in the development of their respective networks. The Commission considered that network carriers only represent one, if an important, part of the industry. It nevertheless conceded, as regards corporate customers concluding contracts with several airlines or alliances, that among other elements, they would not only consider the prices charged on a particular route and the overall discount, but also whether the carrier's network covered the customer's travel needs, which would influence the decision to choose a particular carrier/alliance. In such a case, the customer's choice was driven by network competition and not by competition on individual city pairs.[462]

In its decision on the alliance between British Airways, American Airlines and Iberia, the Commission confirmed the O&D approach, on the basis that while the market investigation showed that some corporate customers (such as large multinationals) attached particular importance to the geographic coverage of airline networks, the demand for air transport services by corporate customers also focused on and was governed by offers of particular city pairs.[463]

Supply-side considerations are taken into account, however, when considering the competitive constraint which individual carriers may exert on a certain market. The hub-and-spoke system determines the network carriers' decision to operate (or not) a passenger air transport service on a particular O&D pair, carriers normally refraining from entering city pairs which are not connected to their respective hubs.[464]

Supply-side substitutability was also considered as of potential relevance by the Commission, in relation to the merger of two carriers each of which had a significant presence at an airport. In *Ryanair/Aer Lingus I*, the question was raised whether the market should be defined as a single relevant market comprising 'short-haul flights out of Dublin', on the basis that Aer Lingus and Ryanair held a share of about 80 per cent of all scheduled European traffic from and to Dublin, and this allowed both airlines to switch between routes and to add other routes out of the airport more easily than other competitors without such a significant base. The Commission did not identify the effects of supply-side substitution strong enough, however, to be equivalent to those of demand-side substitution in terms of effectiveness and immediacy. It thus upheld the use of the traditional O&D approach.[465]

8.4.1.4 Premium Versus Non-premium Passengers

The Commission has traditionally drawn a distinction between passengers travelling on unrestricted tickets – time-sensitive (or premium, generally business) passengers with a need for flexibility – and passengers with restricted tickets – non-time-sensitive (or non-premium, generally leisure) passengers – who are more interested in the price

462. European Commission, Case COMP/M.3280 – Air France/KLM, 11.02.2004, para11 et seq.
463. European Commission Case COMP/39.596 – BA/AA/IB para. 18.
464. Air France/KLM *supra* para. 17.
465. Case No. COMP/M.4439 – Ryanair/Aer Lingus paras 59 – 66.

than the frequency and accept longer journey times.[466] Time-sensitive passengers tend to travel for business purposes, require significant flexibility with their tickets (such as cost-free cancellation and modification of the time of departure), need to maximise their time at their destination and minimise their travel time, requiring a sufficient number of daily flight frequencies so as to allow for a same-day return, with early morning and late afternoon/early evening flights, and preferring full service network carriers with centrally located, as opposed to secondary airports. They tend to pay higher prices for this flexibility.[467] The Commission has, therefore, found that the effects of a merger or alliance may be limited to a single class of customers, such as premium passengers in the SkyTeam joint venture and leisure customers in the *KLM/Martinair* merger.[468]

Non-time-sensitive customers travel predominantly for leisure purposes or to visit friends and relatives, book a long time in advance, do not require flexibility with their booking, and are generally more price sensitive.

This distinction has become less clear on short-haul flights (generally considered to be under 3 hours), with corporate customers becoming more price sensitive and applying lowest fare policies.[469] In *IAG/Aer Lingus*, on the basis of the market investigation, the Commission found there to be no distinction between time-sensitive and non-time-sensitive passengers on routes between airports in Ireland and England, finding that a substantial number of business customers increasingly chose LCCs for their business trips, buying restricted tickets, letting them lapse should they be unable to take the flight originally chosen, and buying a new ticket for another flight instead. It also noted the practice of LCCs adopting strategies to attract corporate customers.[470] A single market comprising all passengers on short-haul routes was, therefore, adopted.

8.4.1.5 Charter Flights

The Commission has found that charter flights – generally speaking, flights bundled with a package holiday – do not belong to the same product market as scheduled/ unbundled flights, on the basis that the final consumer does not consider unbundled flights and package holidays as substitutable. Most customers purchasing unbundled flights cite the independence and the flexibility that unbundled flights offer as the reason for their choice, and similarly, most customers purchasing charter tickets would not switch to unbundled flights. The decision to buy either a package tour or an unbundled flight depends mainly on the specific characteristics of the product rather

466. Commission Decision of 11.08.1999, in Case No. COMP/JV.19, KLM/Alitalia, para. 21. Case No. M.7333 – Alitalia/Etihad, paras 70 and following; Case No. M.7270 – Cesky Aeroholding/ Travel Service/Ceske Aerolinie, para. 20 and following; Case No. M.6663 – Ryanair/Aer Lingus III, para. 382; Case No. M.6607 – US Airways/American Airlines, para. 8; Case No. M.6447 – IAG/bmi, para. 36; Case No. M.6607 – US Airways/American Airlines, para. 8.

467. *See* Nikki Luffhart paras 18 – 22.

468. SkyTeam alliance, Commission Decision Case AT.39964 – Air France/KLM/Alitalia/Delta, 12 May 2015. KLM/Martinair M.5141.

469. Case No. M.7541 IAG/Aer Lingus, paras 22 – 24.

470. *Ibid.*, paras 25 – 28, referring also to the 'Business Plus' offering of Ryanair.

than on pure price considerations.[471] As regards sales by charter airlines of flights not bundled with a package holiday, known as 'dry seats', in *Ryanair/Aer Lingus* it was left open by the Commission whether such sales could exercise any competitive constraint hence form part of the relevant market, as it would not change the competitive assessment.[472]

The wholesale supply of airline seats to tour operators has also been viewed as distinct from the market for the supply of scheduled air transport to end customers and such markets – for wholesale supply of airline seats to tour operators – have tended to be national in scope, though this has been left open.[473]

8.4.1.6 Markets for Direct Flights and Indirect Flights

The O&D market may, in certain cases, be broadened to include indirect flights given that on a particular O&D pair, passengers can travel either by way of a direct flight between the point of origin and the point of destination or by way of an indirect flight on the same O&D pair, but via an intermediate destination.[474] The level of substitutability of indirect flights for direct flights largely depends on the duration of the flight, the longer the flight generally speaking, the higher the likelihood that indirect flights exert a competitive constraint on direct flights.[475]

The Commission has considered that with respect to short-haul routes (generally up to 3 hours flight duration), indirect flights do not generally provide a competitive constraint to direct flights due to the additional time involved and risk of missing a connecting flight, absent exceptional circumstances, as where for example, and even with time-sensitive passengers, the direct connection does not allow for a one-day return trip.[476] It has also found, exceptionally, that indirect services compete with short-haul routes where responses to the market investigation showed significant numbers using them on a small number of routes so that the share of indirect flights was significant.[477]

471. Case No. COMP/M.5141-KLM/Martinair, para. 120.
472. Ryanair/Aer Lingus I paras 300–310.
473. Case No. COMP/M.5440-Lufthansa/Austrian Airlines paras 34–35 – it was left open whether Germany and Austria were a single geographic market due to lack of language barriers, similar customer preferences and minimal price differences between Austria and Germany.
474. Non-stop/one-stop terminology is also used. 'Non-stop' flights are flights that take-off at airport A and land at airport B where they load off passengers without any stops in between. By contrast, 'direct' flights may entail a refuelling stop and/or a disembarking/re-embarking stop, but are marketed under a single flight code and are flown with a single aircraft. 'One-stop' flights include direct flights that do not qualify as 'non-stop', as well as indirect flights which are journeys that require a change of aircraft or a change of flight code (*see* for example IAG/Aer Lingus, *supra*, para. 30).
475. IAG/bmi para. 68.
476. Case No. COMP/M.5403 – Lufthansa/BMI para. 17 Air France/KLM para. 20; Commission Decision of 12 January 2001 in Case No. COMP/M.2041 – United/US Airways, and Commission Decision of 5 March 2002 in Case No. COMP/M.2672 – SAS/Spanair, OJ C 93, 18.4.2002, p. 7.
477. *See* generally Case No. COMP/M.5335 – Lufthansa/SN paras 37–46; Ar France/KLM para. 80 – on the city pairs Bordeaux to Amsterdam and Marseille to Amsterdam, the shares of market of Air France's indirect service (via Paris) indicated that these were a constraint to direct flights.

The Commission has also found that on 'mid-' or 'medium-haul' routes – routes of 3 to 6 hours – where direct flights normally do not provide the option of one-day return trips so that indirect flights are able to compete with direct flights, that indirect flights may be more credible alternatives and in certain circumstances, constitute a competitive alternative.[478]

With respect to long-haul routes (more than 6 hours flight duration), indirect flights will more frequently constitute a competitive alternative to direct services, given that intermediate stops have a lower relative impact on total elapsed time as the total trip duration increases. This will be decided on a case-by-case basis. The Commission has, in certain cases, considered that indirect flights may constitute a competitive alternative to non-stop services, if they are marketed as connecting flights on the city pair on CRSs/GDSs, are operated on a daily basis and cause only a limited extension of the trip (150 minutes waiting time),[479] but there is no hard and fast rule on the point. As regards time-sensitive and non-time-sensitive passengers, while the latter can accept longer connection times, the distinction on basis of passenger types has become less clear, as an increasing number of time-sensitive passengers appear to have become more price sensitive.[480]

8.4.1.7 Airport Substitutability

Airport substitutability will be relevant for determining the extent to which the activities of the parties to an agreement or merger overlap, where they operate from different airports in or adjacent to the same city, or the competitive constraint exercised by competitors which operate from other airports.[481] It will be considered primarily from the point of view of passengers. Factors such as travel time (a preference to minimise the travel time), travel cost (a general preference for the cheapest solution overall), flight times/frequencies/schedules (a preference for specific departure times and dates) and quality of service (whether large shopping facilities, or shorter check-in times) will be relevant.[482]

When considering airport substitutability, the Commission will also examine the catchment area served by airports to determine whether they have sufficiently overlapping catchment areas, so as to be considered as substitutes in the eyes of passengers. If the number of customers on a certain route who live in an overlapping catchment area is sufficiently high, a carrier would take them into account when setting prices.[483] In this assessment, the length of the sector covered may be relevant, as catchment areas increase with sector length, and where the length of the sector is quite short, passengers may be less inclined to change their preferred airport, as the additional time and cost required to get to the alternative airport may be likely to be a greater

478. Case No. COMP/M.5440-LUFTHANSA/AUSTRIAN AIRLINES para. 26; Case No. COMP/M.5335 – Lufthansa/SN Airholding, para. 45 [date].
479. Case No. COMP/M.5403 – LUFTHANSA/BMI para. 16.
480. *Ibid.*, paras 47–50; Case No. COMP/M.3280 –Air France/KLM para. 22.
481. IAG/Aer Lingus, *supra*, para. 47.
482. Ryanair/Aer Lingus I, *supra* para. 73.
483. Case No. COMP/M.3280 – Air France/KLM para. 24.

proportion of the total travel time and cost. In *Air France/KLM*, the Commission found that for flights within Europe, it could be assumed that the radius of an individual airport's catchment area is small, given the overall short travelling time, while for long-haul flights the catchment area is larger.[484]

The Commission has developed, as a first proxy of whether airports are substitutable, the distances from the city to the airport and travelling times, using an indicative benchmark of 100 km or 1 hour driving time. In *Ryanair/Aer Lingus I*, applying this test, the Commission found that scheduled air transport services between Dublin, on the one hand, and Brussels Airport or Charleroi Brussels South airports, on the other, belonged to the same market.[485] The Commission nevertheless noted that total travelling time was probably more important than distance travelled, so issues such as connectivity of the airport, or issues such as parking, would also be relevant. This could only be decided on a route-by-route basis.

The relevance of the catchment area will be only one of several factors, other factors being the characteristics of passengers travelling on the route(s) in question, overall travel time, frequency and times of services, the quality of service and the price of different alternatives. There are cases involving routes served by two network carriers, where the 100 km/1 hour proxy has not been used.[486] It was found that, despite proximity of 53 km from Brussels centre, Antwerp did not exert significant competitive pressure on Brussels' main airport flights, having very few destinations and attracting mainly local business customers, and would not, therefore, be substitutable.[487]

In relation to flights between London airports and Dublin, all six London airports (Heathrow, Gatwick, City, Stansted, Luton and Southend) fell within a 100 km/1 hour radius of the city centre and were found to be prima facie substitutable, but further analysis and responses to the Commission's market investigation showed greater substitutability between flights from Heathrow, Gatwick and City. The Commission therefore assessed the effects of the transaction considering operations at those airports, known as 'London Three'.[488]

As discussed in relation to types of passenger, substitutability may also depend on whether passengers are time or non-time sensitive, for example, London Heathrow, Gatwick and City having been found to be substitutable on routes from London to Madrid and Barcelona for time-sensitive passengers, it being less clear whether Luton and Stansted were substitutable.[489] In *Air France/KLM*, as regards Paris's two main airports, Charles de Gaulle and Orly, it was found that while for many customers the airports were substitutable, this was not the case for corporate customers requiring connections for transfer traffic, since Orly offered fewer connections.[490]

484. *Ibid.*, para. 25.
485. Case No. COMP/M.4439 – Ryanair/Aer Lingus para. 196.
486. *See* case COMP/M.3280 – Air France/KLM, paras 24–35.
487. Case No. COMP/M.5335-Lufthansa/SN Airholding para. 60.
488. Case No. M.7541 – IAG/Aer Lingus paras 257–259.
489. Case No. COMP/M.5747 – Iberia/British Airways paras 21–23.
490. Case No. COMP/M.3280 – Air France/KLM para. 29.

Substitutability from the perspective of airlines providing the transport service i.e., supply-side substitutability, may also be relevant. This would depend on the kind of service airlines wish to provide, a network carrier which provides significant connecting and feeder services having different and greater needs at an airport than a low cost carrier providing mainly point-to-point services. In *IAG/Aer Lingus*, the Commission noted in particular the importance of London Heathrow for network carriers.[491] The Commission has also found that airlines will also have a strong preference in bundling all their activities at one airport, due to fixed overhead and operation costs at the airport.[492]

8.4.1.8 Other Modes of Transport

Other modes of transport, most commonly high speed trains, but also car and ferry, may form part of the relevant O&D markets for air transport services on short-haul routes, where they could be regarded as viable alternatives by customers, in terms of price, frequency, and aggregate travel time. This has been found to be the case with rail services by Eurostar between London and Brussels, which have been found to be substitutable with air services for all passengers, given the comparable aggregate travel times between city centres, frequencies and prices.[493] The O&D pair was thus broader than the direct air services and included rail transport.

In cases where the duration of travel is greater, and the frequencies less, rail has been found not to be substitutable. This was the case with rail transport between Zurich and Frankfurt where the shortest train travel time of almost 4 hours as compared with flight travel time of almost 3 hours was found to be substitutable for non-time-sensitive (leisure) passengers but the extra hour travel distance in each direction, as well as the lower number of daily frequencies (less than half), such that a typical business return trip with the same day, would not be possible, meant that for time-sensitive passengers, it was not substitutable.[494]

Ferry services have only exceptionally been found to be substitutable with air services. In *Olympic/Aegean* the Commission found that for passengers (including time-sensitive), ferry services between Athens and Mykonos formed part of the relevant market, on the basis that they were so close that the total travel time was comparable, as was the frequency of crossings. Services to other islands were not substitutable for time-sensitive passengers and it was left open whether other ferry services were substitutable for non-time-sensitive passengers, as it would not alter the assessment of the transaction.[495]

---

491. IAG/Aer Lingus *supra*, para. 58.
492. Air France/KLM *supra* para. 26.
493. CASE COMP/A.38.477/D2 British Airways/SN Brussels Airways 10 March 2003 para. 19.
494. Lufthansa/Swiss *supra* paras 56–58. A similar conclusion was reached in Air France/KLM in relation to rail travel between Paris and Amsterdam where the rail travel journey was 1 hour longer, with six daily frequencies in contrast with 14 operated by the parties paras 70–71.
495. Olympic/Aegean I and II, *supra*.

8.4.1.9 *Cargo Air Transport Services*

With respect to air cargo transport markets, the O&D approach to market definition is inappropriate, given that cargo is generally less time sensitive than passengers, and is usually transported by different means of transport 'behind' and 'beyond' the origin and destination points. Accordingly, the relevant geographic market has been defined more broadly to be European-wide and, for intra-European cargo transport, would include alternative modes of transport, notably road and train transport, and to a lesser extent sea freight.[496] Further, given cargo may be routed with a higher number of stopovers, any indirect route is substitutable with any direct route.[497]

As regards intercontinental routes, the Commission has found that the corresponding catchment areas broadly correspond to continents, at least for those continents where adequate transport infrastructure allows onward connections (for instance by train, truck, inland waterways, etc.), such as Europe and North America.[498] For continents where local infrastructure is less developed, such as Africa, Asia and the Middle East, these catchment areas would be considered on a country by country basis, air cargo transport from Europe towards Africa, Asia and Middle East being assessed on continent (Europe) to country basis (the respective countries in Asia and Middle East).[499] Air cargo transport markets are also inherently unidirectional as the demand at each end of the route differs substantially, so they must be assessed on a unidirectional basis.[500]

As regards differentiation by reference to types of transported goods (e.g., dangerous or perishable goods), this will generally not be appropriate, save in respect, potentially, of certain products which may require a specific type of carrier, such as oversized cargo or dangerous goods which could not be transported by carriers transporting passengers, due to physical or legal constraints.[501] Such services are, therefore, more likely to be provided by carriers operating full freight aircrafts. It has been found, however, that extremely time-sensitive products (such as perishable goods) would require a high number of frequencies and a better inter-connectivity, which normally only combination airlines (i.e., airlines combining the services of passengers and cargo) could guarantee.[502] The transport of smaller parcels, (grouped by speed of delivery, domestic/international, and quality of service (such as reliability, security, late pick up time, comprehensive track-and-trace ability), has also been found by the Commission to be a separate market in UPS/TNT.[503]

---

496. Case No. COMP/M.5440-Lufthansa/Austrian Airlines para. 28; Case No. COMP/M.5403 – Lufthansa/BMI para. 18.
497. Air France/KLM para. 36.
498. *See* Case No. COMP/M.3280 – Air France/KLM para. 36; Case No. COMP/M.3770 – Lufthansa/ Swiss.
499. In Case No. COMP/M.5403, based on the market investigation, air cargo from Europe to Sierra Leone was found to be a separate market *see* para. 18.
500. Lufthansa/BMI *supra* para. 19.
501. Air France/KLM para. 37.
502. *Ibid.*
503. Commission Decision M.6570 – UPS/TNT 30 Jan 2013 – annulled on appeal Case T-194/13 United Parcel Service *v.* Commission, 7 March 2017.

8.4.2 Competition Assessment of Mergers and Alliances

8.4.2.1 Difference in Legal Tests

There is a difference in the legal test for the assessment of mergers and alliances in that, in the case of mergers, the Commission investigates whether the merger could significantly impede competition, particularly as a result of the creation or strengthening of a dominant position,[504] whereas in the case of alliances under Article 101, the Commission investigates whether the alliance results or is likely to result in the prevention or distortion of competition, and if so, whether the restrictions are justified by efficiencies and consumer benefits under Article 101(3). In practice, the principles applied in the competition assessment and remedies required to address competition concerns in the case of mergers and alliances, are very similar.

Competition will, of course, be eliminated between the parties to a merger. Alliances where the parties cooperate on key parameters of competition such as price, capacity and sharing of revenue, will similarly eliminate competition between the parties. The Commission views such cooperation as by its very nature, harmful to the proper functioning of competition and therefore restrictive 'by object' and, therefore, automatically caught by Article 101(1) (*see* Chapter 4 *Elements of Article 101 TFEU,* section 4.5). Exemption under Article 101(3) is nevertheless possible and the Commission examines the effects, focusing its attention on the routes where there is a high probability that the conditions of Article 101(3) would not be met.[505] As with mergers, commitments may be agreed to address serious competition concerns.

In the *BA/AA/IB* joint venture (oneworld members) and other joint ventures, including within the other two Global alliances (Star and SkyTeam), the parties jointly established fares, regulated capacity, coordinated their respective schedules, cooperated with respect to sales and marketing, shared revenues and sold each other's services, without regard to which party was operating the aircraft. They would, therefore, behave to a large extent, as a single entity on the routes covered by the joint venture, with competition being eliminated between them on markets where these airlines would otherwise compete.[506] Alliances where incentives between the airlines are aligned such that it will be neutral to each carrier whether tickets are sold on its airline or partner airlines, are known as 'metal neutral'.

8.4.2.2 Competitive Assessment of Overlapping Routes

Having identified the relevant markets on which competition should be assessed, which will primarily be on an O&D basis including, as appropriate, indirect as well as direct services and markets for premium and non-premium passengers (*see* section 8.4.1 above), the Commission examines the extent of the competitive overlaps between

504. EUMR Article 2(3).
505. *See* for example, SkyTeam alliance 2015 para. 42; similar assessments were made in BA/AA/IB and the A+ + JV.
506. BA/AA/IB *supra* paras 32, 33, 37; A+ + JV and SkyTeam alliance.

the parties on the markets as identified. This tends to be routes on which the parties actually compete, although if one of the parties is a potential competitor i.e., there is a real possibility of entry – that would be taken into account. In the case of airlines operating a hub-and-spoke network, the General Court has held that an airline would realistically only consider entry on any given O&D city pair if the service was operated from their own hub and if the service could generate sufficient (point-to-point and connecting) traffic to allow operation at a minimum efficient scale.[507]

While the primary focus of competition law is on effects on markets where two or more parties to a merger or alliance operate, if there are effects on other markets, such as other routes where a party has links with a third party, or likely foreclosure of connecting airlines, they will also be considered (*see* sections (3) and (4) below).

Where mergers or alliances are complementary, without overlaps between the parties, issues are unlikely to arise. In the *Air France/KLM* merger, the parties' networks were largely complementary, Air France being more present than KLM in Southern Europe and Africa, whereas KLM operated a higher number of routes to Northern Europe and the Far East. Competition concerns did not arise on such routes.[508]

However, where there are overlap on routes between the parties, there is a route-by-route assessment of the market power held by parties, their competitors and of the extent to which competitors could enter the market or expand existing operations, so as to exercise a significant competitive constraint on the merged entity/alliance. In the case of the *Iberia/British Airways* merger, competition on the London–Madrid route from easyJet, which had taken up slots following a decision exempting an earlier alliance involving some of the parties was found to constrain the parties.[509]

In *Air France/KLM*, there were certain routes between the US and Europe, and routes within Europe including Paris–Amsterdam, both highly congested airports, where market entry by third parties would be unlikely, on which there were significant overlaps and high market shares with insufficient competition to constrain the parties. Commitments from the parties to address such concerns were, therefore, required. This will frequently be the case with one or more routes in the case of mergers of alliances. In *IAG/Aer Lingus*, the parties' combined market shares were high on routes between London and Dublin (60–70 per cent, and similar issues with Belfast) with insufficient competition and limited slots available at London Heathrow and Gatwick.

Closeness of competition is also taken into account. Where the parties are close competitors, the reduction in competition will be greater. Where parties are the largest competitors on a route, it is likely that they will be close, or each other's closest competitors. In the case of the *SkyTeam* alliance, Air France and Delta had high market shares and were found to be closer competitors with each other than with other competitors on the market for premium passengers on the Paris – New York route. This

507. Joined c/ases T-374/94 et ors, European Night Services, [1998] ECR II-3141, para. 137.
508. Air France/KLM, *supra*, upheld on appeal by General Court, Case T-177/04, easyJet Airline Co. Ltd *v.* Commission ECR [2006] II – 1931.
509. Case No. COMP/M.5747 – Iberia/British Airways 14 July 2010.

was also the case in the *British Airways/American Airlines/Iberia alliance*, where the parties were each other's closest competitors on certain routes between London and the US where the alliance would eliminate or significantly reduce competition. Slot and other commitments are used to address such problems.

In *Ryanair/Aer Lingus*, the parties were each other's largest competitors, with a large number of overlapping routes (with a combined share on average of 80 per cent on routes out of Dublin), and both were low-cost airlines operating on a point-to-point basis, which in combination with other barriers to entry, meant that the merger would face insufficient constraint from competitors.[510] If airlines closely monitor one another's prices that will also be evidence of closeness of competition.[511] Similarly, in *Aegean/Olympic* I and II, while there were no serious competition concerns on short-haul international routes, on the domestic market (the parties accounted for more than 90 percent of the market), the merger would create a quasi-monopoly and could result in higher fares.

In both *Ryanair/Aer Lingus* and *Aegean/Olympic*, the overlaps between the parties were concentrated on traffic out of or within one Member State and one airport in particular (Dublin and Athens respectively), where the parties had a significant presence. This was in contrast with previous mergers where the traffic was on a collection of individual routes between various points located in the respective home countries of the parties. These factors were found to deter a new entrant from establishing a base at either airports.

8.4.2.3 Impact of Other Alliances or Agreements on Overlapping and Other Routes

The impact of other arrangements with airlines, such as participation in other alliances, will be taken into account. Where one or more parties are members of Global alliances, their respective alliance partners are not per se considered for the determination of affected markets or calculation of market shares.[512] More far-reaching agreements will be taken into account, however. In *US Airways/American Airlines*,[513] the Commission found that as a result of AA's membership in a metal neutral joint venture with BA and Iberia, the transaction would create a monopoly on the London-Philadelphia route, operated by BA from Heathrow.[514]

510. Ryanair/Aer Lingus I *supra*, paras 57, 59, 71; market shares and number of overlaps had increased from over 30 to over 40 from the first to the second Ryanair/Aer Lingus decision (III).
511. *Ibid.*, s. 7.3.
512. Case No. COMP/M.5747 – Iberia/British Airways para. 55; COMP/M.5440 Lufthansa/Austrian Airlines, COMP/M.5335 Lufthansa/SN. Cooperation within such alliances may include areas such as combined ticket offices, check-in facilities, lounges, boarding experience, cabin crew, meals, seat comfort, punctuality, in-flight entertainment, aircraft cleanliness and baggage handling. Some members may also code-share with each other on certain routes and cooperate in relation to Frequent Flyer Programmes.
513. COMP/M.6607 US Airways/American Airlines 5 August 2013.
514. *Ibid.* Commitments were, there, required. On other transatlantic routes affected by the merger the merged entity would face competition from other metal neutral joint ventures such as the SkyTeam alliance including Delta, Air France/KLM and Alitalia, and the A + + joint venture comprising Lufthansa, Air Canada and United Airlines.

Similarly, if post-merger, there will be close links between one merging party and a close partner of the other merging party, competition on other markets outside of the merger could be affected, with coordination of the parties' respective networks. In such a case, the market shares of the parties will be aggregated with those of their partners.[515] In the *Air France/KLM* merger, the merger was found to be likely to eliminate the incentive for the merged entity and Alitalia to compete on city pairs between the Netherlands and Italy, due to the alliance between Air France and Alitalia.[516]

8.4.2.4 Counterfactual: Other Existing Alliances

When assessing the competitive effects of a merger or alliance, the Commission compares the competitive conditions that would result from the notified merger or alliance, with the conditions that would have prevailed without the merger or alliance, known as the 'counterfactual'. The Commission may also take into account future changes in the market that can reasonably be predicted.[517] In most cases, the competitive conditions existing at the time of the merger constitute the relevant point of comparison. In the case of a merger where the parties are already cooperating in a joint venture agreement, the effect of the merger will merely be to change the contractual link to a permanent structural link. In the *Iberia/British Airways* merger, the pre-existing joint venture with American Airlines whereby the three carriers cooperated and shared revenues on all of their services between North America and Europe was the counterfactual. This joint venture had been approved subject to commitments given to the Commission, so the effects of the proposed merger were found not to give rise to concerns.[518]

In *United Airlines/Continental Airlines*, however, where the parties submitted that since the implementation of the A+ + joint venture, the A+ + partners (United, Continental, Lufthansa and Air Canada) no longer competed on transatlantic routes, and that the proposed merger did not change this situation, the Commission did not accept that claim. It stated that this was on the basis that the merger would remove the possibility that one of them would discontinue the cooperation and start competing again, and, perhaps more significantly, that the Commission was currently investigating the A+ + joint venture, which might lead to a future change in the market, and possibly a situation of actual competition between United and Continental.[519]

Minority shareholdings in other airlines will be taken into account. In *Alitalia/Etihad*, the Commission took into account the interests held by Etihad in Airberlin, Darwin Airline and Jet Airways but these were found not to give rise to concerns.[520]

515. United/US Airways *supra*.
516. Air France/KLM para. 65.
517. Guidelines on the assessment of horizontal mergers under the Council Regulation on the control of concentrations between undertakings ('Horizontal Merger Guidelines'), OJ C 31/5, para. 9.)
518. Case No. COMP/M.5747 – Iberia/British Airways 14 July 2010 paras 68, 96.
519. Case No. COMP/M.5889 United Airlines/Continental Airlines 27 July 2010 paras 36–38.
520. Case M.7333 – Alitalia/Etihad.

8.4.2.5 *Foreclosure of Competing Carriers Connecting to Long-Haul Routes*

Impacts on agreements with competitors, in particular CSAs with other carriers, will also be taken into account, and whether there is a risk that the combined entities could terminate such arrangements so as to deny them access to the hubs from which they operate their own long-haul services. In *IAG/Aer Lingus*, the Commission noted that Aer Lingus, which was then an independent carrier, not a member of any alliance, offered services to large numbers of passengers connecting to a hub airport such as Heathrow, Gatwick or Amsterdam, to flights operated by other carriers. It considered that IAG which was a major long-haul carrier, could have an incentive to discontinue such services, terminating Aer Lingus's feed traffic agreements or otherwise imposing more onerous or restrictive terms, in order to benefit its own services on the long-haul routes. Commitments to ensure that Aer Lingus continued to provide such services were required. Similarly, in the *BA/AA/IB* alliance, anticompetitive effects were likely to arise due to a restriction of competition between the parties and third parties on London–Chicago and London–Miami routes, by means of the parties restricting their competitors' access to connecting traffic, which was important for operations on these transatlantic routes.

8.4.2.6 *Barriers to Entry*

In cases where the parties or merged entry would have high market shares on overlapping routes, competition concerns will be the most serious on routes where there are barriers to entry by airlines who may wish to commence services on a particular route, and thereby exercise a competitive constraint on the parties. These concerns relate to slot availability, the presence of strong parties at airports, entry costs and regulatory factors. These are discussed in the following sections:

(1) Slot Availability

Lack of available slots (the right to take-off and land at an airport) is the most frequent barrier to entry in airline transport cases, given that slots are required for a competitor to enter, or expand services on, a route. The timing of slots will also be an issue, lack of slots during peak times being a serious entry barrier to potential entrants targeting time-sensitive (business) customers.[521]

Lack of slots will be more serious where the airports at both ends are congested. In *BA/AA/IB*, the Commission found that already high shares of the parties (exceeding 50 per cent) were protected by high barriers to entry, in particular the lack of slots at London and New York airports. In *KLM/Alitalia,* this was the case with Schiphol and Malpensa on the Amsterdam – Milan route. Although slots were available at secondary airports like Rotterdam or Orio al Serio, these airports were less attractive for new

521. Case No. COMP/M.3770 – Lufthansa/Swiss, *supra*, para. 33.

entry.[522] Whether other airports may be viewed as substitutable is considered within the assessment of market definition (discussed in section 8.4.1 above).

(2) *Strong Position of Parties at Airports*

Other barriers to entry include the parties' high number of frequencies, extensive FFPs and hub advantage at the end of the routes of concern.

Where parties have a significant presence at a hub airport, this may act as a barrier to entry and expansion for any new entrant or smaller competitor wishing to commence or expand passenger operations. Examples are the Paris – New York route in the *SkyTeam JV*, London and various US cities in *BA/AA/IB*, and Amsterdam – Paris in Air France/KLM, in all of which the parties had hubs at each end of the route. The Commission has stated that a hub operator is able to reap benefits from (a) economies of scale, as it is able to spread its fixed costs at that airport over a large number of routes; (b) better brand recognition and more efficient marketing and advertising expenditure; (c) attractiveness of its frequent flyer programme among the local population; (d) feed traffic from its network flowing through the airport in question; and (e) a better ability to attract corporate customers.[523]

High frequency of services at an airport will represent a barrier to entry, particularly as regards a competitor offering services to more profitable time-sensitive customers, who require early morning flights and a minimum number of frequencies per day to return on the same day. Release of slots in sufficient number to enable a carrier to establish critical mass or a base an airport may be able to address such concerns (*see* discussion of Commitments at section 8.6, below).

In the case of the two mergers that were prohibited, *Ryanair/Aer Lingus* I and III and *Aegean/Olympic* I, the merging parties were both based in the same country and had hubs, high frequencies at the same airport and high national brand recognition, all of which were considered barriers to entry. Likely aggressive action to counter competitors was also found to be a factor which deterred other airlines from indicating a willingness to enter the market.

The General Court in its judgment upholding the *Ryanair/Aer Lingus* decision stated that unlike previous mergers involving active operators which had a home airport in different countries (such as *Air France/KLM* and *Lufthansa/Swiss*), the Commission could not be satisfied that mere slots would ensure access to a route, given the parties operated from the same airport, where they had significant advantages – including the ability of the airlines to switch between routes and to add other routes out of the airport more easily than other competitors without such a significant base – which could not easily be countered by competitors.[524]

The fact that a merger is between two national carriers both of whom have their main bases at an airport does not mean that it will be anticompetitive, however, if there is sufficient competition on the overlapping routes. This was the case with an

522. KLM/Alitalia *supra* para. 30.
523. SkyTeam alliance paras 54–59; Case COMP/M.5335 Lufthansa/Brussels Airlines, para. 160.
524. Case T-342/07 Ryanair Holdings *v.* Commission, [2010] ECR II 3457.

acquisition of joint control over the Czech national carrier České Aerolinie by another Czech carrier which was cleared despite the carriers both having their main bases at Prague airport and all of the overlapping routes being out of Prague airport, given that there was competitive pressure from other carriers.[525]

(3) *Entry Costs*

Establishing a base at an airport requires a significant upfront investment and involves significant commercial risks. Even if slots are available (slots at major airports may of course be extremely costly),[526] entry costs may be significant. These will include costs for ground handling, customer care or offices at the respective airport where they do not yet have operations. They will also include marketing and advertising costs which may be significant, customer information and promotional campaigns being therefore critical to the individual success of airlines.[527] High airport charges will be a further barrier, particularly for low-cost airlines, where the success of the low-cost business model depends to a large extent on a high load factor, i.e., the ability to fill the individual flights with as many passengers as possible.[528]

Entry has also be found to less likely on 'thin' (low volume) routes where there a relatively low average load factor on the route.[529]

(4) *Regulatory Barriers*

National regulatory restrictions have been found to prevent market entry, particularly with regard to long-haul routes between EU and third countries.

In the *SkyTeam* alliance, as regards potential non-stop entrants, the Commission considered it unlikely that any major European or US airline would enter the Paris–New York route, since all three revenue-sharing alliances already operated non-stop services on the route. Further, competition from non-EU or non-US 'fifth freedom' carriers, using the right granted by one State to another State to land and take-off, in the territory of the first State, with traffic coming from or destined to a third State, such as Air India would not be a possibility, given it would not be covered by the EU-US Open Skies Agreement, and would be subject to the regulatory restrictions embodied in the existing bilateral air service agreements.[530]

525. Case No. M.7270 – Cesky Aeroholding/Travel Service/Ceske Aerolinie,
526. The Slot Regulation 95/93 allows airlines to exchange slots with other airlines, often exchanging a slot at a valuable time of day for a 'junk slot' in late evening or early afternoon, which is not particularly useful. A proposal for a revised Regulation would expressly allow airlines to buy and sell slots. Proposal for a regulation of the European Parliament and of the Council on common rules for the allocation of slots at European Union airports, /* COM/2011/0827 final – 2011/0391 (COD).
527. case M.3770 – Lufthansa/Swiss, para. 44.
528. Aegean/Olympic I and II; Ryanair/Aer Lingus Section 7.8.4.3.
529. KLM/Alitalia 1999 para. 30.
530. SkyTeam alliance, para. 64.

When British Airways and American Airlines sought to form an alliance in 1998 and 2002 (before the liberalisation of access between the EU and the US as a result of the EU-US Air Transport Agreement of 2007 as amended in 2010), the then Bermuda II ASA between the UK and the US allowed only two European (BA and Virgin Atlantic) and two US carriers (American Airlines an and United Airlines) to provide transatlantic services between London Heathrow and the US, thus excluding the possibility of market entry. After the entry into force of the EU-US Agreement, the alliance between the two carriers in 2010 was made possible with the surrender of much fewer slots.[531]

In certain cases, undertakings from national authorities have been agreed (*Air France/KLM* and others, *see* 'Commitments' below).

8.4.2.7 *Strengthening of Dominance of Carriers at Slot Restricted Airports*

If a merger or alliance creates or strengthens a dominant position held by a carrier in the market for the holding of slots at a slot restricted airport, that could potentially give rise to competitor foreclosure issues. In *IAG/Aer Lin*gus, this issue was considered when IAG's share of slots at Heathrow was increased from 53 per cent to 56–57 per cent, but the Commission considered that the impact on competitors would be neutral given that the airport was already heavily congested such that the situation would not be fundamentally changed given the relatively limited incremental share.[532]

8.4.2.8 *Efficiencies*

In its consideration of a merger or alliance, the Commission will consider possible efficiencies put forward by the parties and the likelihood that they would counteract the harmful effects on competition which might otherwise result from the merger or alliance.

Benefits will include airlines sharing costs and risks, so being able to extend their network to cover a greater number of destinations which they could not otherwise profitably cover by themselves, increasing the parties' market presence, increasing frequencies and re-scheduling existing services so as to optimise schedules, including connections on indirect routes, and improving load factors hence more efficient use of aircraft. There may also be benefits from mutual recognition of frequent flyer programmes. In its press release on its approval of the *Air France/KLM* merger, the Commission stated 'From a consumer point of view, the combination will allow KLM customers to have access to more than 90 new destinations while Air France customers will be offered 40 new routes. The combination of the two airlines is also expected to bring benefits to consumers and the economy as a whole from costs savings as well as from service improvements resulting from combined networks.'[533]

531. BA/AA/IB *supra*.
532. IAG/Aer Lingus paras 440–441.
533. Commission Press Release IP/04/194, 11 February 2004.

There is debate as to whether mergers and alliances result in lower prices. According to the EU/Department of Transport Alliance Report, alliances (and the same argument would apply to mergers) could reduce prices for interlining passengers, the reduction being greater the more integrated the cooperation.[534] This would be due to the elimination of 'double marginalisation'. In traditional types of code-sharing, a marketing airline sells the seats of an operating airline for a 'transfer' price, which often includes a considerable mark-up over an operating party's marginal costs. Elimination of the double marginalisation requires the transfer price to be equal to marginal costs, thus generating savings (*see also* 'out-of-market' efficiencies discussed below).[535] A study of the US Department of Justice disputes these price reduction effects:[536]

(1) Burden of Proving Efficiencies

The test for proving efficiencies is high and parties may not always submit efficiency arguments. In the case of mergers, according to the Horizontal Merger Guidelines, efficiencies must be verifiable, merger-specific and pass on benefits to consumers. As regards verifiability, the Commission must be reasonably certain that the efficiencies are likely to materialise, and be substantial enough to counteract a merger's potential harm to consumers. Efficiencies must also be merger-specific – a direct consequence of the notified merger and they cannot be achieved to a similar extent by less anticompetitive alternatives. Efficiencies also have to benefit consumers – but if there is little competitive pressure on the parties, there will be little incentive on the part of the merged entity to pass efficiency gains on to consumers.[537] In the case of a merger leading to a market position approaching that of a monopoly, the Commission guidelines provide that it is highly unlikely that efficiency gains would be sufficient to counteract its potential anticompetitive effects.[538]

Similarly, in the case of alliances caught by Article 101(1), the burden will be on the parties to demonstrate that the four cumulative criteria of Article 10(3) are met. In summary, they are: (i) the agreement must create efficiencies, (ii) the restrictions imposed by this agreement must be indispensable to the creation of these efficiencies, (iii) consumers must receive a fair share of these efficiencies, and (iv) the agreement must not create the possibility to eliminate competition in respect of a substantial part of the market. These are discussed in greater detail in Chapter 4 section 4.7.[539]

534. Transatlantic Airline Alliances: Competitive Issues and Regulatory Approaches: A report by the European Commission and the United States Department of Transportation 16 November 2010, ec.europa.eu/competition/sectors/transport/.../joint_alliance_report.pdf, paras 43 et seq.
535. Star Alliance A + + para. 64, 67.
536. *See* OECD Paper on Airline Competition 18–19 June 2014 DAF/COMP(2014)14, para. 98; Brueckner et al (2014); Gillespie and Richard 2010.
537. Horizontal Merger Guidelines, paras 78–88.
538. Horizontal Merger Guidelines para. 84; *see also* Ryanair/Aer Lingus I in which there was an extensive discussion of efficiencies; *see also* Commission Competition Policy Newsletter 2007 No. 3 p. 65.
539. *See also* Communication from the Commission – Guidelines on the application of Article 101(3) of the Treaty OJ C 101, 27 April 2004 p. 97, also discussed in Chapter 4.

(2) *Out-of-Market Efficiencies: 'Behind and Beyond' Routes*

In long-haul cases, destinations connecting to the route being assessed, known as 'behind and beyond' routes, may be taken into account in the consideration of efficiencies under Article 101(3) (and potentially also under the EUMR). This has been a novel feature of the consideration of efficiencies, applied in the A+ + joint venture, where the Commission departed from the practice whereby it conducts its analysis of anticompetitive effects and efficiencies within the same market, namely on routes affected by the cooperation.

According to the Commission Guidelines on Article 101(3), benefits should in principle be enjoyed by the consumers affected by the restrictions, but where markets are related and the group of consumers affected by the restriction and benefiting from the efficiency gains, are substantially the same, benefits may be taken into account.[540] In the context of air transport alliances, in the A+ + joint venture, the Commission accepted that when assessing the Frankfurt-New York route, it could also take account of efficiencies generated on 'behind and beyond' routes, namely travel from Prague-Frankfurt-New York or Frankfurt-New York-Seattle.[541] The Commission found that there was a considerable commonality between the passengers travelling on the Frankfurt-New York route - the group that suffered from the likely competitive harm under Article 101(1) of the Treaty and who enjoyed the 'in-market' efficiencies - and the passengers who flew on related behind and beyond routes and benefited from the 'out-of-market' efficiencies on those routes. It also concluded that out-of-market efficiencies on the related behind and beyond routes could be credited to passengers who travelled on the Frankfurt–New York route.

The efficiencies referred to by the Commission in this regard were the saving of costs through the elimination or reduction of the 'double marginalisation' (discussed above). This would increase the number of passengers on the behind and beyond routes and, therefore, on the route of concern (Frankfurt - New York), and would allow the parties to add non-stop frequency (or increase the size of the aircraft) on the route of concern, which would result in higher time-savings and economies of density for the passengers on the Frankfurt-New York route. The Commission found, however, that the level of demonstrated efficiencies, was insufficient to outweigh the likely significant negative effects resulting from the elimination of competition between Lufthansa and Continental on the Frankfurt-New York premium market and from the inability of competitors of the parties to provide a competitive constraint, due to substantial barriers to entry and expansion.[542]

540. Guidelines on Article 101(3), para. 43).
541. CASE COMP/AT.39595 - Continental/United/Lufthansa/Air Canada Star Alliance 23 May 2013 para. 55 et seq.
542. *Ibid.*, paras 74–78.

8.4.2.9 *'Failing Firm' Defence*

A merger that could significantly impede effective competition may nevertheless be found compatible with the internal market if it can be proved that without the merger, the failing firm would simply disappear from the market. The basic requirement is that the deterioration of the competitive structure that follows the merger cannot be said to be caused by the merger and that it would deteriorate to at least the same extent in the absence of the merger.[543] The conditions to invoke the defence are very strict, however, so the defence is almost never accepted.[544]

In 2011, in *Aegean/Olympic I*, the Commission had prohibited the merger due to the market power of the parties in the Greek market and the uncertainty that a new airline of a sufficient size would enter the market and restrain the merged entity's pricing. It also rejected the 'failing firm' defence. In 2013, at the time of the decision in *Aegean/Olympic II*, Aegean and Olympic were, as before, the two closest competitors on the Greek market for transport of passengers, and entry in the immediate future by other airlines was unlikely on any of the routes of concern (now five as opposed to nine, and with the economic crisis in Greece having deteriorated). However, the Commission concluded that the conditions for the failing firm defence applied, namely first, Olympic would have gone out of business shortly; second, there was no other credible purchaser other than Aegean interested in acquiring Olympic; and third there had also been no expression of any credible interest in the acquisition of Olympic's assets including its brand. Consequently, the most likely scenario was that absent the transaction, Olympic's assets would leave the market completely.

The Commission, therefore, concluded that any competitive harm caused by Olympic's disappearance as an independent competitor would not be caused by the merger. The Commission granted approval without conditions, albeit there would be monitoring of the dominant position held by Aegean on the routes of concern.[545]

The filing firm defence was also invoked by the parties in the *IAG/bmi* merger, without success. While accepting that the most likely outcome if it was not acquired by IAG would be insolvency, the tests for the defence to apply were not met. While bmi was a separate entity which was separately managed, it was a fully owned subsidiary of Lufthansa, which was not facing overall financial difficulties. Further, there was little likelihood that the assets that it owned (56 slot pairs at Heathrow), would exit the market, given the severe congestion affecting Heathrow, but rather, would be reallocated to other carriers. For competition assessment purposes, the counterfactual against which to assess the transaction absent the merger was, however, the scenario whereby bmi would have exited all markets.[546]

543. Horizontal Merger Guidelines, para. 89.
544. The defence has been successfully invoked in Commission merger decisions: Case No. IV/M.308 Kali + Salz/MDK/Treuhand 14 December 1993; M.2314 BASF/Pantochim/Eurodiol 11 July 2001; and Aegean/Olympic II *supra.*
545. Case No. COMP/M.6796 – Aegean/Olympic II Decision followed a Phase II investigation; Commission press release Statement on Aegean/Olympic Air merger 9 October 2013.
546. Case No. COMP/M.6447 IAG/BMI para. 133.

8.5 MERGERS AFFECTING CARGO MARKETS

Given the generally wide market definition in cargo transport, concerns tend not to arise in the case of cargo markets. In the more specialised sector of transport of smaller parcels which includes differentiated markets (*see* section 8.4.1 above), the Commission prohibited the proposed acquisition by UPS of TNT Express, a merger between 'integrators' which would have reduced the number of market players from four to three. The merger was approved in the US and is an example of the respective authorities, despite cooperation in antitrust and mergers, reaching differing conclusions.[547] The Commission decision was, however, annulled on appeal by the General Court on the gounds that, in its decision, the Commission made non-negligible changes to the econometric analysis model previously discussed with UPS, which it should have communicated to UPS before adopting the decision, thus infringing its rights of defence. TNT had completed a merger with Fedex before the Court's judgment.[548]

8.6 COMMITMENTS

The EUMR and Regulation 1/2003 (in the case of alliances) enable commitments to be accepted by the Commission as a condition of approving a merger or allowing an alliance to proceed.[549] The Commission must be satisfied that commitments will eliminate the competition concerns entirely and will be capable of being implemented effectively within a short period.[550] Further, the principle of proportionality requires that commitments must be suitable and not exceed what is appropriate and necessary for attaining the objective pursued, so they must not, for example, disproportionately disrupt the parties' operations.[551]

Unlike other industry sectors, very high market shares in O&D markets have been accepted by the Commission in mergers and alliances between airlines given their network benefits, but commitments are required. Generally, the aim of commitments is to ensure that competitive market structures are preserved. EU competition law, therefore, has a preference for structural commitments, such as commitments to divest a business unit as opposed to behavioural commitments which require monitoring.[552]

547. COMP/M.6570 UPS/TNT Express 30 January 2013; annulled on appeal Case T-194/13 United Parcel Services *v.* Commission 7 March 2017.
548. Case M.7630 Fecex / TNT Express 8 January 2016.
549. EUMR Article 6(2), *see also* Commission Regulation 802/2004 and the Commission Remedies Notice *supra*; Regulation 1/2003 Article 9(1.)
550. Remedies Notice para. 9; similar principles apply to alliances commitments under Regulation 1/2003.
551. easyJet *v.* Commission, *supra* para. 133; BA/AA/IB *supra*.
552. Commission notice on remedies acceptable under Council Regulation (EC) No. 139/2004 and under Commission Regulation (EC) No. 802/2004 OJ C 267, 22.10.2008, p. 1 (' Remedies Notice'), para. 15.

8.6.1 Slot Commitments

The commitment most frequently required in the case of airline mergers or alliances is the release of slots. Within the air transport services sector, structural commitments such as divestiture of a business have not been employed, though their use is not necessarily excluded.[553] While divestiture is the remedy preferred by the Commission, it may accept others where divestiture of a business is impossible, provided they can restore effective competition, achieving effects equivalent to divestiture.[554] In easyJet *v.* Commission, the General Court rejected the argument that divestiture of slots in the *Air France/KLM* merger was inadequate.[555] It also stated that the divestiture of slots required, may be regarded as a structural remedy.[556] Commitments in airline merger or alliance cases seek to facilitate market entry or expansion of services by existing competitors, mainly by way of a release of slots to replace the loss of competition as a result of the merger or alliance.[557]

Before approving slot releases offered by the parties, the Commission has to be able to conclude that it will be possible to implement the commitments and that they will be effective to prevent competition being restricted. It therefore market tests the commitments, publishing them to gauge competitors' willingness to enter the market, and in cases where competitors are unwilling to do so, they will be unlikely to be accepted as a remedy. This was the case in the mergers prohibited thus far, *Aegean/Olympic I, Ryanair/Aer Lingus I* and *III*.

Slot commitments have developed over the years so as to encourage competitors to apply for slots released. In older cases, slots had to be released within 90 minutes of the time requested on long-haul and 30 minutes on short-haul, or if the parties had no such slots available, the slots closest in time to the request.[558] The time limit on short-haul routes is now more usually 20 minutes within the time requested[559] and on long-haul generally 60 minutes from the applicant's requested time.[560]

Further, in contrast with the older cases where monetary compensation payable by the prospective entrant was prohibited, this is now permitted at airports where secondary trading takes place, so long as such contractual provisions are clearly disclosed. This reflects the Commission's approach in its 2008 Communication on the allocation of slots at EU airports, where it took into account the specific situation at

553. Divestiture of a business including assets and comprising 43 overlap routes to a competitor, Flybe, was among remedies offered in Ryanair/Aer Lingus III. The Commission, however, considered the remedy package unlikely to enable Flybe or other carriers to effectively enter and build a presence on all the overlap routes in the short term or to constrain the merged entity to a sufficient extent - Ryanair/Aer Lingus III *supra*, paras 1733 et seq; *see also* Aegean/Olympic I.
554. Remedies Notice para. 61.
555. easyJet *v.* Commission *supra* para. 154.
556. *Ibid.*, para. 183.
557. Remedies Notice para. 63 and footnote 69.
558. Case No. COMP/M.3770 Lufthansa/Swiss of 20.8.2005; Commission Decision of 11 February 2004 in Case No. COMP/M.3280 Air France/KLM.
559. IAG/Aer Lingus para. 562; Case No. COMP/M.644 IAG/BMI.
560. BA/AA/IB, London - New York, CASE COMP/AT.39595 - Continental/United/Lufthansa/Air Canada, Frankfurt - New York).

airports such as London Heathrow, where an active secondary market for slots had existed for many years, with slots costing millions of Euros.[561]

Further, the surrender of slots is for an unlimited duration in the case of mergers, and typically 10 years for alliances (as opposed to six years in early cases) and the slots must be returned to the slot coordinator, as opposed to the airline partners as previously, if they are underused by the new entrant.

To make the slots more attractive, a new entrant may also be granted 'grandfather' rights, once they have operated on a route for a period such as six IATA seasons, thereby being able to use them for other destinations.[562]

Slots granted will be for a specified number of flights and generally seek to replace the loss of competition resulting from the merger or alliance. In *Air France/KLM,* the Commission authorised the merger but required the parties to surrender 47 pairs of slots (94 single take-off and landing slots) per day to enable for example, a competitor to start six new daily return flights between Paris and Amsterdam and the same or another competitor to also offer one daily return flight between Amsterdam and New York. In *US Airways/American Airlines*, to address the monopoly on the London-Philadelphia route, operated by BA, the parties committed to release one daily slot pair at London Heathrow and Philadelphia airports and other measures to encourage market entry, such as the possibility for a new entrant to acquire 'grandfathering' rights after a certain period (discussed below). The parties (and their other joint venture partners) also committed to entering into special feed traffic agreements with the likely entrant airline (discussed below).

In *IAG/Aer Lingus*, a total five daily slot pair releases were required at London Gatwick airport to facilitate new entry to Dublin and Belfast routes, and these were taken up by Ryanair. In *British Airways/Iberia/GB Airways,* the market investigation found that for routes from London to Madrid, corporate customers on average required at least four daily frequencies out of Heathrow or Gatwick, so the Commission required up to a maximum of four daily slot pairs at London Gatwick and at Madrid for one single competitor.[563] The maximum of four daily slot pairs to be provided would be reduced by the number of services already operated by such competitor on this route. These were allocated to easyJet.

In some cases, where parties have high frequencies at an airport, the Commission has found that competitors would tend not to operate routes to a significant extent, without a base at either end of a given route – so concentrating aircraft and traffic at a single airport and enabling early departures and late arrivals – so as to generate

561. Commission's Communication COM(2008)227 final on the application of Regulation (EEC) No. 95/93 on common rules for the allocation of slots at Community airports, as amended, 30 April 2008, p6; British Airways/American Airlines/Iberia; IAG/Aer Lingus para. 567.

562. Case No. COMP/M.3770 – Lufthansa/Swiss. These are common in mergers and alliances and the utilisation period after which grandfather rights are acquired may be longer where slots are very valuable. *See* Lufthansa/Austrian *supra* – Vienna – Frankfurt eight seasons were required para. 342.

563. CASE COMP/D2/38.479: British Airways/Iberia/GB Airways 10 December 2003.

considerable cost savings through economies of scale and greater flexibility to react to changes in supply and demand on routes out of this base.[564] In *Lufthanasa/Austrian*, where there were concerns on routes between Vienna and five other destinations, the Commission required the parties to make a large number of slots available at Vienna so as to facilitate the establishment of a base by a new entrant and/or the enlargement of the bases of the competitors already present at Vienna airport.[565]

The EUMR and Regulation 1/2003 do not require the parties to a merger or alliance to identify a new entrant to claim slots, but the General Court has stated this may be necessary, in particular, where no competitor shows any interest in entering an affected market, and the Commission has required this in certain cases.[566]

If there are competing applications for slots, the Commission must evaluate the bids and allocate the slots on the basis of which carrier will exercise the most effective competitive constraint. Like all decisions, these decisions may be the subject of appeal. Aer Lingus appealed against the decision whereby slots were allocated to Virgin after *IAG/bmi*, though the action was later withdrawn at the time of its merger with IAG.[567] While competitors may choose to offer compensation for requested slots, the Commission has stated that compensation is not a factor in the Commission's competitive assessment of applicants' requests for slots: it would only be taken into consideration if two or more applicants were deemed to impose a similarly effective competitive constraint.[568]

Duration and efficacy of slot commitments: Commitments to release slots in merger cases are unlimited in duration, so that even if slots are not taken up by another airline, they may be claimed at any time in the future.[569] In the case of alliances, commitments are generally of 10 years' duration.[570] There is a variable record of slots being claimed following slot releases in merger and alliance cases, with substantial numbers of slots not claimed, despite the Commission introducing changes discussed above and other remedies (section 8.6.2–8.6.6), to encourage greater take-up of slots. The fact that slots are not actually claimed, does not rule out the threat of potential competition should the merged entity or alliance partners raise prices or reduce the quality of services, however.

564. Ryanair/Aer Lingus I para. 381–382; 939; *see also* Aegean/Olympic were similar issues arose.
565. Lufthansa/Austrian Phase II clearance, paras 329, 397.
566. Lufthansa/Austrian *supra*.
567. Case T-101/13 Aer Lingus *v.* Commission, application dated 14 February 2013 for the annulment of the decision of the European Commission of 14 November 2012 on the assessment of the viability of Applicants and evaluation of their formal bids pursuant to Clause 1.4.9 of the Commitments attached to the Commission Decision of 30 March 2012 declaring a concentration compatible with the common market (Case COMP/M.6447 – IAG/bmi) following the Monitoring Trustee's opinion of 29 October 2012 – Summer 2013 IATA Season. *See also* removal from the register by which the appeal was withdrawn on 21 September 2015.)
568. British Airways/American Airlines/Iberia *supra*.
569. *See* for example, Case No. COMP/M.5440-Lufthansa/Austrian Airline; Air France/KLM, *supra*.
570. BA/AA/IB *supra*.

Slot commitments are accompanied by a variety of other measures to encourage the take-up of slots and to address other competition issues arising. The following types of remedy will routinely be used alongside commitments to release slots.

8.6.2 Fare Combinability

The parties will frequently be required to enter into fare combinability agreements with competitors on the routes of concern. These provide for the possibility for competitors to offer a return trip comprising a non-stop service provided by that competitor in one direction, and a service in the other direction by the parties. This seeks to increase the number of frequencies the competitor is able to offer, thus reducing the parties' frequency advantage.[571] The Commission has limited this remedy to competitors who do not themselves, or through another alliance, operate a hub (or a focus city) at both ends of the route.[572] Commitments have provided for fare combinability agreements on the route of concern irrespective of whether a new service is being operated using slots released. They have also provided for the Commission to approve the terms of the agreement to check that they are reasonable.[573]

8.6.3 Interlining: Special Prorate Agreements

Special Prorate Agreements (SPAs) set out the terms of interlining, providing for the allocation of revenue between the parties on journeys with two or more legs operated by different airlines. In cases where there is a possibility that the parties may wish to exclude other carriers who have feed traffic agreements with one of the parties i.e., which they use to connect to services which they operate on long-haul routes in competition with the parties, the Commission will require the parties to enter into SPAs to allow such carriers (or would-be carriers) to use those connecting services if they so request.[574] The terms should be no worse than the terms of any SPA between the relevant party and any other third party carrier.[575] As with fare combinability agreements, the Commission has stipulated that SPAs should only be available for carriers who do not, alone or through alliance partners, operate hubs (or focus cities) at both ends of the route of concern. Commitments have provided for the Commission to approve the terms of the agreement to check that they are reasonable.[576] In *IAG/Aer Lingus*, IAG made a commitment to enter into agreements with competing airlines which operate long-haul flights out of London Heathrow, Gatwick, Amsterdam (and other airports) so that Aer Lingus would continue to provide these airlines with connecting passengers.[577]

571. BA/AA/IB *supra*; SkyTeam Alliance *supra*; Air France/KLM; IAG/Aer Lingus.
572. Skyteam alliance, *supra* para. 119.
573. *Ibid.*, para. 120.
574. Air France/KLM; IAG/Aer Lingus; BA/AA/IB.
575. SkyTeam JV, *supra*.
576. *Ibid.*, paras 120.
577. IAG/Aer Lingus, paras 568–583.

8.6.4 Access to Frequent Flyer Programmes

The Commission often requires that if a carrier operating services on routes of concern requests to be hosted on the parties' frequent flyer programme (loyalty programmes offered by airlines under which customers enrolled in the programme accrue points for travel on that airline that can be redeemed for free air travel and other products or services), it must be allowed to participate on equal terms as compared to other members of the alliance of which the parties are members, so that the requesting carrier's customers may accrue points, and benefit from other services such as airport lounge access or priority bookings.[578]

8.6.5 Intermodal Agreements

Where there is competition from another mode of transport (usually rail), the parties may agree to enter into 'intermodal' agreements if requested to do so. In *Air France/KLM*, such commitments were given so that the rail operator Thalys could conclude intermodal agreements, allowing it to offer time-sensitive customers a combination of a one-way railway trip with a return flight, thus increasing the attractiveness of the railway link between Paris and Amsterdam.[579]

8.6.6 Other Commitments Less Frequently Agreed

8.6.6.1 Regulatory Commitments

In the case of concerns arising on intercontinental O&D markets, where the Commission has found regulatory barriers from third party ASAs, it has in some cases obtained declarations from the national aviation authorities to ensure that third party competition will not be excluded. In *Air France/KLM*, the French and Dutch authorities gave declarations to remove fifth and sixth freedom restrictions, so as to give traffic rights to other carriers wishing to stop over in Paris and Amsterdam, en route to the US and would refrain from regulating prices on long-haul routes. These were considered important given the account taken by Commission of the existence of indirect, or network, competition on long-haul routes as a factor moderating the finding of dominance.[580]

8.6.6.2 Frequency Freeze and Price Remedies

The Commission has required parties to agree to frequency freezes and restrictions on price reductions to prevent predatory practices to exclude new entrants to markets of concern. Undertaking on slots have been accompanied by measures requiring the

578. SkyTeam Alliance; Air France/KLM.
579. KLM *supra* para. 165; *see also* Lufthansa/Swiss *supra*, para. 197.
580. Air France/KLM, *supra* paras 97–104, 155; *see also* Lufthansa/Swiss paras 188–189.

airline partners to refrain from increasing their offer of flights ('frequency freeze') on the affected routes to give the new entrant(s) a fair chance to establish itself/themselves as a credible competitor.[581] In *KLM/Alitalia,* there was also an obligation on the parties to reduce their frequencies when a new entrant started operating on a given route for two years after entry and to freeze frequencies at this level for four consecutive IATA seasons.[582] Such commitments have not tended to appear in later cases.

The Commission has similarly imposed restrictions on price reductions, requiring parties to agree that if they reduce a published fare on a given route, they will offer a similar reduction on another route. In *Air France/KLM* the Commission required the parties to apply an equivalent reduction (in percentage terms) on the corresponding fare on the Lyon–Amsterdam route whenever they reduced the Paris–Amsterdam fare. This commitment applied only as long as the reduction on Paris–Amsterdam remained effective and as long as there was no competing service on Lyon–Amsterdam.[583]

8.6.7 Monitoring Trustee

Where commitments are given, the decision provides for the appointment by the merged entity/parties of a monitoring trustee who has the duty to monitor the parties' compliance with the commitments. The monitoring trustee is appointed by the parties, but independent from the parties and subject to Commission approval.

581. Lufthansa/Swiss; Air France/KLM.
582. KLM/Alitalia *supra*.
583. In Faull & Nikpay EU Law of Competition 3rd Edition, it is suggested that the frequency freeze remedy may not be used by the Commission due to possible negative effects on airlines' freedom to respond to market changes and that caution may equally be required with pricing remedies which may be difficult to apply in practice 15.127–128.

CHAPTER 9

Enforcement of EU Competition Law

9.1 OVERVIEW

The Commission has extensive powers to investigate infringements of EU competition law, to order termination of infringements and to impose fines of up to 10 per cent of worldwide turnover on undertakings. Commission decisions are subject to appeal by interested parties to the General Court and the Court of Justice. National competition authorities (NCAs) have similar powers and there are procedures for cooperation with the Commission and other competition authorities. There is also private enforcement of competition law through national courts, whether by way of a 'follow-on' claim for damages pursuant to a decision of the Commission or other competition authority, or by way of a stand-alone action. An EU Directive harmonises conditions for the conduct of such actions.

9.2 ENFORCEMENT AUTHORITIES AND INTERACTION OF EU AND NATIONAL LAW

There is cooperation at international level between competition authorities. Both the Commission and NCAs have the power to enforce Articles 101 and 102, and national courts in the case of private enforcement in the context of litigation. Traditionally, the Commission was the sole enforcer of EU competition law operating under Regulation 17/62, the application of which to the air transport sector was delayed until the late 1980s and which until 1 May 2004, was restricted to routes within the EU only.[584]

584. *See also* discussion in Chapter 2 of the ECJ Ahmed Saeed case and pre-1/5/2004 limitation acknowledged by the Commission in the Airfreight cartel decision.

Since 1 May 2004, with the entry into force of Regulation 1/2003[585] the Commission has had the power to investigate agreements between EU and non-EU carriers.[586] Further, with the expansion of the EU and to enable the Commission to concentrate its enforcement activities on the most serious cases, the pre-1 May 2004 system of notification of agreements to the Commission, which conferred immunity from fines from the date of filing, has been abolished. This has been replaced by a system based on assessment by individual companies of the compatibility of their agreements with the competition rules, subject to possible enforcement by the Commission, and NCAs and courts, which have also been granted the power to apply Articles 101 and 102, including to determine if an agreement qualifies for exemption under Article 101(3).

There is Commission guidance on allocation of cases and cooperation between the Commission and national courts and competition authorities.[587] According to this guidance, cases may be handled by one or more NCAs acting in parallel - where an agreement or practice has substantial effects on competition mainly in their respective territories and where the action of only one authority would not be sufficient to bring the entire infringement to an end and/or to sanction it adequately. The Commission, however, is considered best placed to handle suspected infringements which affect competition in more than three EU countries, where other EU laws are affected, or the EU interest requires the adoption of a Commission decision to develop Community competition policy in a new area or to ensure effective enforcement.

There are also guidelines to ensure coordination and information between authorities and the Commission[588] and to avoid decisions which conflict with EU competition law[589]

9.3 COMMISSION POWERS OF INVESTIGATION

The Commission has wide powers of investigation. NCAs of the Member States have similar powers and there is extensive NCA enforcement of EU and/or national competition law at Member State level.[590] Commission or NCA investigations may be prompted by a complaint by a third party such as competitor or customer, by a leniency

585. Council Regulation (EC) No. 1/2003 of 16 December 2002 on the implementation of the rules on competition laid down in Articles 81 and 82 of the Treaty, OJ L 1, 4.1.2003, p. 1.
586. Council Regulation (EC) No. 411/2004 of 26 February 2004 repealing Regulation (EEC) No. 3975/87 and amending Regulations (EEC) No. 3976/87 and (EC) No. 1/2003, in connection with air transport between the Community and third countries, OJ L 68, 6 March 2004 p. 1 *See* Chapter 2.
587. Commission Notice on the cooperation between the Commission and the courts of the EU Member States in the application of Articles 81 [101] and 82 [102] EC OJ C 101, 27.04.2004, pp. 54–64; Commission Notice on cooperation within the Network of Competition Authorities OJ C 101, 27.04.2004, pp. 43–53.
588. Articles 11–12 Reg 1/2003.
589. Reg 1/2003, Articles 3,16; ECN Notice *supra* para. 43.
590. For example, OFT decision 19 April 2012 pursuant to UK law and/or Article 101 imposing a fine of GBP 58.5 million, reduced from GBP 121 million imposed in August 2007.

application (whistleblower), by the Commission or an NCA of its own initiative or by a request from another competition authority (which could be within, or outside, the EU).[591]

There is a limitation period of five years from the date on which the infringement is committed, or in the case of a continuing or repeated infringements, which may be the case with a cartel - the burden of proof being on the Commission to show the infringement was single and continuous - from the date on which the infringement ceases.[592]

9.3.1 Request for Information

The Commission may gather information by means of a written request for information, addressed to the company(ies) under investigation as well as third parties. The request will either be a simple request or in the form of a decision, and will state the deadline and penalties imposed for failure to supply correct information.[593] It will frequently be drafted in general terms, though requests may be or may become more specific.[594] There is an obligation to respond to a request by Decision, but not a simple request, though if a response is not forthcoming, the request may be re-issued in the form of a Decision.

9.3.2 Dawn Raids

In cases of covert infringements, namely cartels, where there is a risk that evidence could be withheld or destroyed, the Commission and/or NCA will be more likely to proceed by means of an unannounced inspection within the EU (or in the case of Iceland, Liechtenstein or Norway, conducted by the EFTA Surveillance Authority).[595] This may be at company premises, company cars, and if prior authorisation is obtained from the local court on the basis of reasonable suspicion that information may be stored there, at the homes of directors or other employees.[596] NCA officials may accompany the Commission officials, and NCAs may also conduct similar investigations.[597] If dawn raids take place at different undertakings, they will usually be coordinated to take place simultaneously, including those in different countries, as was the case in 2006 with the airlines investigated for alleged cartels in the air freight sector. Where an undertaking is dawn raided, it will be appropriate for it to contact its head office, but not to tip off other implicated parties.

591. The Commission investigation of discrimination against Sabre in 1999 followed a request by the US authorities. *See* Chapter 7 *Abuse of a Dominant Position.*
592. Reg 1/2003 Article 25.
593. Regulation 1/203, Article 18.
594. The ECJ annulled Commission RFIs which were excessively vague and imposing a disproportionate burden on the recipients having regard to the volume of information requested – Judgments in Cases C-247/14 P et ors Heidelberg Cement *v.* Commission 10 March 2016.
595. Regulation 1/3003, Article 20.
596. *Ibid.* Article 21.
597. *Ibid.* Article 22.

The Commission has the power to examine and take copies of records on computers, laptops, tablets, and ask for oral explanations of documents disclosed (such as factual questions relating to documents). Companies have a right against self-incrimination and general questions the answers to which would involve an admission of an infringement, such as the object of meetings, could breach this right.[598] The Commission has the right to seal areas of premises if a day is not sufficient to conclude their investigation, and breaking the seal will attract fines.[599]

9.3.3 Legal Professional Privilege

Communications between the company and its external EEA qualified lawyers for the purpose of seeking or giving advice on the possible application of Articles 101 and 102, are subject to legal professional privilege i.e., are protected from disclosure to the Commission or other NCA conducting an investigation, or to an adverse party in litigation before the Court of Justice or national courts.[600] The relevant communications must be made 'for the purposes and in the interests of the client's right of defence', which includes not only communications after the initiation of Commission proceedings, but also earlier communications which have a relationship to the subject matter of investigation.[601] Such documents should be clearly marked 'Legally privileged and confidential' or similar wording. There have been challenges to the exclusion of in-house communications from legal professional privilege, but the Court of Justice confirmed in *Akzo Nobel*, that communications from in-house lawyers to the company and from non-EU qualified lawyers are not protected.[602] Internal communications confined to summarising external advice or internal documents preparatory to seeking, or discussing, advice may be privileged provided it can be proved that they were prepared exclusively for the purpose of seeking legal advice from an external lawyer.[603]

9.3.4 Extraterritoriality

Articles 101 and 102 TFEU focus on the effect on competition and trade within the EU and apply irrespective of where an undertaking is located or where the agreement has been concluded.[604] Since the *Wood Pulp* case, transatlantic alliances and the *Airfreight*

598. Case 374/87 Orkem *v.* Commission [1989] ECR 3283.
599. Reg 1/2003, Article 20(1)(d).
600. Case C-155/75 AM & S Europe Ltd *v.* Commission [1982] ECR 1575.
601. *Ibid.*, para. 21, 23. In AM & S, communications made six years prior to the Commission proceedings were protected.
602. C-550/07 P Akzo Nobel *v.* Commission [2010] ECR I 8301. The European Parliament also proposed to recognise in-house privilege within Regulation 1/2003 but this was rejected, EP document A5-0229/2001.
603. *See* Kerse & Kahn EU Antitrust Procedure 6th edition, for a detailed discussion.
604. Guidelines on the effect on trade concept contained in Articles 81 and 82 of the Treaty, 2004 OJ C 101/81, para. 100.

cartel more generally, it has been clear that agreements between non-EU undertakings or between EU and non-EU undertakings which affect trade within the EU will be caught by EU competition law.[605] This will also be the case with abuse of a dominant position by an entity outside the EU (*see Intel* discussed below). The EU Merger Regulation 139/2004 also applies to mergers where global and EEA turnover thresholds are met, irrespective of where the merging parties are based.

It is not clear that the Commission has the power to request information from companies located outside the EEA. The Commission has the power to issue requests for information and must copy the NCA of the Member State 'in whose territory the seat of the undertaking is situated'.[606] The Commission does address requests to undertakings outside the EU, but does so without mentioning sanctions for failure to respond, unlike with undertakings located within the EU where sanctions are set out, and the response of such an undertaking will be a matter for the recipient's corporate strategy.[607] Jurisdictional difficulties would not arise if the company has a subsidiary or a branch within the EU, or if there is a bilateral agreement between the EU and the country in question providing for cooperation in the field of competition law, as is the case with the US.[608] There is also cooperation between competition authorities worldwide within the International Competition Network. The Commission has also addressed Statements of Objections and Decisions directly to companies located outside the EU.[609]

9.4 INTER-JURISDICTIONAL COOPERATION BETWEEN COMPETITION AUTHORITIES

Given the international dimension of air transport, EU and non-EU jurisdictions may be affected by a single cartel, merger or alliance, so cooperation between authorities is important. Communication takes place between competition authorities worldwide within the framework of the International Competition Network, and in the air transport sector there are also EU – third country agreements which provide for cooperation on competition law both as regards enforcement and to minimise differences in the application of the law, with consultation on individual cases and notification of individual proceedings.[610]

The notable examples of these are agreements between the EU and the US and Canada, which provide for cooperation between the respective competition authorities to avoid conflicts, and 'to promote compatible regulatory results and to minimise

605. Case C-85/89, Ahlström osakeyhtiö and others *v.* Commission ('Wood Pulp').
606. According to Article 18(5) of Regulation 1/2003.
607. In Marine Hoses, [2009] OJ C186/6 and Seamless Tubes [2003] OJ L140/1, companies located outside the EU responded to Commission requests.
608. Decision in US based Intel addressed to Intel, care of its Irish subsidiary. Case COMP/37/7990.
609. Dyestuffs Joined Cases 48/69 ICI *v.* Commission [1972] ECR 619; Power Transformers COMP/39.129.
610. The EU agreements with Canada and US contain such provisions contain cooperation and positive comity agreements to coordinate enforcement and avoid conflicting decisions. In practice, this will involve notification to one another of mergers which impact on the other and consultation at the investigative stages.

differences in approach with respect to their respective competition reviews of inter-carrier agreements'.[611] There is consultation, therefore, on transatlantic alliances (*see* for example the discussion in the Joint EU – DoT Paper generally and with reference to the oneworld alliance BA/AA/IB on assessment and ensuring compatibility of remedies to be agreed; *see also* the discussion of EU and third country agreements in Chapter 2 *Liberalisation of Air Transport* and Chapter 8 *Mergers and Alliances*).[612]

An example of coordination in the case of cartels was the *Airfreight* cartel investigation, in which investigations which included dawn raids were coordinated between authorities internationally. As regards fining policy, in the *Airfreight* cartel decision, the Commission reduced fines by 50 per cent on the basis that only half of the harm took place in the EU (*see* Chapter 5 *Article 101 TFEU: Horizontal Agreements*, section 5.2.4.2, for discussion of the Commission decision, subsequent annulment on procedural grounds by the General Court and re-issued decision).

9.5 COMPLAINTS

Any person or business with a legitimate interest, or a Member State, can submit a complaint to the Commission or NCA and it may be made in anonymity which the Commission is obliged to respect, though in practice, it may be more useful if the Commission knows the identity. The complainant will be informed of the Commission's reasons if it decides to reject a complaint and documents on which the rejection is based. It is an appealable decision though the Commission has a wide discretion, also being able to reject complaints on grounds of administrative priorities or if another NCA has dealt with the case.[613] In easyJet *v.* Commission, the General Court held that the Commission had been justified in rejecting a complaint lodged by easyJet against Schiphol airport's pricing, on the basis that that complaint to the Dutch NCA had been closed.[614] If a complaint is pursued, the complainant will play an active role in the proceedings, receiving a non-confidential copy of the SO and may request (albeit not have the guaranteed right) to attend any oral hearing.[615]

9.6 COMMISSION PROCEDURE: PROCEEDINGS

If, following investigations, the Commission decides to pursue proceedings it issues a Statement of Objections (SO) setting out its case to the parties (this is not a pubic

611. Article 20 of the EU-US Agreement. Procedures are set out in Annex 2 to the Agreement.
612. *See* generally Transatlantic Airline Alliances: Competitive Issues and Regulatory Approaches – A report by the European Commission and the United States Department of Transportation 16 November 2010; *see also* Agreement on Air Transport Between Canada and the European Community and Its Member States Article 14, referring to Agreement between the Government of Canada and the European Communities regarding the Application of their Competition Laws 1999.
613. Regulation 1/2003, Article 13(1).
614. Case T-355/13, Judgment of the General Court of 21 January 2015.
615. *See* generally Commission Regulation 773/2004 relating to the conduct of proceedings by the Commission pursuant to Articles [101] and [102] of the EC Treaty OJ L 123, 27/04/2004 p. 18.

document), to which they have usually two months in which to respond, also having access to documents on the Commission's file, and if they so request, there will be an oral hearing with the Commission. If the case has been instigated by a complaint the complainant will also receive a non-confidential copy of the SO. The burden of proof to show an infringement rests with the Commission and in Article 101 cases, the burden shifts to the company to prove that the conditions of Article 101(3) (efficiencies and consumer benefits) are satisfied (*see* Chapter 4 *Elements of Article 101 TFEU, section 4.6*).

9.6.1 Commission Decisions

The Commission may issue a prohibition decision, a commitments decision or in certain cartel cases, a settlement decision, which will be published in the EU's Official Journal. Other decisions finding there to be no infringement, imposing periodic penalties or rejecting a complaint (or summary thereof) will also be published.

9.6.1.1 Prohibition Decision

In a prohibition decision, the Commission formally finds an infringement, which will generally require the company concerned to stop the infringement, will impose remedies and/or impose a fine.[616]

9.6.1.2 Commitment Decision

Alternatively, in 'commitment decisions',[617] parties may offer commitments that are intended to address the competition concerns identified by the Commission, but without the decision making a finding of an infringement. These are frequently used in airline alliance investigations.[618] The decision makes legally binding commitments offered by undertakings under investigation and is desirable for the company(ies) in question, in that there is no finding of an infringement – which could potentially form the basis of potential damages actions by third parties – and for the Commission, in that it should result in a more speedy resolution of competition concerns. The resolution of competition issues in airline alliances through commitment decisions have generally, however, taken many years. Commitment decisions are not appropriate in cases where the Commission considers that the very nature of the infringement calls for a fine. Undertakings under investigation are free to contact the Commission at any time during an investigation to discuss a possible commitment decision. The procedure is that the Commission drafts a Preliminary Assessment summarising the facts and identifying the competition concerns, on the basis of which the parties may put forward appropriate commitments. If the Commission is satisfied, it market tests the offered

616. Regulation 1/2003, Article 7.
617. Regulation 1/2003, Article 9.
618. For a discussion of the Commission's approach to commitments in alliances, *see* Faull & Nikpay, 3rd edition, Chapter 15.

commitments, publishing a summary in the Official Journal of the European Union, depending on the results of which it may require undertaking(s) to amend the commitments before the Commission makes them binding through a commitment decision (*see also* Chapter 8 *Mergers and Alliances*).

9.6.1.3 *Settlement Decision (Cartel Cases)*

Since 2008, many cartel decisions have been settlement decisions.[619] In cartel cases, where an SO has not yet been issued, in the interests of shortening the procedure, the Commission has a discretion to invite the parties to enter into settlement discussions. In so doing, the Commission will have regard, among other things, to the likelihood of reaching a settlement within a reasonable time frame.[620] The settlement procedure may proceed with the parties (and not necessarily all the parties, known as 'hybrid' cases) who agree to engage in such discussions.[621] The Commission has the discretion to discontinue discussions at any stage.

Discussions will cover issues such as the facts, gravity and duration of the infringement and the potential maximum fine, and parties must keep discussions confidential. A settlement submission will be submitted by each party acknowledging its liability for the infringement. An SO will be issued after the discussions which, if agreed by the parties and if they wish to settle, will be followed by a settlement decision. The parties will receive a reduction of 10 per cent of their fine after other factors relevant to setting the fine have been taken into account.[622] The content of the decision may also be less detailed than in cases which have not been settled. Settlements under the Settlement Procedure are distinct from 'commitment decisions' under Article 9 of Regulation 1/2003 which are designed to close investigations of a breach of Article 101 and/or 102, by making remedies offered by the parties legally binding and without a finding of an infringement.

9.7 FINES

9.7.1 Level of Fines

There are no criminal sanctions under EU competition law. This should be treated with caution as certain Member States and non-EU jurisdictions impose criminal sanctions such as imprisonment and personal fines, with the possibility of extradition of EU

619. Between 2008 and 2016, there have been 20 settlement decisions.
620. Commission Regulation (EC) No. 773/2004, relating to the conduct of proceedings by the European Commission pursuant to Articles 81 and 82 of the EC Treaty, 2004 OJ L 123 p. 18; Commission Notice on the Conduct of settlement procedures in view of the adoption of decisions under Articles 7 and 23 of Council Regulation (EC) No. 1/2003, 2008 OJ C 167 p. 1.
621. The first hybrid decision was Commission Decision C(2010) 5001 final - Case COMP/38866 — Animal feed phosphates; upheld by the EU General Court in Case T-456/10 Judgment of the General Court of 20 May 2015 — Timab Industries and CFPR *v.* Commission, OJ C 221, 6 July 2015, pp. 6-7.
622. *See* 'Fines' below.

citizens to countries such as the US.[623] The sanction for competition infringements by the Commission is the imposition of fines. Fines may imposed, first, if an undertaking refuses to submit to an investigation or provides incorrect or misleading information, further to a request for information or a dawn raid. In such a case, the Commission may impose a fine of up to 1 per cent of group worldwide turnover in the preceding year, and may impose periodic penalties until the information is provided.[624]

Second, if an undertaking is found guilty of negligently or deliberately committing an infringement, the Commission may impose a fine of up to 10 per cent of group worldwide turnover in the preceding financial year.[625] In fixing the amount of the fine, regard will be had both to the gravity and to the duration of the infringement. The Commission enjoys a wide discretion in the assessment of fines but applies a process whereby, in summary: (i) it applies a fine of up to 30 per cent of sales in the affected market(s); (ii) multiplies this by the number of years of the infringement; (iii) in cartel cases, it may add a further 15–20 per cent of the value of sales affected; and (iv) the resulting figure, known as the 'base amount', may then be increased or decreased, to reflect aggravating or mitigating factors, such as recidivism (for which a 100 per cent increase will be applied), benefits realised by the offender, or a reduction to reflect leniency.[626] Leniency applications are discussed in Chapter 5 section 5.2.

Fines in recent years have become very substantial. The highest fine on a single company to date has been on Intel for abuse of a dominant position – EUR 1.06 billion,[627] and for a cartel EUR 2.9 billion in the trucks sector[628] (*see* generally Chapter 5 section 5.2 for fines in the air transport sector).

9.7.2 Liability of Parent to Pay Fines for Infringement Committed by Subsidiary

Given that fines are calculated as a percentage of turnover, establishing parental liability can have a significant impact on fines. The Commission and the Court readily assume a parent to share liability for infringements by a subsidiary. When a parent company is found to exert 'decisive influence' over the conduct of its subsidiary, it can be held jointly and severally liable for the fines imposed on that subsidiary. The 10

623. Jail sentences were imposed on individuals in the case of investigations of the Airfreight cartel in the US and Australia.
624. Reg 1/2003 Article 23(1), Article 24(2).
625. *Ibid.*, Article 23(3).
626. Commission Guidelines on the method of setting fines imposed pursuant to Article 23(2)(a) of Regulation (EC) No. 1/2003, OJ 2006 C 210 p. 2, which have led to increased fines. In the Airfreight cartel decision, fines in respect of routes between the EEA and third countries were reduced by 50 per cent on the basis that part of the harm on such routes was likely to fall outside the EEA, by 15 per cent on the basis that carriers were encouraged to concert on prices on certain routes under bilateral Air Services Agreements with third countries, and an uplift for recidivism was imposed on SAS (*see* Chapter 5 for discussion of the Decision, which was annulled.)
627. T-286/09 – Intel *v.* Commission 12 June 2014, appeal pending before the ECJ C-413/14 P.
628. Commission press release IP/16/2582 19 July 2016. The Commission published statistics on fines, available on its website: http://ec.europa.eu/competition/cartels/statistics/statistics.pdf.

per cent limit on fines, therefore, applies to the turnover of the parent company, increasing the level of the fines as well as the risk of recidivism, for which fines are increased. The General Court has ruled that the Commission can generally assume that a wholly owned subsidiary essentially follows the instructions given to it by its parent company, without needing to check whether the parent company has in fact exercised such power.[629] The burden would then be on the parent company to rebut this presumption by producing evidence that the subsidiary does not, in essence, comply with the instructions which it issues and, as a consequence, acts autonomously on the market.[630]

The Commission and Court have also found parent companies to be jointly and severally liable for the anticompetitive conduct of a joint venture company (approved by the Commission as a full-function JV under the EU Merger Regulation) in which they each had a 50 per cent interest. Personal involvement by the parent(s) in any infringement was not required.[631]

9.7.3 Compliance Programmes and Commission Fining Policy

Historically, the Commission offered reductions in fines if it found that a party which had committed a competition infringement had a competition compliance programme in place.[632] The Commission encourages companies to implement such programmes, which comprise measures to minimise the risk of an infringement of competition law, and may variously include an audit of existing agreements and practices, guidelines for senior management and employees, training and disciplinary sanctions for breach. They may also include guidelines for the conduct of meetings with competitors and on dawn raids. The Commission has, however, changed its position of taking a compliance programme into account as a mitigating factor when setting fines.[633] Many NCAs take a similar approach in their national law, with exceptions such as the UK which reduces fines if there is a clear and unambiguous commitment to compliance throughout the organisation.[634]

---

629. Case T-39/07, Eni SpA *v.* European Commission.
630. *Ibid.*, *see also* Case T-112/05, Akzo Nobel NV *v.* Commission [2007] ECR II 5049, para. 62.
631. C-499/11 P, upholding Case T-42/07 Dow Chemical and Others *v.* Commission [2011] ECR II-4531, upholding Commission Decision of 29 November 2006 relating to a proceeding under Article 101, Case COMP/F/38.638 – Butadiene Rubber. The decision refers to parental liability for fines, but states that whether group companies form part of the same 'undertaking' or are separate 'undertakings' for the purposes of deciding if there is an 'agreement' within the meaning of Article 101(1) may be different.
632. Commission Decision National Panasonic [1982] OJ L354/28.
633. Case C-501/11 P Schindler Holdings *v.* Commission REF – the Court upheld the decision not to offer a reduction of a fine for participation in a cartel which nevertheless took place, para. 142.
634. *See also* Wouter Wils: 'Antitrust compliance programmes and optimal antitrust enforcement; Journal of Antitrust Enforcement, Vol. 1, No. 1 (2013) pp. 52–81. Guidance on compliance programmes is available on the Commission's website:http://ec.europa.eu/competition/antitrust/compliance/index_en.html).

9.8 APPEALS

Appeals to the General Court may be brought against decisions by the addressees of decisions or by third parties who have sufficient interest, and they may appeal against the whole decision (liability and fines), or fines only.[635] Appeals may also be brought against decisions of the General Court to the Court of Justice, though the latter appeals may be on points of law only. The procedures of the General Court and Court of Justice are summarised in Chapter 1 *Introduction to the European Union and Competition Law* sections 1.4.4–1.4.5.

9.9 DAMAGES AND PRIVATE ENFORCEMENT

9.9.1 Stand-Alone Actions in National Courts

The right to compensation for loss suffered as a result of a breach of competition law is well established. Actions to claim damages to compensate for loss caused by an infringement of EU competition law, as well as to seek an injunction to prevent future loss being caused, are possible by way of 'stand-alone' actions in national courts i.e., without proof of an infringement by the Commission or an NCA. This is because Articles 101 and 102 create direct effects in national law in relations between individuals, and the Court of Justice has held that the full effectiveness of the competition rules would be put at risk if it were not open to any individual to claim damages for loss caused to it by a contract or by conduct liable to restrict or distort competition.[636] The direct effect of Articles 101 and 102 is discussed in Chapter 1 section 1.6.4 and section 9.9.1 below. The claimant must prove that there has been not only a breach of competition law, but also quantify loss and establish that the loss claimed was caused by the infringement, which can be a complex exercise. As regards injunctions to bring anticompetitive practices or conduct to an end, the Commission has powers to order interim measures but this is likely to be a lengthy procedure, whereas national courts may offer more rapid injunctive relief. 'Follow-on' damages claims are also possible, further to a decision finding an infringement. Findings by the EU Commission in decisions are binding, so can be relied on in follow-on private actions for damages.[637] Loss and causation have to be established, however.

Actions for recovery of damages and/or injunctive relief are governed by national laws which vary across the EU.[638] Jurisdiction in the case of actions based on breach of competition law, whether stand-alone claims or follow-on damages claims, is

635. The General Court upheld appeals brought by addresses of the Airfreight decision, discussed in Chapter cartels.
636. Case C-453/99, Courage *v.* Crehan ECR [2001] I-6297, para. 26.
637. Regulation 1/2003, Article 16.
638. The preferred forums for the bringing of actions for breach of competition law in the EU tend to be Germany, the Netherlands and the UK. In each of these countries, actions were brought by claimants against airlines fined by the Commission in the Airfreight cartel decision.

governed by the EU Judgments Regulation, under which the jurisdiction shall be as laid down by the contract, or on the basis of factors such as the domicile of the defendant, where the contract was performed or activity (such as cartel activity) took place, or where damage was suffered. A detailed discussion is beyond the scope of this work.[639]

9.9.2 Damages Directive

The Commission found that EU Member State laws made it costly and difficult to bring actions to obtain compensation suffered as a result of a reach of competition law, particularly in the case of SMEs and consumers, and that this area of the law across the EU Member States presented a picture of 'total underdevelopment'.[640]

An EU Directive has, therefore, been adopted to harmonise rules on actions for damages.[641] The Directive establishes a presumption of harm in cartel cases i.e., that the cartel increased prices – quantification of that harm would still have to be assessed. It also provides: that a decision of an NCA that there has been an infringement will be binding on courts of that Member State, and prima facie evidence of an infringement in the courts of other Member States; that there must be a minimum limitation period of five years from the date the claimant reasonably became aware of the infringement (this covers the case where there has been concealment of the infringement); and that a defendant in a cartel damages action can argue that where a claimant is a purchaser who has passed on any overcharge to its own customers, damages should be reduced accordingly (known as the 'passing-on' defence').

The Directive also provides rights for national courts to order the disclosure of evidence from a defendant or a third party, including the competition authority. However, it seeks to prevent disclosure of leniency applications or settlement discussions in damages litigation, so as not to discourage such applications. It also changes the normal principle of joint and several liability of cartel participants for loss caused as a result of the cartel, by providing that immunity recipients can be liable only to their own customers.[642]

639. Regulation 44/2001 Council Regulation of 22 December 2000 on jurisdiction and the recognition and enforcement of judgments in civil and commercial matters, as amended – *see* http://eur-lex.europa.eu/legal-content/EN/TXT/HTML/?uri=CELEX:02001R0044-20150110&rid=1; *see* Case C-302/13 flyLAL-Lithuanian Airlines *v.* Starptautiskā lidosta Rīga VAS And Air Baltic Corporation AS, 23 October 2014.
640. Green Paper – Damages actions for breach of the EC antitrust rules (SEC(2005) 1732) COM/2005/0672 final.
641. Directive 2014/104/EU on certain rules governing actions for damages under national law for infringements of the competition law provisions of the Member States and of the European Union, OJ L 349, 5.12.2014, pp. 1–19.
642. The Commission has also issued a Recommendation urging Member States to introduce mechanisms for injunctive and compensatory collective redress OJ L 201, 26.7.2013, pp. 60–65, Guidance on quantifying harm in damages actions for breach of Articles 101 and 102 (OJ 2013 C 167 p. 7, and has stated that Guidelines for national courts on the passing on of overcharges will also be issued.) The Directive had to be implemented in Member States' national laws by 27 December 2016.

CHAPTER 10

EU State Aid Rules

Article 107 provides:

> 1. *Save as otherwise provided in the Treaties, any aid granted by a Member State or through State resources in any form whatsoever which distorts or threatens to distort competition by favouring certain undertakings or the production of certain goods shall, in so far as it affects trade between Member States, be incompatible with the internal market.*
> 2. *The following shall be compatible with the internal market:*
>   (a) *aid having a social character, granted to individual consumers, provided that such aid is granted without discrimination related to the origin of the products concerned;*
>   (b) *aid to make good the damage caused by natural disasters or exceptional occurrences;*
>   (c) *aid granted to the economy of certain areas of the Federal Republic of Germany affected by the division of Germany, in so far as such aid is required in order to compensate for the economic disadvantages caused by that division. Five years after the entry into force of the Treaty of Lisbon, the Council, acting on a proposal from the Commission, may adopt a decision repealing this point.*
> 3. *The following may be considered to be compatible with the internal market:*
>   (a) *aid to promote the economic development of areas where the standard of living is abnormally low or where there is serious underemployment, and of the regions referred to in Article 349, in view of their structural, economic and social situation;*
>   (b) *aid to promote the execution of an important project of common European interest or to remedy a serious disturbance in the economy of a Member State;*
>   (c) *aid to facilitate the development of certain economic activities or of certain economic areas, where such aid does not adversely affect trading conditions to an extent contrary to the common interest;*

(d) *aid to promote culture and heritage conservation where such aid does not affect trading conditions and competition in the Union to an extent that is contrary to the common interest;*
(e) *such other categories of aid as may be specified by decision of the Council on a proposal from the Commission.*

10.1 OVERVIEW

Articles 107–109 TFEU lay down the principles for the control of State aids in order to prevent the distortion of competition by State subsidies and other aids. The Commission has sole competence to determine whether aid breaches Article 107 and can order governments to recover aid that has been illegally granted. Aid must generally be pre-notified to the Commission for approval and national courts have power to declare unnotified aid unlawful under Article 108(3). Articles 107 and 108 have been implemented by Regulations,[643] the Decision 2012/21 on services of a general economic interest [644] and are the subject of three sets of Guidelines, namely the Rescue and Restructuring Guidelines 2014,[645] the Aviation Guidelines 2014[646] and the Commission Notice on the notion of State aid 2016.[647]

In the air transport sector, aid was traditionally granted in the years following liberalisation from the early 1990s onwards by Governments to their flag carrier airlines, notably in the form of restructuring aid, with some substantial capital injections being authorised, though in more recent years aid has also been granted by publicly owned airports in the form of reductions in airport charges and other grants granted by airports to low-cost airlines on start-up routes.

The EU State aid principles - the notion of 'aid', the conditions for aid to be compatible with the internal market - and enforcement by the Commission and national courts are discussed below. A final section discusses third country subsidies to airlines where rules are limited in their scope and have never been applied in practice.

---

643. Council Regulation (EU) 2015/1589 of 13 July 2015 laying down detailed rules for the application of Article 108 of the Treaty on the Functioning of the European Union, OJ L 248, 24.9.2015, p. 9 ('Procedural Regulation'); Commission Regulation 2015/2282 of 27 November 2015 amending Regulation (EC) No. 794/2004 as regards the notification forms and information sheets OJ L 325, 10.12.2015, p. 1 ('Implementing Regulation'); Regulation 1407/2013 of 18 December 2013 on the application of Articles 107 and 108 TFEU to *de minimis* aid OJ L 352, 24 December 2013 p. 1.
644. Commission Decision 2012/21/EU of 20 December 2011 on the application of Article 106(2) of the Treaty on the Functioning of the European Union to State aid in the form of public service compensation granted to certain undertakings entrusted with the operation of services of general economic interest OJ L 7, 11.1.2012, pp. 3–10.
645. Communication from the Commission — Guidelines on State aid for rescuing and restructuring non-financial undertakings in difficulty OJ C 249, 31.7.2014, pp. 1–28.
646. Communication from the Commission — Guidelines on State aid to airports and airlines OJ C 99, 4.4.2014, pp. 3–34 (the 'Aviation Guidelines').
647. Commission Notice on the notion of State aid as referred to in Article 107(1) of the Treaty on the Functioning of the European Union OJ C 262, 19.7.2016, pp. 1–50. There are other Commission Notices a discussion of which is beyond the scope of this work.

10.2 DEFINITION OF STATE AID

Article 107(1) provides:

> Save as otherwise provided in the Treaties, any aid granted by a Member State or through State resources in any form whatsoever which distorts or threatens to distort competition by favouring certain undertakings or the production of certain goods shall, in so far as it affects trade between Member States, be incompatible with the internal market.

For a measure to constitute 'aid' within the meaning of Article 107(1), there must be aid granted by the State or through State resources and which confers an advantage on the recipient, the intervention must be liable to affect trade between Member States and it must distort or threaten to distort competition.

10.2.1 Aid Granted by the State or Through State Resources Which Confers an Advantage

10.2.1.1 Recipient Must Be an 'Undertaking'

The recipient must be an undertaking. This will be the case whenever an entity is engaged in an economic activity, which means the offering of goods or services on a market, regardless of the entity's legal status and the way in which it is financed. The notion of undertaking is the same as under Articles 101 and 102 and is discussed in Chapter 4 section 4.2. In relation to airports, the provision of airport services to airlines and service providers in exchange for airport charges, constitutes an economic activity, so that public financing of such activities is subject to the State aid rules, as is the construction or upgrade or extension of airport infrastructure which is commercially exploited.[648] Therefore, the entity carrying out such an activity, regardless of whether it is public or private, is considered as an undertaking for the purposes of EU law. Public, non-economic functions such as air-traffic control, police and customs are outside the scope of the State aid rules.[649] The public funding of such activities should, however, be strictly limited to compensating the costs to which they give rise and may not be used to finance other activities.[650] Overcompensation of non-economic activities

648. Case T-128/98 Aéroports de Paris *v.* Commission ECR [2000] II 3929; Communication from the Commission — Guidelines on State aid to airports and airlines OJ C 99, 4.4.2014, pp. 3–34 ('Aviation Guidelines 2014'); Joined Cases T-443/08 and T-455/08 Mitteldeutsche Flughafen AG and Flughafen Leipzig Halle GmbH *v.* Commission, ('Leipzig-Halle airport' judgment), [2011] ECR II-1311, in particular paras 93 and 94; Case T-196/04 Ryanair *v.* Commission [2008] ECR II-3643; Aid to Berlin Brandenburg airport SA.41342, 3 August 2016 – cleared on the basis of the market economy investor principle hence no aid.
649. *Ibid., see also* Aviation Guidelines para. 35; Commission Notice on the notion of State aid as referred to in Article 107(1) of the Treaty on the Functioning of the European Union OJ C 262, 19.7.2016, p. 1 paras 201–209, 214.
650. Aviation Guidelines para 36.

may constitute aid. Further, public financing of non-economic activities must not lead to undue discrimination between airports.[651]

10.2.1.2 Through State Resources or Imputable to the State

The transfer of State resources must result from financial advantages received directly from the State or from State resources such as from local authorities,[652] or any intermediary body acting by virtue of powers conferred on it, and potentially from a company owned or controlled by the State.[653]

10.2.1.3 Types of Aid

Aid may take a wide variety of forms, which include direct grants, loans on preferential terms, State guarantees and the making of investments, such as the taking on of shareholdings in companies which may be experiencing financial difficulties. It may also include measures which mitigate charges which would normally be payable, and thus similar in character to subsidies, such as preferential tax treatment[654] or the provision of airport services to airlines at discounted rates.[655] Misuse of aid, for example, aid authorised for the provision of infrastructure then being used for the benefit of a single or specific undertakings, may also constitute aid.[656] The determining factor is whether the recipient receives a benefit which it could not obtain under normal market conditions.[657] This is discussed in the following section.

10.2.1.4 Economic Advantage and the Market Economy Operator Principle

The aid measure must directly or indirectly favour an undertaking (or undertakings) so as to constitute an economic advantage which the recipient would not have obtained in normal market conditions.[658]

651. Ibid para 37
652. Joined Cases T-267/08 and T-279/08, Nord-Pas-de-Calais [2011] ECR II 1999, para. 108.
653. Case C-482/99 France *v.* Commission ('Stardust Marine') [2002] ECR I 4397; Case C-284/12 Deutsche Lufthansa AG *v.* Flughafen Frankfurt-Hahn GmbH, 21 November 2013.
654. Commission Decision 2013/199/EU of 25 July 2012 on State aid Case SA.29064 – Differentiated air travel tax rates implemented by Ireland – Commission concluded that an Irish air travel tax applicable to flights from Irish airports allowing a lower rate for destinations up to 300 km from Dublin breached State aid rules; Case T-473/12 Aer Lingus *v.* Commission, T-500/12 Ryanair *v.* Commission, General Court judgments 5 February 2015; appeal to Court of Justice pending C-164/15 P; Commission Decision Olympic Airways – Greek State's toleration of Olympic Airways' failure to pay more than €350 million in tax and social security liabilities (Commission Press Release IP/05/1139 14 September 2005).
655. *See* Generally Guidelines on the notion of aid para. 51–54; Ryanair *v.* Commission *supra*.
656. Aviation Guidelines-requirement of non-discriminatory access-para. 108.
657. Commission Notice on the notion of aid, *supra*, para. 66.
658. Case C-39/94 SFEI and Others [1996] ECR I-3547, para. 60, and Case C-342/96 Spain *v.* Commission [1999] ECR I-2459, para. 41; Ryanair *v.* Commission *supra* para. 38.

If the State can show that it has acted under the same terms and conditions as a commercial investor when providing the necessary funding, known as the 'market economy operator principle' (also known as the 'market economy investor principle' or 'market economy lender principle' in the case of loans) then State aid is not involved. This involves a complex assessment of all the circumstances so as to decide whether a rational private investor would have entered into the transaction in question on the same terms. Investments by commercial operators on the same terms and conditions as the public authority, and/or the presence of a business plan demonstrating that the investment provides an adequate rate of return for the investors, in line with the normal market rate of return that would be expected by commercial operators on comparable projects, would be required (*see also* discussion at sections 10.3.2.2–10.3.2.3).[659]

To the extent that aid can be justified from a commercial point of view in the light of the market economy operator test, it falls outside Article 107(1), and it follows that to the extent that it exceeds what the market economy operator would accept, it would constitute State aid. If that is the case, the Commission then examines whether the aid can be found compatible with the internal market (*see* section 10.3 below). In the case of loans and guarantees, the aid element is the difference between the rate which the borrower should pay, having regard to the aid recipient's financial position and security offered, and that actually paid.[660]

Following the emergence of low cost carriers and the conclusion of arrangements on favourable terms with regional airports, most commonly by Ryanair, the Commission found such deals to constitute State aid. Following the decision of the General Court in *Ryanair v. Commission*[661] and the Aviation Guidelines, it is now clear that such arrangements may fall outside the definition of 'aid' on the basis that they may satisfy the private investor principle. Aid to start-ups is discussed below (*see* section 10.3.2.3).

10.2.2 Effect on Trade Between Member States

10.2.2.1 Low Threshold for 'Effect on Trade Between Member States'

Under the EU State aid rules, there is no requirement, as is the case with Articles 101 and 102 TFEU, that the effect on trade between Member States be appreciable. Further, as regards aid that is purely local, the Court has held that that it is not impossible that a public subsidy granted to an undertaking which provides only local or regional transport services and does not provide any transport services outside its State of origin, may nonetheless have an effect on trade between Member States. This is because the supply of transport services by that undertaking may, therefore, be

659. *See* generally Guidelines on notion of aid paras 83–105.
660. *Ibid.*, paras 108–114.
661. T-196/04 – Ryanair *v.* Commission ECR [2008] II 3643 (Charleroi case).

maintained or increased, with the result that undertakings established in other Member States have less chance of providing transport services in the market in that Member State.[662]

In the case of small airports that predominately serve local users and for which the impact on cross-border investment is marginal, Commission Guidelines on the notion of aid state that such aid is unlikely to have an effect on trade between Member States.[663] Where there is competition with another airport, however, this can give the subsidised project a selective economic advantage over its rivals and is, therefore, likely to fall within the State aid rules.

10.2.2.2 De Minimis Aid

The notable case where an effect on trade between Member States is deemed not to arise is the '*de minimis*' principle. The Commission is empowered by Regulation 994/98[664] to lay down by way of block exemption a threshold below which aid measures are considered not to meet all the criteria laid down in Article 107(1) and, therefore, do not fall under the notification obligation.[665] The Commission has adopted two *de minimis* block exemptions, applying to *de minimis* aid generally, and to services of a general economic interest below), respectively (the latter of which is discussed at section 10.3.2.5).

The *de minimis* aid block exemption Regulation 1407/2013 provides that aid to an undertaking not exceeding EUR 200,000 over a period of three fiscal years is deemed outside the State aid rules, so that notification of such aid is not required.[666] Different companies within the same group cannot each receive *de minimis* aid.[667] Loans secured as to a minimum of 50 per cent are also permitted if the recipient is not subject to insolvency proceedings, or would not fulfil the criteria under its national law to be placed in insolvency and the loan does not exceed either EUR 1 million and a duration of 5 years or EUR 500,000 and a duration of 10 years.[668] Guarantees are *de minimis* if they do not exceed 80 per cent of the underlying loan and the amount guaranteed does

662. *Altmark* case, *supra* paras 77–78.
663. Commission Notice on the notion of State aid as referred to in Article 107(1) of the Treaty on the Functioning of the European Union C/2016/2946 OJ C 262, 19.7.2016, pp. 1–50 para. 197, 210; Commission Decision in State aid in case SA.38441 — United Kingdom — Isles of Scilly Air links (OJ C 5, 9.1.2015, p. 4).
664. Council Regulation (EC) No. 994/98 of 7 May 1998 on the application of Articles 92 and 93 of the Treaty establishing the European Community to certain categories of horizontal State aid OJ L 142, 14.5.1998, p. 1.
665. Council Regulation (EC) No. 994/98 of 7 May 1998 on the application of Articles [107 and 108] of the Treaty on the Functioning of the European Union to certain categories of horizontal State aid OJ L 142, 14.5.1998, pp. 1–4.
666. Commission Regulation (EU) No. 1407/2013 of 18 December 2013 on the application of Articles 107 and 108 of the Treaty on the Functioning of the European Union to *de minimis* aid OJ L 352, 24.12.2013, p. 1, Article 3.
667. Under previous *de minimis* Regulations, the term 'enterprise' had been used to denote 'recipient'. Commission Regulation (EC) No. 69/2001 of 12 January 2001 on the application of Articles [107] and [108] of the EC Treaty to *de minimis* aid, Article 1. Recipient as 'undertaking' was introduced by Regulation 1998/2006).
668. *Ibid.* Article 4(3).

not exceed EUR 1.5 million.[669] There are rules on the cumulation of aid, whereby it is possible to receive *de minimis* aid alongside aid under a notified scheme or under the General Block Exemption Regulation[670] (the application of which to air transport is currently limited), provided that the total aid would not exceed the maximum permitted aid intensity for that particular project under the notified scheme or the General Block Exemption Regulation.

10.2.3 Distort or Threaten to Distort Competition

The Court has held that when State aid strengthens the position of an undertaking compared with other undertakings competing in intra-EU trade, the latter must be regarded as affected by that aid.[671] It is, therefore, sufficient that the recipient of the aid competes with other undertakings on markets which are open to competition.[672]

10.3 COMPATIBILITY OF STATE AID WITH THE INTERNAL MARKET

If a measure constitutes State aid, it is in principle prohibited by Article 107(1). However, Article 107(2)–(3) list a number of grounds of exemption on which aid could nevertheless be authorised by the Commission, which has exclusive competence to declare State aid compatible with the internal market. Aid measures within the meaning of Article 107(1) must be notified to the Commission in advance and approved before being granted, with the exemption of aid which is exempt by block exemptions (such as *de minimis* aid and certain services of general economic interest (SGEI) cases). In making its assessment, the Commission will consider a wide range of factors, including the justification for the aid, the objective of common interest it serves, by preventing social hardship or addressing market failure,[673] and the likelihood of restoring the long-term viability of the undertaking.[674] It also takes into account the nature of the aid (whether it is a loan, or grant), the amount of aid and the size of the recipient, hence the market impact on competitors having to compete with the subsidised goods and/or services.[675]

10.3.1 Article 107(2): 'Mandatory' Grounds of Compatibility

Article 107(2) lists a number of grounds on which the Commission must declare aid compatible with the internal market. Such measures nevertheless have to be notified to

669. *Ibid.* Article 4(6).
670. Commission Regulation (EU) No. 651/2014 of 17 June 2014 declaring certain categories of aid compatible with the internal market in application of Articles 107 and 108 of the Treaty OJ L 187, 26.6.2014, p. 1 ('GBER').
671. Case C-730/79 Philip Morris *v.* Commission ECR [1980] 2671 para. 11.
672. Case T-214/95 Het Vlaamse Gewest *v.* Commission [1998] ECR II-717.
673. *See* R&R Guidelines section 3.1.1.
674. *Ibid.* section 3.1.2.
675. *Ibid.* 3.6.2.2.

the Commission to enable it to ensure that the conditions are indeed met. These are of generally limited relevance to the air transport sector, save for two cases discussed below.

(1) Article 107(2)(a) Aid Having a Social Character

This includes, for example, aid measures in favour of persons living in remote or sparsely populated regions such as islands or for categories of passengers such as children, people with disabilities, low incomes, or elderly.[676]

(2) Article 107(2)(b) Aid to Make Good the Damage Caused by Natural Disasters or Exceptional Occurrences

Aid was authorised under this ground in the form of emergency aid by Member States to airlines for a limited period following the September 2001 terrorist attacks – to compensate for the costs to airlines of American airspace being closed for four days and to help airlines meet the extra costs of insurance.[677] Schemes had to be notified to the Commission to demonstrate that that the amounts granted did not exceed the losses.

10.3.2 Article 107(3): 'Discretionary' Grounds of Compatibility

Article 107(3) provides:

The following may be considered to be compatible with the internal market:

(a) aid to promote the economic development of areas where the standard of living is abnormally low or where there is serious underemployment, and of the regions referred to in Article 349, in view of their structural, economic and social situation;
(b) aid to promote the execution of an important project of common European interest or to remedy a serious disturbance in the economy of a Member State;
(c) aid to facilitate the development of certain economic activities or of certain economic areas, where such aid does not adversely affect trading conditions to an extent contrary to the common interest;

...

(e) such other categories of aid as may be specified by decision of the Council on a proposal from the Commission

Article 107(3) lists grounds on which the Commission may declare aid compatible with the internal market. The ground which is invoked in the case of aid to airports and airlines is Article 107(3)(c). The application of Article 107(3)(c) to types of aid granted in the air transport sector is discussed below.

676. Aviation Guidelines paras 156–157.
677. Communication from the Commission to the European Parliament and the Council COM(2001) 574 final 10 October 2001.

10.3.2.1 Operating Aid

Operating aid - aid to cover operating costs - can only be authorised under exceptional circumstances. The Commission considers that airports and airlines should normally bear their own operating costs. Examples of types of permissible aid which may include operating aid are aid of a social character (section 10.3.1.1 above), aid for start-up airlines (section 10.3.2.3 below), certain aid to airports which have been granted a temporary derogation from the prohibition of operating aid for a period of 10 years (section (4) below) and aid to fund services of a general economic interest (section 10.3.2.5 below).

10.3.2.2 Rescue and Restructuring Aid

Rescue and restructuring aid - which is granted to firms in financial difficulty - can be highly distortive of competition as it artificially keeps a company in the market that would otherwise have exited. The years following the liberalisation of air transport from the early 1990s onwards saw substantial aid to rescue and/or restructure the major flag carrier airlines given the removal of commercial restrictions on and application of competition law to air transport in the EU.[678] The Commission issued guidelines in 1994 for the assessment of such funding, but these were revised in 2014 so as to make the rules more strict, for example as regards the definition of firms in difficulty, the requirement of a well-defined common interest for the grant of aid and requiring greater funding by the recipient of aid (discussed below).[679]

In general, rescue and/or restructuring aid to firms in difficulty may be authorised by the Commission, but subject to conditions to ensure that aid is granted only to companies that have a realistic prospect of viability and that take measures to alleviate the distortions of competition brought about by the State support. A firm is-regarded as being in difficulty where, without State intervention, it would almost certainly be condemned to go out of business in the short or medium term.[680] A company will be ineligible for rescue and/or restructuring aid in the first three years from its creation.[681]

Rescue aid is by nature temporary assistance, the purpose of which is to keep an ailing firm afloat for the time needed to work out a restructuring or liquidation plan. In accordance with the R&R Guidelines rescue aid may only be granted in the form of loans at market rates which must be repaid, or guarantees which must be terminated, at the end of the rescue period which cannot exceed six months.[682] The measures must have no adverse effects on other Member States and must be accompanied by an undertaking to submit a restructuring plan or a liquidation plan or proof that the loan

678. These included Sabena, Iberia, Aer Lingus, TAP, Air France, Olympic Airways, Alitalia, and later, in 2009, Austrian Airlines pre-merger with Lufthansa. Airlines in other Member States have latterly been granted such aid.
679. Communication from the Commission - Guidelines on State aid for rescuing and restructuring non-financial undertakings in difficulty OJ C 249, 31.7.2014, pp. 1–28 ('R&R Guidelines').
680. *See* R&R Guidelines para. 20(a)-(d)
681. *Ibid.*, para. 21.
682. *Ibid.*, para. 55.

has been repaid and/or any guarantee granted has been terminated. The Commission endeavours to reach a decision within one month from the notification of such aid.[683]

Restructuring aid, involves permanent assistance and is granted only where there is a feasible plan to restore long-term viability, such as asset sales, reductions in capacity and/or workforce, while minimising the distortion of competition.[684] Restructuring aid can take any form, whether loans, capital injections, equity participation of the State, and can be particularly contentious, with challenges by competitors arguing that less efficient firms are surviving with the benefit of State aid. There is a 'one time, last time' principle, whereby there can be no further restructuring aid for at least 10 years.[685] This does not, however, prevent an undertaking which has received rescue aid from subsequently being granted restructuring aid, or vice versa. Aid granted to Sabena in 2001 in the form of a bridging loan from the Belgian Government was acceptable as rescue aid, even though it had already benefited from restructuring aid. The aid, however, could not be used for restructuring, so as to recapitalise the company.[686]

There was a breach of the 'one time, last time' principle in the case of Alitalia which was the subject of a Commission decision ordering recovery of a loan of EUR 300 million by the Italian State to Alitalia in 2008. Previous aid of EUR 1.4 billion had been authorised in 1997, with a further capital increase in 2001 and rescue aid of EUR 400 million loan in 2004. The EUR 300 million loan was found not to meet the market investor principle, the State not acting as a prudent shareholder, and it breached the 'one time, last time' rule, restructuring and rescue aid having been granted in 2001 and in 2004, respectively.

Following the Commission decision in Alitalia requiring repayment of the loan, there was a special administration procedure involving the sale of Alitalia's assets to a new company CAI. The Commission concluded that the loan was recoverable from Alitalia, not CAI, on the basis that the sale did not involve aid, being subject to independent valuation, nor was there continuity between the two companies, and the new company would reduce capacity.[687] Issues were similarly resolved in the case of Olympic Airways, where conditions on the authorisation aid of EUR 2 billion in 1994 were breached, leading to Commission enforcement action, and findings that further aid had been granted. In 2008, the airline was privatised, with 65 per cent of flight

683. Commission Notice on a simplified procedure for treatment of certain types of State Aid OJ C 136, 16.6.2009, p. 3 – on the basis that meeting all substantive conditions the R&R Guidelines, notably a threshold of **EUR** 10 million and the implementation of a restructuring plan approved by the Commission – paras 121–123.

684. R&R Guidelines paras 78–82.

685. *Ibid.*, paras 70–75.

686. Commission Press Release IP/01/1432, 17 October 2001. Sabena went into liquidation before the aid in the form of **EUR** 125 million was used and it was allocated as rescue aid to a wholly owned subsidiary, *see* Commission Press Release IP/01/1558 9 November 2001.

687. Commission Decision 2009/155/EC of 12 November 2008 on the loan of EUR 300 million granted by Italy to Alitalia No. 26/8 (OJ 2009 L 52 p3) and Decision C(2008) 6745 final 12 November 2008, concerning State aid (N 510/2008 – Italy - Sale of assets if the airline Alitalia; upheld on appeal by General Court Case T-123/09 Ryanair *v.* Commission ECR [2012] 164, and by Court of Justice Case C-287/12 P Ryanair *v.* Commission 13 June 2013. *See* European State Aid Law Quarterly 2014 Vol. 13 Issue 1 p. 98 Milligan, Sales.

capacity, groundhandling and maintenance operations being transferred to new entities, the remaining parts being liquidated.[688]

A further restructuring case involving a major airline was the privatisation of Austrian Airlines in 2009, with the Austrian State recapitalising the airline with EUR 500 million to compensate the buyer, Lufthansa, for the high level of debt. Bankruptcy would have been a cheaper option, so the cash injection constituted 'aid'. This was authorised on the basis that the aid was kept to the minimum required and there was a reduction in capacity.[689]

It is a requirement that in any restructuring, the recipient, its shareholders, creditors of the group or new investors, make a significant contribution to the restructuring costs, which should be comparable to the aid in terms of the effects on the recipient's position. The R&R Guidelines indicate that a threshold of 50 per cent of the restructuring would normally be required, unless in exceptional cases where the government in question can demonstrate particular hardship.[690] The R&R Guidelines also require that if the restructuring plan succeeds, the State must receive a fair share of the benefits.

Recent decisions prohibiting the grant of restructuring aid include aid to Cyprus Airways and Estonian air, concluded that repeated support breached the 'one time, last time' principle, that the airlines had no credible plans ensuring their long-term viability and, in the case of Cyprus Airways, it did not provide a sufficient own contribution to the restructuring.[691] Restructuring aid has been authorised in favour of Adria Airways, airBaltic, Air Malta and LOT Polish Airlines.[692]

Commission State aid Decisions include, in chronological order (*see* Shawcross & Beaumont Air law 4th edition (2015), Chapter 41, for summaries): Sabena,[693] Iberia,[694] Aer Lingus,[695] TAP,[696] Air France,[697] Olympic,[698] Sabena,[699] LTU,[700] Alitalia,[701] Cyprus

688. Commission Press Release IP/08/1336, 17 September 2008.
689. Commission Decision of 28 August 2009 on State aid C 6/09 (ex N 663/08) — Austria Austrian Airlines — Restructuring Plan (notified under document C(2009) 6686) OJ L 59, 9.3.2010, pp. 1-38; upheld, along with Commission decision approving the merger, by General Court in Cases T-511/09 and T-162/10 Niki Luftfahrt GmbH *v.* Commission 13 May 2015.
690. R&R Guidelines paras 62-64.
691. Commission Press Releases IP/15/3121 9 January 2015, IP/15/6023 7 November 2015.
692. *See* Commission Competition Policy Brief Issue 10 July 2014.
693. Commission Decision of 24 July 1991, OJ L 300/48.
694. Commission press release IP(92) 606.
695. Commission Decision of 21 December 1993, OJ L 54/30.
696. Commission Decision of 6 July 1994, OJ L 279/29.
697. Commission Decision of 27 July 1994, OJ L 254/73 (decision annulled by ECJ, but aid decision amended and aid granted).
698. Commission Decision of 7 October 1994, OJ L 273/22 (and *see* discussion above in this section).
699. Commission Decision of 20 October 2001, OJ C 67/14, 17.3.2004; case N 636/2004.
700. Commission Decisions of 20 December 2001, OJ C 68/20 2003; case N 723/2001, 19 March 2003, OJ C 148/8 2003.
701. Commission Decision of 20 July 2004, OJ C 125/6; case N279/2004 (and *see* discussion in this section).

Airways,[702] Volare,[703] Alpi Eagles,[704] Austrian Airlines,[705] Air Malta,[706] Czech Airlines,[707] Malév,[708] Adria Airways,[709] LOT Polish Airlines,[710] airBaltic,[711] Blue Panorama Airlines[712] and Estonian Air.[713]

10.3.2.3 *Arrangements Between Airports and Airlines:* Start-Up Aid

Where an airport has public resources at its disposal, the existence of aid to an airline can be excluded where the arrangement satisfies the market economy operator test. This will be the case if the price for airport services corresponds to the market price or it can be demonstrated through an *ex ante* analysis that the arrangement will generate a profit for the airport.[714] The Aviation Guidelines offer further specific guidance on arrangements entered into by regional airports, which are predominantly publicly owned. The leading case where these issues first arose is discussed below:

(1) Start-Up Aid to Airlines: Charleroi Case

In 2004, the Commission widely interpreted the notion of 'aid' so as to prohibit favourable deals between low-cost airlines and smaller airports or regional authorities,[715] but following the decision of the General Court in *Ryanair v. Commission*,[716] reflected by the Aviation Guidelines, it is now clear that such arrangements may fall outside the definition of 'aid' if the market investor principle is satisfied.

Acting on a complaint from Brussels Airport, the Commission investigated the deal with the Walloon Region, which granted Ryanair a reduction of some 50 per cent on landing charges as compared with the standard level and undertook to compensate

702. Commission Decisions of 3 May 2005, OJ C 191/4, case N 69/2005; of 7 March 2007, OJ l 49/25, 22.2.2008; case C 10/2006; of 27 June 2012, OJ C 230/1, case SA 32523; of 6 March 2013, OJ C 152/12, 30.5.2013, case SA 35888; Case SA 38225; Case SA 37220; Commission Decisions of 4 February 2014, OJ C 117/125; of 9 January 2015, OJ L 179/83.
703. Commission Decision of 8 March 2006, OJ C 204/3; case N512/2005.
704. Commission Decision of 12 November 2008, OJ C 53/2 2009; case N388/2008.
705. Commission Decisions of 19 January 2009; case NN 72/2009 and 28 August 2009, OJ L 59/1; case C 6/2009.
706. Commission Decisions of 15 November 2011, OJ C 102/4 2011; case N 504/2010 and of 27 June 2012, OJ L 301/29 2012; case SA.33015.
707. Commission Decision of 19 September 2012, OJ L 92/16 2013; case SA.30908.
708. Commission Decision of 9 January 2012, OJ L 92/1.
709. Commission Decision of 9 July 2014; case SA 32715.
710. Commission Decision of 15 May 2013, OJ C 204/4; case SA 35900; OJ C 37/55 2014; Commission Decision of 29 July 2014; case SA 36874.
711. Commission Decision of 20.11.2012, OJ C 69/40, 8.3.2013; Commission Decision of 9 July 2014; case SA 34191.
712. Commission Decision of 11 June 2014, OJ C/251, 1.8.2014; case SA.38634.
713. Commission Decision of 7 November 2015; cases SA.35956 and SA.36868, Commission press release IP/15/6023.
714. Aviation Guidelines para. 53.
715. Commission Decision 2004/393/EC of 12 February 2004 concerning advantages granted by the Walloon Region and Brussels South Charleroi Airport to the airline Ryanair in connection with its establishment at Charleroi OJ L 137 30.4.2004 p. 1 (the 'Charleroi case').
716. T-196/04 – Ryanair *v.* Commission ECR [2008] II 3643.

Ryanair for any loss of profit arising from any subsequent change in airport charges. Ryanair undertook to base between two and four aircraft at Charleroi Airport and to operate, over a 15-year period, at least three rotations a day per aircraft, in return for which the airport manager BSCA (controlled by the Walloon Region) undertook to contribute to the costs incurred by Ryanair in establishing its base and to invoice Ryanair 1 EUR per passenger for the provision of groundhandling services, rather than 10 EUR collected for those services from other users.

The Commission found that the reduced airport charges placed Ryanair in a more advantageous position than its competitors flying out of Charleroi, while the compensation guarantee allowed it to operate in a commercial environment which was safe from any commercial risk. The Commission decided, in particular, that the Walloon Region had entered into the agreement with Ryanair in its capacity as a public authority, and that its role in that agreement could not be examined by applying the market economy investor principle. According to that principle, a State measure does not constitute State aid where the advantage received by recipient undertaking is one which it could have obtained under normal market conditions. That principle cannot be applied if the State acts in its capacity as a public authority, when its conduct can never be compared to that of a private operator in a market economy. On this basis, the advantages constituted State aid which could distort competition and the Commission ordered that Charleroi Airport demand repayment of the aid, quantified at EUR 4 million. Following the case, the Commission issued Guidelines on financing of airports and start-up aid to airlines departing from regional airports 2005.[717]

On appeal, the Commission's decision was annulled by the General Court in 2008, on the grounds that the Walloon Region's fixing of landing charges and the accompanying indemnity were directly connected with the management of airport infrastructure, which constituted an economic activity, so that the private investor test should apply. The Court held that the airport charges were to be regarded as consideration for services rendered at Charleroi Airport and it remitted the case to the Commission to consider in the light of the private investor principle.

The Charleroi aid was eventually approved by the Commission in 2014.[718] The Commission had a significant number of similar investigations related to these issues which had to be assessed in the light of the market economy investor principle. The Commission's approach to such aid is now set out in the Aviation Guidelines paragraphs 138–155 discussed below.

(2) Aviation Guidelines Provisions on Aid to Start-Up Routes

The Aviation Guidelines now lay down principles for the assessment of such aid, replacing those set out in the 2005 Guidelines, and these have been applied in the assessment of a number of cases. To determine whether arrangements involve State aid, the market economy operator test applies, with it having to be demonstrated that

717. OJ C 312, 9.12.2005, pp. 1–14.
718. Commission Decision of 1 October 2014 concerning measures SA.14093 implemented by Belgium in favour of Brussels South Charleroi Airport and Ryanair.

the revenue from the airline's operations (airport charges and non-aeronautical revenues) at the airport will cover the costs of the arrangements with the airline, with a reasonable profit margin. Where arrangements involve aid, the Guidelines provide that start-up aid will be permitted where it increases the connectivity of the regions by opening new routes, or facilitates regional development of remote regions. If there is a high-speed rail link on the route in question or services from another airport in the same catchment area, set at around 100 kilometres or around 60 minutes travelling time by car, bus, train or high-speed train from the airport in question, this will not be the case.[719]

Airlines operating at airports with fewer than 3 million passengers per year may receive start-up aid for three years following the launching of a new route. Aid for airports serving 3–5 million passengers will only exceptionally be considered compatible with the internal market. Start-up aid for routes in a remote region may be permitted irrespective of the size of the airport concerned, however. The aid may cover up to 50 per cent of the airport charges and should be allocated on a non-discriminatory basis.[720]

As regards notification, the Commission encourages Member States to notify national schemes rather than individual airport measures, with the exception of airports of 3–5 million passengers not located in remote areas, which must be notified individually.[721]

10.3.2.4 State Aid to Airports

Following the *Aéroports de Paris* case, the provision of airport services to airlines and service providers in exchange for airport charges has been considered to be an economic activity. Since that case, therefore, public financing of such activities, as well as the construction or upgrade of airport infrastructure which is commercially exploited is considered to be an economic activity, and therefore, must comply with the State aid rules.[722] Public – non-economic – functions such as air-traffic control, police and customs will be outside the scope of the rules (*see also* section 10.2.1.1 above and generally Chapter 4 section 4.2.3).[723] The principles on the grant of aid to airports are outlined below.

---

719. Aviation Guidelines paras 25, 138–140, 151.
720. *Ibid.*, para. 152.
721. *Ibid.*, paras 154–155.
722. Case T-128/98 Aéroports de Paris *v.* Commission ECR [2000] II 3929; Communication from the Commission — Guidelines on State aid to airports and airlines OJ C 99, 4.4.2014, pp. 3–34 ('Aviation Guidelines 2014'); Joined Cases T-443/08 and T-455/08 Mitteldeutsche Flughafen AG and Flughafen Leipzig Halle GmbH *v.* Commission, ('Leipzig-Halle airport' judgment), [2011] ECR II 1311, in particular paras 93 and 94; Case T-196/04 Ryanair *v.* Commission [2008] ECR II-3643; Aid to Berlin Brandenburg airport SA.41342, 3 August 2016 – cleared on the basis of the market economy investor principle hence no aid.
723. *Ibid., see also* Aviation Guidelines para. 35; Commission Notice on the notion of State aid as referred to in Article 107(1) of the Treaty on the Functioning of the European Union OJ C 262, 19.7.2016, p. 1 paras 201–209, 214.

Investment aid to airports may be permitted for costs relating to construction costs of airport infrastructure (excluding non-aeronautical activities[724]) which the market cannot deliver. The funding gap is considered greatest for smaller airports. On this basis, the Aviation Guidelines provide that the proportion of costs relating to the investments (aid intensity) shall not exceed 25 per cent in the case of airports handling 3–5 million passengers per year, 50 per cent for airports handling 1–3 million passengers, and 75 per cent for airports handling less than 1 million passengers (potentially more in exceptional circumstances). These may be increased by 20 per cent if the airport is in a remote region.[725]

For airports handling more than 5 million passengers, aid may be permissible in only very exceptional circumstances where there is a clear market failure and other external factors.[726] To be eligible for aid, the infrastructure must contribute to the connectivity of regions, combat traffic congestion at major hub airports or facilitate regional development. Investment to create unused capacity infrastructure, namely, within the catchment of an existing airport which has capacity, is unlikely to be permitted, therefore.[727] If aid is granted, the airport must be available to interested users on non-discriminatory terms.[728] The guidelines lay down provisions on the notification of aid to the Commission.[729]

Operating aid. In the case of airports serving less than 3 million passengers a year, the Commission has required that operating aid must be phased out by the end of a transitional period of 10 years ending in April 2024, with a business plan submitted to the Commission to assess the aid. The maximum aid that may be granted is 50 per cent of operating costs.[730] Aid after this date will not be permitted, unless it falls within the rules applicable to financing of services of a general economic interest.[731] To be permissible, it has to be shown that the services contribute to the objectives of connectivity described in relation to investment aid and that the airport does not fall within the catchment area of another airport.

In the case of airports serving up to 700,000 passengers per year, aid may be granted up to a higher limit of 80 per cent of the funding gap, for a period of five years.[732]

724. Aviation Guidelines paras 97–98.
725. *Ibid.*, para. 100–103.
726. *Ibid.*, para. 105.
727. *Ibid.*, para. 106; *see also* Commission decision prohibiting aid of EUR 47 million by Germany to Zweibrucken airport, on the basis it duplicated capacity provided by another airport located 40 km away. Commission Press Release MEMO 14-544 1 October 2014.
728. *Ibid.*, para. 108.
729. *Ibid.*, para. 111.
730. *See* Commission Press Release IP/15/474 1 7 April 2015 – authorisation of aid to certain French airports.
731. Aviation Guidelines paras 121, 127–129.
732. *Ibid.*, para. 130.

10.3.2.5 Services of General Economic Interest (*SGEI*): *Article 106(2) TFEU*

An exception to the prohibition of operating aid is State aid intended to support the operation of SGEI – such as air transport services on public service obligation (PSO) routes, or management of airports in peripheral and/or sparsely populated regions. These may fall outside Article 107(1) on the basis that no economic advantage is conferred. Article 106(2) provides:

> *Undertakings entrusted with the operation of services of general economic interest*[733]*... shall be subject to the rules contained in the Treaties, in particular to the rules on competition, in so far as the application of such rules does not obstruct the performance, in law or in fact, of the particular tasks assigned to them.*[734] *The development of trade must not be affected to such an extent as would be contrary to the interests of the Union*

According to the *Altmark* case,[735] where public subsidies are granted to undertakings expressly required to discharge public service obligations in order to compensate for the costs incurred in discharging those obligations, the existence of an economic advantage may be excluded if they comply with the following principles:

(i) the project is necessary for the provision of services that can be considered as genuine services of general economic interest (SGEI) for which the public service obligations (PSO) have been clearly defined. As regards air transport services, a PSO can only be imposed under Regulation 1008/2008[736] and only in respect of a route where transport needs cannot be fulfilled by an existing air route or other means of transport. Article 16(1) provides that a Member State may impose a PSO 'in respect of scheduled air services between an airport in the EU and an airport serving a peripheral or development region in its territory or on a thin route to any airport on its territory any such route being considered vital for the economic and social development of the region which the airport serves.'[737] As regards airports, this would be possible if the area to be served (such as islands or peripheral regions) would otherwise be isolated to an extent that it would prejudice its social and economic development.[738]

733. There must be a measure entrusting the undertaking with the operation of the service in question, *see* Case 127/73 Belgische Radio en Televisie v SABAM [1974] ECR 313.
734. The burden of proof that the performance of the service would be obstructed is on the undertaking and the requirement is strictly construed, it not being sufficient that the performance of the tasks would be merely hindered or made more difficult: Case T-260/94 Air Inter v Commission [1997] ECR II 997.
735. Case C-280/00 Altmark Trans and Regierungspräsidium Magdeburg GmbH [2003] ECR I-7747, paras 89–93; Communication from the Commission on the application of the European Union State aid rules to compensation granted for the provision of services of general economic interest, OJ C 8, 11.1.2012, p. 4.
736. Council Regulation 1008/2008 of 24 September 2008 on common rules for the operation of air services in the Community (Recast) OJ L 293, 31.10.2008, pp. 3–20, Articles 15–17.
737. *See also* Aviation Guidelines paras 69–70.
738. *Ibid.*, para. 72.

(ii) the parameters of compensation have been established in advance in an objective and transparent manner;

(iii) there is no compensation paid beyond the net costs of providing the public service and a reasonable profit;[739] and

(iv) the SGEI have been either assigned through a public procurement procedure that ensures the provision of the service at the least cost to the community or the compensation does not exceed what an efficient company would require.[740]

If any one of the *Altmark* criteria is not fulfilled, public service compensation provides an economic advantage to its recipient and may constitute State aid within the meaning of Article 107(1). Such aid may nevertheless be compatible with the internal market under Article 106(2). Further, notification will not be required if the requirements set out in the Commission Decision 2012/21 are met. This covers public service compensation granted to: (i) airports where the average annual traffic does not exceed 200,000 passengers over the duration of the SGEI entrustment; and (ii) airlines, as regards air links to islands where the average annual traffic does not exceed 300,000 passengers.[741]

Finally, there is a *de minimis* exemption for SGEI of aid of up to EUR 500,000 per undertaking over a three-year period.[742]

The Aviation Guidelines also provide for the award of public service compensation for the management of an airport, provided it serves areas that would otherwise be isolated from the rest of the EU to an extent detrimental to their development.[743]

10.4 GENERAL BLOCK EXEMPTION REGULATION: PROPOSED EXTENSION TO AIRPORTS

The most significant block exemption under the EU State rules is EU State Aid General Block Exemption Regulation 651/2014 (the 'GBER').[744] This has limited application to air transport but is discussed briefly given there are proposals to extend it to aid to airports.

739. *See also* Council Regulation 1008/2008, Article 17(8).
740. Regulation 1008/2008 requires that the right may be granted only through a public procurement process (Article 17). *See also* Commission Communication on the application of the European Union State aid rules to compensation granted for the provision of services of general economic interest OJ C 8 of 11.1.2012, p. 4.
741. Commission Decision 2012/21 of 20 December 2011 on the application of Article 106(2) of the Treaty on the Functioning of the European Union to State aid in the form of public service compensation granted to certain undertakings entrusted with the operation of services of general economic interest OJ L 7, 11.1.2012, p. 3; Aviation Guidelines para. 74–76.
742. Commission Regulation (EU) No. 360/2012 of 25 April 2012 on the application of Articles 107 and 108 of the Treaty on the Functioning of the European Union to *de minimis* aid granted to undertakings providing services of general economic interest, OJ L 114, 26.4.2012, pp. 8–13.
743. Aviation Guidelines para. 72.
744. Commission Regulation (EU) No. 651/2014 of 17 June 2014 declaring certain categories of aid compatible with the internal market in application of Articles 107 and 108 of the Treaty OJ L 187, 26.6.2014, pp. 1–78.

The Commission adopted a revised GBER in 2014 as part of its State aid modernisation. This declares certain aid measures compatible with the internal market and exempt from prior notification to the Commission, so as to reduce the administrative burden and costs, and the number of notifications handled by the Commission, and to speed up the implementation of projects. The criteria of the GBER specify, in particular, eligible beneficiaries, maximum aid intensities (i.e., the maximum proportion of the eligible costs of a project that can benefit from State aid) and eligible expenses. These criteria are derived from the Commission's decision-making practice. The GBER does not apply to aid to air transport, save to the extent some other category of aid, such as training aid, is granted to entities in the air transport field. This was stated to be due to the Commission's lack of experience in the area but Recital 1 to the GBER provided that the Commission envisaged including ports and airports in the GBER as soon as sufficient case experience has been collected. The proposed new provisions are GBER will, if adopted, apply to regional airports with annual passenger traffic of up to 3 million.[745]

10.5 PROCEDURE AND ENFORCEMENT: ARTICLE 108

Article 108 TFEU sets out the principles for notification and enforcement of the State aid rules and Council Regulation 2015/1589 (the 'Procedural Regulation') lays down the rules for the application of Article 108, such as review and investigation of aid, notification of aid and recovery of incompatible aid.[746]

Article 108 provides:

> *1. The Commission shall, in cooperation with Member States, keep under constant review all systems of aid existing in those States. It shall propose to the latter any appropriate measures required by the progressive development or by the functioning of the internal market.*
>
> *2. If, after giving notice to the parties concerned to submit their comments, the Commission finds that aid granted by a State or through State resources is not compatible with the internal market having regard to Article 107, or that such aid is being misused, it shall decide that the State concerned shall abolish or alter such aid within a period of time to be determined by the Commission.*
>
> *If the State concerned does not comply with this decision within the prescribed time, the Commission or any other interested State may, in derogation from the provisions of Articles 258 and 259, refer the matter to the Court of Justice of the European Union direct.*
>
> *On application by a Member State, the Council may, acting unanimously, decide that aid which that State is granting or intends to grant shall be considered to be compatible with the internal market, in derogation from the provisions of Article 107 or from the regulations provided for in Article 109, if such a decision is justified*

745. The draft amending Regulation is available at: http://ec.europa.eu/competition/consultations/2016_gber_review/index_en.html.

746. Council Regulation (EU) 2015/1589 of 13 July 2015 laying down detailed rules for the application of Article 108 of the Treaty on the Functioning of the European Union OJ L 248, 24.9.2015, p. 9.

> *by exceptional circumstances. If, as regards the aid in question, the Commission has already initiated the procedure provided for in the first subparagraph of this paragraph, the fact that the State concerned has made its application to the Council shall have the effect of suspending that procedure until the Council has made its attitude known.*
>
> *If, however, the Council has not made its attitude known within three months of the said application being made, the Commission shall give its decision on the case.*
>
> *3. The Commission shall be informed, in sufficient time to enable it to submit its comments, of any plans to grant or alter aid. If it considers that any such plan is not compatible with the internal market having regard to Article 107, it shall without delay initiate the procedure provided for in paragraph 2. The Member State concerned shall not put its proposed measures into effect until this procedure has resulted in a final decision.*
>
> *4. The Commission may adopt regulations relating to the categories of State aid that the Council has, pursuant to Article 109, determined may be exempted from the procedure provided for by paragraph 3 of this Article*

10.5.1 Notification of Aid: Article 108(3)

The EU State aid rules require prior notification of any aid to the Commission, and Member States must wait for approval before aid can be put into effect. There are exceptions to the requirement that aid be notified but in the air transport sector they are currently very limited, the principal exceptions being small amounts aid within the *de minimis* thresholds (discussed above at section 10.2.2) and SGEI cases (discussed above at section 10.3.2.5).

From receipt of notification, the Commission has two months (one month in the case of rescue aid) in which to issue a decision either approving the aid or stating that a formal investigation will be carried out as to whether the aid being granted is 'compatible with the internal market' within the meaning of Article 107(3). Notification will be preceded by discussions between the Member State and the Commission. The Commission issues a Notice in the Official Journal of the EU to inform other Member States and interested parties. This further investigation can take up to 18 months, or longer if agreed with the Member State.

10.5.2 Commission Review of Unnotified and Existing Aid

Article 108(3) prohibits Member States from putting State aid into effect without prior Commission approval. Such aid will be unlawful. Article 108(1) requires the Commission, whether of its own initiative or following a complaint, to investigate unlawful aid – aid which has not been notified [747] – and to monitor existing aids, in case aid which it has authorised has been misused or the terms of the authorisation breached.[748]

747. Procedural Regulation, *supra*, Article 12.
748. *Ibid.* Article 21.

Under Regulation 2015/1589[749] the Commission has powers to request information from Member States and beneficiaries of aid and to conduct site visits to gather information.[750] It can also suspend unlawful aid and order provisional recovery pending the outcome of its investigation, as well as order recovery of aid found to breach Article 107 (*see* section 10.5.3 below).

Since unlawfulness refers to procedural issues only (non-notification), it is still possible that the measure may be assessed as compatible and the aid therefore be approved. This is a question which the Commission has sole competence to determine.[751]

10.5.3 Recovery of Aid

Where aid is not notified and is subsequently found to be illegal (or existing aid misused) under Article 108(3), the Commission issues a decision finding that aid breaches the State aid rules and requires the Member State to recover the aid with interest payable from the date on which the unlawful aid was granted until the date of its recovery.[752] The purpose of the recovery is to re-establish the situation that existed on the market prior to the granting of the aid. There is a substantial time limit of 10 years from the grant of aid for a decision ordering recovery.[753] If the Commission orders a Member State to recover aid, it must implement the decision in accordance with national law, but must not apply national laws if they stand in the way of effective and immediate implementation of the Commission decision.[754] The Commission referred France to the Court of Justice under Article 108(2), however, for failure to implement a decision ordering it to recover aid which it decided had been illegally granted to Ryanair by three airports. While the French authorities had sent out recovery demands, they were unable to execute them due to French laws under which recovery orders are automatically suspended if there are appeals. Under EU law, the appeals do not have a suspensory effect, meaning France would be obliged to recover the aid. [755]

749. *Supra.*
750. Articles 10 and 20. In the latter case, the Commission has power to make on-site monitoring visits.
751. Joined Cases C-261/01 and C-262/01 van Calster and Others [2003] ECR I 12249, para. 75; Case C-284/12, Deutsche Lufthansa AG v Flughafen Frankfurt-Hahn GmbH, 21 November 2013, para. 28.
752. *See* Council Regulation (EC) No. 2015/1589 of 13 July 2015 laying down detailed rules for the application of Article 108 TFEU – the Procedural Regulation. Article 16. The Commission has published the 'Recovery Notice: Towards an effective implementation of Commission decisions ordering Member States to recover unlawful and incompatible State aid; Commission Regulation (EC) 271/2008 lays down rules with respect to the method for fixing the recovery interest rate; rates are published on the Commission website: http://ec.europa.eu/competition/state_aid/legislation/base_rates_eu28tris_en.pdf) from the aid recipient.)
753. Procedural Regulation, Article 17.
754. *Ibid.* Article 16(3).
755. Commission Press Release IP/15/5442 27 July 2015.

If the recipient is unable to repay the funds, the Member State is in practice obliged to institute winding-up proceedings and pursue the recipient as an unsecured creditor.[756] In certain cases where orders for recovery of aid have been made in restructuring cases, the aid recipient's assets have been transferred to a new entity, without circumventing the obligation to recover aid illegally granted (*see* section 10.3.2.2).[757]

10.5.4 Role of National Courts

Only the Commission, subject to review by the General Court and Court of Justice, can adjudicate on the compatibility of aid with the internal market. Article 108(3), which requires the notification of aid, is directly effective, however, and can, therefore, be invoked directly by individuals who may sue in the national courts to challenge aid which either has not been notified or has been paid before securing Commission approval.[758] In such a case, the remit of the national court is to determine if 'aid' has been granted, and if so, it must order the cessation and recovery of the unnotified aid, save in exceptional circumstances.[759] Unnotified aid is not automatically incompatible with the internal market, but as the question of incompatibility is a separate question, that does not prevent national courts overturning unnotified aid.[760]

To determine whether a particular measure constitutes 'aid' within the meaning of Article 107 can be a complex exercise for a national court. The Procedural Regulation, therefore, enables national courts to ask the Commission for information or for its opinion on points concerning the application of the State aid rules, though this does not legally bind the national courts.[761] The scope of the national court's obligations in dealing with such a case has been clarified by the Court of Justice on a preliminary ruling requested by the German court in the case of Frankfurt-Hahn airport (FFH), Lufthansa AG *v.* Flughafen Frankfurt-Hahn GmbH.[762] FFH, a public company majority owned by the German Government, had a package of arrangements with Ryanair, which was responsible for 95 per cent of its traffic, comprising reduced fees and marketing support for the opening of new routes. Lufthansa challenged the measures before the national court, asking it to order cessation and recovery from Ryanair of aid which the airport had allegedly paid.

The Commission then commenced a formal investigation under Article 108(2), having reached a preliminary opinion that the measures (which also included grants and a guarantee by the regional authority to FFH), constituted 'aid'. The national court, given its duty to consider whether the measures constituted State aid, then requested

756. Case C-499/99, Commission *v.* Spain, [2002] ECR I-06301; Commission Recovery Notice *supra*, para. 20. Such proceedings may not be required if recovery is an absolute impossibility, namely, where the recipient has no assets.
757. *See* discussion of Alitalia, Olympic and Sabena cases at section 10.3.2.2 above.
758. Case C-301/87 France *v.* Commission (Boussac), [1990] ECR I-307.
759. *See also* Commission notice on the enforcement of State aid law by national courts OJ C 85, 9.4.2009, pp. 1–22.
760. Ibid, para. 30.
761. Procedural Regulation, recitals 37–38.
762. Case C-284/12, Deutsche Lufthansa AG *v.* Flughafen Frankfurt-Hahn GmbH, 21 November 2013.

a ruling from the Court of Justice as to whether, in proceedings for cessation and recovery of aid, it was bound by this preliminary opinion. The Court held that where the Commission had opened a formal investigation, the national court need not consider whether the measure in question constituted aid but could presume that it was aid, relying on the fact that a Commission investigation had been commenced. This would be the case even though the Commission has not reached a final view. The national court was required to '*adopt all the necessary measures with a view to drawing the appropriate conclusions from an infringement of the obligation to suspend the implementation of that measure*'.[763] It follows that a national court may order the cessation and recovery of allegedly unlawful State aid where the Commission has launched an investigation. Where no such investigation has been commenced, it is then for the national court to consider whether the measures constitute State aid - in particular whether they constitute an advantage and are selective.[764]

The FFH - Ryanair arrangements were ultimately found by the Commission to be compatible with the EU State aid rules on the basis that any differences in airport charges actually paid for the use of the infrastructure were based on commercially justified differentiation.[765] Aid to FFH in the form of a guarantee on loans was found to breach the State aid rules, however.[766] Lufthansa subsequently challenged the Commission's assessment that public grants given to FFH did not constitute illegal State aid and argued that State aid granted to the airport in the form of a guarantee on loans had in effect been passed on to Ryanair as the most important user of that airport.[767]

10.6 SUBSIDIES TO THIRD COUNTRY AIRLINES

The EU State rules do not apply to aid granted by third countries to airlines or airports within their territory, nor do the WTO rules apply in the air transport sector. Air transport continues to be excluded from the WTO General Agreement on Trade in Services (GATS), the Annex on Air Transport Services excluding traffic rights and traffic related services.[768]

10.6.1 Regulation 868/2004

To create a framework to protect the competitive position of EU carriers adversely affected by third country subsidies to airlines, the Council adopted Regulation

763. *Ibid.*, para. 45.
764. *Ibid.*, para. 34.
765. Commission Decision 2016/789 of 1 October 2014 on the State aid SA.21121 implemented by Germany concerning the financing of Frankfurt Hahn airport and the financial relations between the airport and Ryanair OJ L 134, 24.5.2016, p. 46.
766. Commission Decision of 1 October 2014 on the State aid SA.32833 implemented by Germany concerning the financing arrangements for Frankfurt Hahn airport put into place in 2009 to 2011).
767. Deutsche Lufthansa *v.* Commission (T-764/15).] Case T-764/15: Action brought on 29 December 2015 — Deutsche Lufthansa *v.* Commission OJ C 68, 22.2.2016, p. 43, pending.
768. WTO General Agreement on Trade in Services (GATs) Annex of Air Transport Services 1994.

868/2004 concerning protection against subsidisation and unfair pricing practices causing injury to EU air carriers in the supply of air services from countries not members of the EU.[769] The Regulation was prompted by significant subsidies granted by the US Government to airlines following the September 2001 events (*see* section 10.3.1.2 above, for a brief discussion of other EU measures).

Under this Regulation, an unfair pricing practice is deemed to exist on a particular service to or from the EU where non-EU carriers benefit from a non-commercial advantage, and charge air fares which are sufficiently below those offered by competing EU air carriers to cause injury.[770] Subsidies may be a financial contribution or the foregoing of revenue that would otherwise be due by the Government of the country in question.[771] Whether there is injury depends on evidence of the level of fares, the effect of such services on those offered by EU air carriers, and the impact of those services on the EU industry in terms of number of flights, utilisation of capacity, passenger bookings, market share, return on capital, investment and employment.[772]

Non-EU airlines can be subject to an investigation into an unfair pricing practice either following a written complaint to the Commission (the investigation to be commenced within 45 days of the complaint) or on its own initiative, if there is sufficient evidence of subsidies or unfair pricing practices, injury, and of course a causal link between the allegedly subsidised or unfairly priced air services and the alleged injury. This may be extended by 30 days if the issue is being discussed within the framework of a bilateral agreement with the country in question. The air carriers and Government concerned must be informed of the commencement of an investigation and be invited to make comments.[773]

The investigation must be carried out 'expeditiously' and normally be concluded within nine months of the initiation of proceedings.[774] If the Commission concludes that pricing is unfair, it can impose duties (provisional pending full investigation, or definitive following a full investigation, on the subsidised airlines equivalent to the damage suffered by European carriers. The 'redressive measures' imposed by the European Commission on the carrier guilty of the discriminatory practice cannot exceed the non-commercial advantage granted to the non-EU air carrier and can remain in force only as long as it is necessary to offset the subsidies or unfair pricing practices which are causing injury.[775]

This Regulation was never used, nor has any complaint concerning a non-EU carrier been made.[776] Difficulties in the application of the Regulation would include

769. OJ L162 30 April 2004, p. 1.
770. Regulation 868/2004, *supra,* Article 5.
771. *Ibid., see* generally Article 4.
772. *Ibid.* Article 6.
773. *Ibid.* Article 7.
774. *Ibid.* Article 8.
775. *Ibid.* Articles, 9, 10, 12.
776. In the shipping sector, the EU imposed duties on container cargoes transported from the EU to Australia by Hyundai, under Regulation 4057/86 of 22 December 1986 on unfair pricing practices in maritime transport OJ No. L 179, 11. 7. 1985, p. 4. *See* Council Regulation 15/89 of 4 January 1989 introducing a redressive duty on containerised cargo to be transported in liner service between the Community and Australia by Hyundai Merchant Marine Company Ltd of

matters such as proving the existence of subsidies or favourable treatment of a non-EU airline, and the ability in practice to carry out an investigation in the non-EU country in question given that consent of the government concerned would be required.

10.6.2 Consultation on Regulation 868/2004

In 2012, the Commission issued a Communication discussing the impact of foreign air carriers (including the Gulf carriers) and considering how best to ensure fair competition in international air transport.[777] This was followed by the launch of a consultation on revision or replacement of the Regulation, given it has appeared unsuitable for its purpose, with discussion of options such as dealing with the issue in the framework of air services with third countries.[778] A proposal for a revised Regulation is expected in 2017.

Seoul, Republic of Korea OJ L4 06/01/1989 p. 1. *See* generally EALA article: http://eala.aero/wp-content/uploads/2016/11/EU-Regulation-868-of-2004-Report-of-a-unilateral-approach-in-regulating-unfair-subsidisation-and-unfair-pricing-practies-and-its-failure.pdf.

777. Commission Communication COM (2012) 556 'The EU External Aviation Policy – Addressing Future Challenges' September 2012.

778. *See*: http://ec.europa.eu/smart-regulation/impact/planned_ia/docs/2014_move_009_unfair_pricing_practices_en.pdf.

Annexes

ANNEX I

TREATY ON THE FUNCTIONING OF THE EUROPEAN UNION – PROVISIONS ON COMPETITION AND STATE AID

Article 101

1. The following shall be prohibited as incompatible with the internal market: all agreements between undertakings, decisions by associations of undertakings and concerted practices which may affect trade between Member States and which have as their object or effect the prevention, restriction or distortion of competition within the internal market, and in particular those which:
   (a) directly or indirectly fix purchase or selling prices or any other trading conditions;
   (b) limit or control production, markets, technical development, or investment;
   (c) share markets or sources of supply;
   (d) apply dissimilar conditions to equivalent transactions with other trading parties, thereby placing them at a competitive disadvantage;
   (e) make the conclusion of contracts subject to acceptance by the other parties of supplementary obligations which, by their nature or according to commercial usage, have no connection with the subject of such contracts.
2. Any agreements or decisions prohibited pursuant to this Article shall be automatically void.
3. The provisions of paragraph 1 may, however, be declared inapplicable in the case of:
   - any agreement or category of agreements between undertakings,
   - any decision or category of decisions by associations of undertakings,

- any concerted practice or category of concerted practices, which contributes to improving the production or distribution of goods or to promoting technical or economic progress, while allowing consumers a fair share of the resulting benefit, and which does not:
  (a) impose on the undertakings concerned restrictions which are not indispensable to the attainment of these objectives;
  (b) afford such undertakings the possibility of eliminating competition in respect of a substantial part of the products in question.

Article 102

Any abuse by one or more undertakings of a dominant position within the internal market or in a substantial part of it shall be prohibited as incompatible with the internal market in so far as it may affect trade between Member States.

Such abuse may, in particular, consist in:

(a) directly or indirectly imposing unfair purchase or selling prices or other unfair trading conditions;
(b) limiting production, markets or technical development to the prejudice of consumers;
(c) applying dissimilar conditions to equivalent transactions with other trading parties, thereby placing them at a competitive disadvantage;
(d) making the conclusion of contracts subject to acceptance by the other parties of supplementary obligations which, by their nature or according to commercial usage, have no connection with the subject of such contracts.

Article 103

1. The appropriate regulations or directives to give effect to the principles set out in Articles 101 and 102 shall be laid down by the Council, on a proposal from the Commission and after consulting the European Parliament.
2. The regulations or directives referred to in paragraph 1 shall be designed in particular:
   (a) to ensure compliance with the prohibitions laid down in Article 101(1) and in Article 102 by making provision for fines and periodic penalty payments;
   (b) to lay down detailed rules for the application of Article 101(3), taking into account the need to ensure effective supervision on the one hand, and to simplify administration to the greatest possible extent on the other;
   (c) to define, if need be, in the various branches of the economy, the scope of the provisions of Articles 101 and 102;
   (d) to define the respective functions of the Commission and of the Court of Justice of the European Union in applying the provisions laid down in this paragraph;

(e) to determine the relationship between national laws and the provisions contained in this section or adopted pursuant to this Article.

Article 104

Until the entry into force of the provisions adopted in pursuance of Article 103, the authorities in

Member States shall rule on the admissibility of agreements, decisions and concerted practices and on abuse of a dominant position in the internal market in accordance with the law of their country and with the provisions of Article 101, in particular paragraph 3, and of Article 102.

Article 105

1. Without prejudice to Article 104, the Commission shall ensure the application of the principles laid down in Articles 101 and 102. On application by a Member State or on its own initiative, and in cooperation with the competent authorities in the Member States, which shall give it their assistance, the Commission shall investigate cases of suspected infringement of these principles. If it finds that there has been an infringement, it shall propose appropriate measures to bring it to an end.
2. If the infringement is not brought to an end, the Commission shall record such infringement of the principles in a reasoned decision. The Commission may publish its decision and authorise Member States to take the measures, the conditions and details of which it shall determine, needed to remedy the situation.
3. The Commission may adopt regulations relating to the categories of agreement in respect of which the Council has adopted a regulation or a directive pursuant to Article 103(2)(b).

Article 106

1. In the case of public undertakings and undertakings to which Member States grant special or exclusive rights, Member States shall neither enact nor maintain in force any measure contrary to the rules contained in the Treaties, in particular to those rules provided for in Article 18 and Articles 101 to 109.
2. Undertakings entrusted with the operation of services of general economic interest or having the character of a revenue-producing monopoly shall be subject to the rules contained in the Treaties, in particular to the rules on competition, in so far as the application of such rules does not obstruct the performance, in law or in fact, of the particular tasks assigned to them. The development of trade must not be affected to such an extent as would be contrary to the interests of the Union.

3. The Commission shall ensure the application of the provisions of this Article and shall, where necessary, address appropriate directives or decisions to Member States.

Article 107

1. Save as otherwise provided in the Treaties, any aid granted by a Member State or through State resources in any form whatsoever which distorts or threatens to distort competition by favouring certain undertakings or the production of certain goods shall, in so far as it affects trade between Member States, be incompatible with the internal market.
2. The following shall be compatible with the internal market:
   (a) aid having a social character, granted to individual consumers, provided that such aid is granted without discrimination related to the origin of the products concerned;
   (b) aid to make good the damage caused by natural disasters or exceptional occurrences;
   (c) aid granted to the economy of certain areas of the Federal Republic of Germany affected by the division of Germany, in so far as such aid is required in order to compensate for the economic disadvantages caused by that division. Five years after the entry into force of the Treaty of Lisbon, the Council, acting on a proposal from the Commission, may adopt a decision repealing this point.
3. The following may be considered to be compatible with the internal market:
   (a) aid to promote the economic development of areas where the standard of living is abnormally low or where there is serious underemployment, and of the regions referred to in Article 349, in view of their structural, economic and social situation;
   (b) aid to promote the execution of an important project of common European interest or to remedy a serious disturbance in the economy of a Member State;
   (c) aid to facilitate the development of certain economic activities or of certain economic areas, where such aid does not adversely affect trading conditions to an extent contrary to the common interest;
   (d) aid to promote culture and heritage conservation where such aid does not affect trading conditions and competition in the Union to an extent that is contrary to the common interest;
   (e) such other categories of aid as may be specified by decision of the Council on a proposal from the Commission.

Article 108

1. The Commission shall, in cooperation with Member States, keep under constant review all systems of aid existing in those States. It shall propose to

the latter any appropriate measures required by the progressive development or by the functioning of the internal market.

2. If, after giving notice to the parties concerned to submit their comments, the Commission finds that aid granted by a State or through State resources is not compatible with the internal market having regard to Article 107, or that such aid is being misused, it shall decide that the State concerned shall abolish or alter such aid within a period of time to be determined by the Commission.
If the State concerned does not comply with this decision within the prescribed time, the Commission or any other interested State may, in derogation from the provisions of Articles 258 and 259, refer the matter to the Court of Justice of the European Union direct.
On application by a Member State, the Council may, acting unanimously, decide that aid which that State is granting or intends to grant shall be considered to be compatible with the internal market, in derogation from the provisions of Article 107 or from the regulations provided for in Article 109, if such a decision is justified by exceptional circumstances. If, as regards the aid in question, the Commission has already initiated the procedure provided for in the first subparagraph of this paragraph, the fact that the State concerned has made its application to the Council shall have the effect of suspending that procedure until the Council has made its attitude known.
If, however, the Council has not made its attitude known within three months of the said application being made, the Commission shall give its decision on the case.
3. The Commission shall be informed, in sufficient time to enable it to submit its comments, of any plans to grant or alter aid. If it considers that any such plan is not compatible with the internal market having regard to Article 107, it shall without delay initiate the procedure provided for in paragraph 2. The Member State concerned shall not put its proposed measures into effect until this procedure has resulted in a final decision.
4. The Commission may adopt regulations relating to the categories of State aid that the Council has, pursuant to Article 109, determined may be exempted from the procedure provided for by paragraph 3 of this Article.

Article 109

The Council, on a proposal from the Commission and after consulting the European Parliament, may make any appropriate regulations for the application of Articles 107 and 108 and may in particular determine the conditions in which Article 108(3) shall apply and the categories of aid exempted from this procedure.

ANNEX II

OTHER RELEVANT PROVISIONS OF THE TREATY ON THE FUNCTIONING OF THE EUROPEAN UNION

COMPETENCES OF THE EUROPEAN UNION

Article 3

1. The Union shall have exclusive competence in the following areas:
   (a) customs union;
   (b) the establishing of the competition rules necessary for the functioning of the internal market;
   (c) monetary policy for the Member States whose currency is the euro;
   (d) the conservation of marine biological resources under the common fisheries policy;
   (e) common commercial policy.
2. The Union shall also have exclusive competence for the conclusion of an international agreement when its conclusion is provided for in a legislative act of the Union or is necessary to enable the Union to exercise its internal competence, or in so far as its conclusion may affect common rules or alter their scope.

SERVICES OF GENERAL ECONOMIC INTEREST

Article 14

Without prejudice to Article 4 of the Treaty on European Union or to Articles 93, 106 and 107 of this Treaty, and given the place occupied by services of general economic interest in the shared values of the Union as well as their role in promoting social and territorial cohesion, the Union and the Member States, each within their respective powers and within the scope of application of the Treaties, shall take care that such services operate on the basis of principles and conditions, particularly economic and financial conditions, which enable them to fulfil their missions. The European Parliament and the Council, acting by means of regulations in accordance with the ordinary legislative procedure, shall establish these principles and set these conditions without prejudice to the competence of Member States, in compliance with the Treaties, to provide, to commission and to fund such services.

FREEDOM OF ESTABLISHMENT

Article 49

Within the framework of the provisions set out below, restrictions on the freedom of establishment of nationals of a Member State in the territory of another Member State shall be prohibited. Such prohibition shall also apply to restrictions on the setting-up of agencies, branches or subsidiaries by nationals of any Member State established in the territory of any Member State.

Freedom of establishment shall include the right to take up and pursue activities as self-employed persons and to set up and manage undertakings, in particular companies or firms within the meaning of the second paragraph of Article 54, under the conditions laid down for its own nationals by the law of the country where such establishment is effected, subject to the provisions of the Chapter relating to capital.

Article 50

1. In order to attain freedom of establishment as regards a particular activity, the European Parliament and the Council, acting in accordance with the ordinary legislative procedure and after consulting the Economic and Social Committee, shall act by means of directives.
2. The European Parliament, the Council and the Commission shall carry out the duties devolving upon them under the preceding provisions, in particular:
   (a) by according, as a general rule, priority treatment to activities where freedom of establishment makes a particularly valuable contribution to the development of production and trade;
   (b) by ensuring close cooperation between the competent authorities in the Member States in order to ascertain the particular situation within the Union of the various activities concerned;
   (c) by abolishing those administrative procedures and practices, whether resulting from national legislation or from agreements previously concluded between Member States, the maintenance of which would form an obstacle to freedom of establishment;
   (d) by ensuring that workers of one Member State employed in the territory of another Member State may remain in that territory for the purpose of

taking up activities therein as self-employed persons, where they satisfy the conditions which they would be required to satisfy if they were entering that State at the time when they intended to take up such activities;

(e) by enabling a national of one Member State to acquire and use land and buildings situated in the territory of another Member State, in so far as this does not conflict with the principles laid down in Article 39(2);

(f) by effecting the progressive abolition of restrictions on freedom of establishment in every branch of activity under consideration, both as regards the conditions for setting up agencies, branches or subsidiaries in the territory of a Member State and as regards the subsidiaries in the territory of a Member State and as regards the conditions governing the entry of personnel belonging to the main establishment into managerial or supervisory posts in such agencies, branches or subsidiaries;

(g) by coordinating to the necessary extent the safeguards which, for the protection of the interests of members and others, are required by Member States of companies or firms within the meaning of the second paragraph of Article 54 with a view to making such safeguards equivalent throughout the Union;

(h) by satisfying themselves that the conditions of establishment are not distorted by aids granted by Member States.

ECONOMIC AND MONETARY POLICY

Article 119

1. For the purposes set out in Article 3 of the Treaty on European Union, the activities of the Member States and the Union shall include, as provided in the Treaties, the adoption of an economic policy which is based on the close coordination of Member States' economic policies, on the internal market and on the definition of common objectives, and conducted in accordance with the principle of an open market economy with free competition.
2. Concurrently with the foregoing, and as provided in the Treaties and in accordance with the procedures set out therein, these activities shall include a single currency, the euro, and the definition and conduct of a single monetary policy and exchange-rate policy the primary objective of both of which shall be to maintain price stability and, without prejudice to this objective, to support the general economic policies in the Union, in accordance with the principle of an open market economy with free competition.
3. These activities of the Member States and the Union shall entail compliance with the following guiding principles: stable prices, sound public finances and monetary conditions and a sustainable balance of payments.

ANNEX III
TREATY ON EUROPEAN UNION PROVISIONS

SINCERE COOPERATION – ARTICLE 4(3)

Article 4

1. In accordance with Article 5, competences not conferred upon the Union in the Treaties remain with the Member States.
2. The Union shall respect the equality of Member States before the Treaties as well as their national identities, inherent in their fundamental structures, political and constitutional, inclusive of regional and local self-government. It shall respect their essential State functions, including ensuring the territorial integrity of the State, maintaining law and order and safeguarding national security. In particular, national security remains the sole responsibility of each Member State.
3. Pursuant to the principle of sincere cooperation, the Union and the Member States shall, in full mutual respect, assist each other in carrying out tasks which flow from the Treaties.
   The Member States shall take any appropriate measure, general or particular, to ensure fulfilment of the obligations arising out of the Treaties or resulting from the acts of the institutions of the Union.
   The Member States shall facilitate the achievement of the Union's tasks and refrain from any measure which could jeopardise the attainment of the Union's objectives.

WITHDRAWAL FROM THE EUROPEAN UNION

Article 50

1. Any Member State may decide to withdraw from the Union in accordance with its own constitutional requirements.
2. A Member State which decides to withdraw shall notify the European Council of its intention. In the light of the guidelines provided by the European Council, the Union shall negotiate and conclude an agreement with that State, setting out the arrangements for its withdrawal, taking account of the framework for its future relationship with the Union. That agreement shall be negotiated in accordance with Article 218(3) of the Treaty on the Functioning of the European Union. It shall be concluded on behalf of the Union by the Council, acting by a qualified majority, after obtaining the consent of the European Parliament.
3. The Treaties shall cease to apply to the State in question from the date of entry into force of the withdrawal agreement or, failing that, two years after the notification referred to in paragraph 2, unless the European Council, in agreement with the Member State concerned, unanimously decides to extend this period.
4. For the purposes of paragraphs 2 and 3, the member of the European Council or of the Council representing the withdrawing Member State shall not participate in the discussions of the European Council or Council or in decisions concerning it.
   A qualified majority shall be defined in accordance with Article 238(3)(b) of the Treaty on the Functioning of the European Union.
5. If a State which has withdrawn from the Union asks to rejoin, its request shall be subject to the procedure referred to in Article 49.

Index

D

E

AEROSPACE LAW AND POLICY SERIES

1. Erwin von den Steinen, *National Interest and International Aviation* (ISBN 90-411-2455-1).
2. Ludwig Weber, *International Civil Aviation Organisation: An Introduction* (ISBN 978-90-411-2622-1).
3. Niels van Antwerpen, *Cross-Border Provision of Air Navigation Services with Specific Reference to Europe: Safeguarding Transparent Lines of Responsibility and Liability* (ISBN 978-90-411-2688-7).
4. Brian F. Havel, *Beyond Open Skies: A New Regime for International Aviation* (ISBN 978-90-411-2389-3).
5. Jiefang Huang, *Aviation Safety through the Rule of Law: ICAO's Mechanisms and Practices* (ISBN 978-90-411-3115-7).
6. Marian Hoeks, *Multimodal Transport Law: The Law Applicable to the Multimodal Contract for the Carriage of Goods* (ISBN 978-90-411-3246-8).
7. George N. Tompkins, Jr., *Liability Rules Applicable to International Air Transportation as Developed by the Courts in the United States: From Warsaw 1929 to Montreal 1999* (ISBN 978-90-411-2646-7).
8. Daniel Calleja Crespo and Pablo Mendes de Leon (eds), *Achieving the Single European Sky: Goals and Challenges* (ISBN 978-90-411-3730-2).
9. Donal Patrick Hanley, *Aircraft Operating Leasing: A Legal and Practical Analysis in the Context of Public and Private International Air Law*, Second Edition, (ISBN 978-90-411-6050-8).
10. Mikołaj Ratajczyk, *Regional Aviation Safety Organisations: Enhancing Air Transport Safety through Regional Cooperation* (ISBN 978-90-411-5861-1).
11. Benjamyn I. Scott (ed.), *The Law of Unmanned Aircraft Systems: An Introduction to the Current and Future Regulation under National, Regional and International Law* (ISBN 978-90-411-6126-0).
12. Stamatis Varsamos, *Airport Competition Regulation in Europe* (ISBN 978-90-411-6831-3).
13. Katarzyna Malinowska, *Space Insurance: International Legal Aspects* (ISBN 978-90-411-6784-2).
14. John Milligan, *European Union Competition Law in the Airline Industry* (ISBN 978-90-411-6618-0).

www.ingramcontent.com/pod-product-compliance
Lightning Source LLC
Chambersburg PA
CBHW071244230926
51849CB00001B/225
9789041166180